Journey to Become a Google Cloud Machine Learning Engineer

Build the mind and hand of a Google Certified ML professional

Dr. Logan Song

BIRMINGHAM—MUMBAI

Journey to Become a Google Cloud Machine Learning Engineer

Publishing Product Manager: Dhruv Jagdish Kataria
Content Development Editor: Sean Lobo
Technical Editor: Rahul Limbachiya
Copy Editor: Safis Editing
Project Coordinator: Farheen Fathima
Proofreader: Safis Editing
Indexer: Pratik Shirodkar
Production Designer: Prashant Ghare
Marketing Coordinators: Shifa Ansari and Abeer Riyaz Dawe

First published: September 2022
Production reference: 1300822

Published by Packt Publishing Ltd.
Livery Place
35 Livery Street
Birmingham
B3 2PB, UK.

ISBN 978-1-80323-372-7

www.packt.com

To Grandpa and Grandma, your love made this book possible.

To Dad and Mom, your DNA is in the book.

To Peiying, Peihua, Peixing, and Hengping, your encouragement is visible on each page of the book.

To Nancy, Neil, and Nicole, you are the driving force of the book.

To Tracey, thank you for allowing me to spend so much time on machine learning in the cloud.

- Logan Song

Contributors

About the author

Dr. Logan Song is the enterprise cloud director and chief cloud architect at Dito (www.ditoweb.com). With 25+ years of professional experience, Dr. Song is highly skilled in enterprise information technologies, specializing in cloud computing and machine learning. He is a Google Cloud-certified professional solution architect and machine learning engineer, an AWS-certified professional solution architect and machine learning specialist, and a Microsoft-certified Azure solution architect expert. Dr. Song holds a Ph.D. in industrial engineering, an MS in computer science, and an ME in management engineering. Currently, he is also an adjunct professor at the University of Texas at Dallas, teaching cloud computing and machine learning courses.

From Thanksgiving of 2021 to August of 2022, it took nine months to complete this book. I want to thank God for the amazing grace that made this book possible.

This book would not have been possible without the great support and collaboration from the Packt team: Sean Lobo, Prashant Ghare, Aparna Nair, Dhruv J. Kataria, the technical reviewer, the copy editors, and the whole Packt production team. It's been such a great pleasure working with the team!

I also want to thank my friend Farukh Khalilov, and the graduate student assistants at the University of Texas at Dallas, for their tremendous help in developing and verifying the Google Cloud practices and Python labs in this book. My gratitude is beyond words.

About the reviewer

Vijender Singh is a certified multi-cloud expert having 5+ years of experience and currently working with the Amazon Alexa AI team to tackle the effective use of AI on Alexa. He has completed an MSc with Distinction from Liverpool John Moores University with research work on keyphrase extraction. He has completed MLPE GCP, 5x Azure, 2x AWS certification, and TensorFlow certification. Vijender is instrumental in co-mentoring and teaching colleagues with machine learning and TensorFlow, which is a fundamental tool for the ML journey. He believes in working toward a better tomorrow.

Before starting the Google Cloud Machine Learning journey, you need to ask yourself a serious question: am I committed to taking this path?

In the summer of 2015, I was facing the same question: do I really want to get out of my comfort zone and pursue a new career called "cloud computing and machine learning"? At that time, I had been working in the traditional IT industry for over 20 years and was very comfortable with my professional life. Starting a new journey meant that I would have to learn from scratch!

For the whole summer, I was thinking about this question, along with another fundamental question: what do I really want to do in my life?

And one day, I came across Steve Jobs' famous commencement speech at Stanford University in 2005 (https://news.stanford.edu/2005/06/14/jobs-061505/), and suddenly I heard a voice:
"Stay hungry, stay foolish!"

At that moment, I made up my mind.

Today, I am so thankful to God for what happened in that summer and on that day!

Now, if you are determined as I was in 2015, let's march on our journey, together.

- Logan Song

Table of Contents

2

Part 2: Introducing Machine Learning

3

4

Developing and Deploying ML Models   51

5

Understanding Neural Networks and Deep Learning   73

Part 3: Mastering ML in GCP

6

Learning BQ/BQML, TensorFlow, and Keras   89

Part 4: Accomplishing GCP ML Certification

10

Part 5: Appendices

Appendix 1

Appendix 2

Appendix 3

Practicing with Scikit-Learn   197

Appendix 4

Practicing with Google Vertex AI   215

Appendix 5

Practicing with Google Cloud ML API   259

Index   297

Other Books You May Enjoy   308

Preface

Since the first programmable digital computer called ENIAC came to our world in 1946, computers have been so widely used and have become an integral part of our lives. It's impossible to imagine a world without computers.

Entering the 21st century, the so-called *ABC Triangle* stands out in the computer world, and its three vertices represent today's most advanced computer technologies – A for Artificial intelligence, B for Big data, and C for Cloud computing, as you can see from the following figure. These technologies are reshaping our world and changing our lives every day.

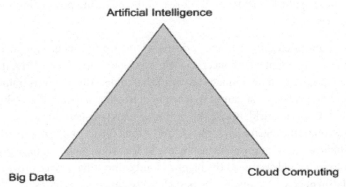

It is very interesting to look at these advanced computer technologies from a historical point of view, to understand what they are and how they have developed with each other:

- **Artificial intelligence (AI)** is a technology that enables a machine (computer) to simulate human behavior. **Machine learning (ML)** is a subset of AI that lets a machine automatically learn from past data and predict based on the data. AI was introduced to the world around 1956, shortly after the invention of ENIAC, but in recent years, AI has gained momentum because of the accumulation of big data and the development of cloud computing.

- **Big data** refers to the steady exponentially increasing data generated and stored in the past years. In 2018, the total amount of data created and consumed was about 33 zettabytes (1 ZB =8,000,000,000,000,000,000,000 bits) worldwide. This number grew to 59 ZB in 2020 and is predicted to reach a mind-boggling 175 ZB by 2025. To process these big data sets, huge amounts of computing power are needed. It is inconceivable to process these huge data sets on commodity computers, not to mention the time it takes for a company to deploy traditional data centers to place these computers. Big data processing calls for new ways to provision computing powers.

- **Cloud computing** came into our world in 2006, about half a century after the idea of AI. Cloud computing provides computing powers featuring elastic, self-provisioning, and on-demand services. In a traditional computing model, infrastructure is conceived as hardware. Hardware solutions are physical – they require space, staff, planning, physical security, and capital expenditure – thus they have a long hardware procurement cycle that involves acquiring, provisioning, and maintaining. The cloud computing model made the infrastructure as software – choose the cloud computing services that best match your business needs, provision and terminate those resources on-demand, scale the resources up and down elastically in an automated fashion based on demand, deploy the infrastructure/resources as immutable codes that are managed with version control, and pay for what you use. With the cloud computing model, computing resources are treated as temporary and disposable: they can be used much more quickly, easily, and cost-effectively. The cloud computing model made AI computing feasible.

AI, big data, and cloud computing work with each other and thrive – more data results in more AI/ML applications, more applications demand more cloud computing power, and more applications will generate more data.

Famous for its innovation-led mindsets and industry-trend-led products, Google is a leader in the *ABC Triangle* technologies. As an ML pioneer, Google developed AlphaGo in 2017, the first computer program that defeated a professional human Go world champion. AlphaGo was trained on thousands of human amateur and professional games to learn how to play Go. AlphaZero skips this step and learns to play against itself – it quickly surpassed the human level of play and defeated AlphaGo by 100 games to 0. In addition to the legendary AlphaGo and AlphaZero, Google has developed numerous ML models and applications in many areas, including vision, voice, and language processing. In the cloud computing arena, Google is one of the biggest cloud computing service providers in the world. **Google Cloud Platform (GCP)** provides the best cloud services on earth, especially in the areas of big data and ML. Many companies are keen to use Google Cloud and leverage the GCP ML services for their business use cases. And this is the purpose of our book. We aim to learn about and master *the best of the best* – ML in Google Cloud.

Who this book is for

This book is for anyone that not only wants to better understand the concept of ML in the cloud, but also those that have a decent grasp and want to dive deep to become a professional Google-certified cloud ML engineer.

What this book covers

Chapter 1, *Comprehending Google Cloud Services*, provides an overview of the GCP services with the practice examples detailed in *Appendix 1*.

Chapter 2, *Learning Python Programming*, delves into the Python basic knowledge and programming skills. The Python data science libraries are explored, with practice examples detailed in *Appendix 2*.

Chapter 3, Preparing for ML Development, covers preparations for the ML process, including ML problem definition and data preparation.

Chapter 4, Developing and Deploying ML Models, dives into the ML process, including platform preparation, dataset splitting, model training, validation, testing, and deployment with the practice examples detailed in *Appendix 3*.

Chapter 5, Understanding Neural Networks and Deep Learning, introduces the modern AI methods of deep learning with neural network modeling.

Chapter 6, Learning BQML, TensorFlow, and Keras, discover Google's BigQuery machine learning for structured data, and Google's ML framework of TensorFlow and Keras.

Chapter 7, Exploring Google Cloud Vertex AI, examines Google's end-to-end ML suite of Vertex AI and its ML services with the practice examples detailed in *Appendix 4*.

Chapter 8, Discovering Google Cloud ML API, looks at how you can leverage Google's pre-trained model APIs for ML development with the practice examples detailed in *Appendix 5*.

Chapter 9, Using Google Cloud ML Best Practices, summarizes the best practices in ML development in Google Cloud.

Chapter 10, Achieving the GCP ML Certification, studies GCP ML certification exam questions by integrating the knowledge and skills learned from previous chapters.

Appendix 1, Practicing with Basic GCP Services, provides examples for provisioning basic GCP services.

Appendix 2, Practicing with Python Data Library, provides examples of Python data library practices, including NumPy, Pandas, Matpotlib, and Seaborn.

Appendix 3, Practicing with ScikitLearn, provides examples of scikit-learn library practices.

Appendix 4, Practicing with Google Vertex AI, provides examples for practicing Google Cloud Vertex AI services.

Appendix 5, Practicing with Google Cloud ML API, provides examples for Google Cloud ML API practicing.

To get the most out of this book

It is a best practice to learn machine learning in Google Cloud in two folds: studying the chapters to master the basic concepts, and learning by doing all the lab examples in the chapters, especially the labs in the appendices.

While some basic computer technical knowledge is expected to start, being a cloud developer or cloud engineer is not a necessity. You can read this book from beginning to end, or you can jump to the chapters that seem most relevant to you.

If you are using the digital version of this book, we advise you to type the code yourself or access the code from the book's GitHub repository (a link is available in the next section). Doing so will help you avoid any potential errors related to the copying and pasting of code.

Download the example code files

You can download the example code files for this book from GitHub at `https://github.com/PacktPublishing/Journey-to-a-Google-Cloud-Professional-Machine-Learning-Engineer`. If there's an update to the code, it will be updated in the GitHub repository.

We also have other code bundles from our rich catalog of books and videos available at `https://github.com/PacktPublishing/`. Check them out!

Download the color images

We also provide a PDF file that has color images of the screenshots and diagrams used in this book. You can download it here: `https://packt.link/ugTOg`.

Conventions used

There are a number of text conventions used throughout this book.

`Code in text`: Indicates code words in text, database table names, folder names, filenames, file extensions, pathnames, dummy URLs, user input, and Twitter handles. Here is an example: "Mount the downloaded `WebStorm-10*.dmg` disk image file as another disk in your system."

A block of code is set as follows:

```
html, body, #map {
  height: 100%;
  margin: 0;
  padding: 0
}
```

When we wish to draw your attention to a particular part of a code block, the relevant lines or items are set in bold:

```
[default]
exten => s,1,Dial(Zap/1|30)
exten => s,2,Voicemail(u100)
```

```
exten => s,102,Voicemail(b100)
exten => i,1,Voicemail(s0)
```

Any command-line input or output is written as follows:

```
$ mkdir css
$ cd css
```

Bold: Indicates a new term, an important word, or words that you see onscreen. For instance, words in menus or dialog boxes appear in **bold**. Here is an example: "Select **System info** from the **Administration** panel."

Tips or Important Notes
Appear like this.

Get in touch

Feedback from our readers is always welcome.

General feedback: If you have questions about any aspect of this book, email us at customercare@packtpub.com and mention the book title in the subject of your message.

Errata: Although we have taken every care to ensure the accuracy of our content, mistakes do happen. If you have found a mistake in this book, we would be grateful if you would report this to us. Please visit www.packtpub.com/support/errata and fill in the form.

Piracy: If you come across any illegal copies of our works in any form on the internet, we would be grateful if you would provide us with the location address or website name. Please contact us at copyright@packt.com with a link to the material.

If you are interested in becoming an author: If there is a topic that you have expertise in and you are interested in either writing or contributing to a book, please visit authors.packtpub.com.

Share Your Thoughts

Once you've read Journey to Become a Google Cloud Machine Learning Engineer, we'd love to hear your thoughts! Scan the QR code below to go straight to the Amazon review page for this book and share your feedback.

https://packt.link/r/1-803-23372-9

Your review is important to us and the tech community and will help us make sure we're delivering excellent quality content.

Part 1: Starting with GCP and Python

This part provides a general background of Google Cloud Platform (GCP) and the Python programming language. We introduce the concept of cloud computing and GCP, and briefly look at the basic GCP services including compute, storage, networking, database, big data, and machine learning. We go through an overview of the Python language basics, programming structures, and control flows. We then discuss the Python data science libraries, including NumPy, Pandas, Matpotlib, and Seaborn, to better understand their functions and use cases.

This part comprises the following chapters:

- Chapter 1, Comprehending Google Cloud Services
- Chapter 2, Learning Python Programming

1

Comprehending Google Cloud Services

In Part 1 of this book, we will be building a foundation by focusing on Google Cloud and Python, the essential platform and tool for our learning journey, respectively.

In this chapter, we will dive into **Google Cloud Platform** (GCP) and discuss the Google Cloud services that are closely related to **Google Cloud Machine Learning**. Mastering these services will provide us with a solid background.

The following topics will be covered in this chapter:

- Understanding the GCP global infrastructure
- Getting started with GCP
- GCP organization structure
- GCP Identity and Access Management
- GCP compute spectrum
- GCP storage and database services
- GCP big data and analytics services
- GCP artificial intelligence services

Let's get started.

Understanding the GCP global infrastructure

Google is one of the biggest cloud service providers in the world. With the physical computing infrastructures such as computers, hard disk drives, routers, and switches in Google's worldwide data centers, which are connected by Google's global backbone network, Google provides a full spectrum of cloud services in GCP, including compute, network, database, security, and advanced services such as big data, **machine learning** (**ML**), and many, many more.

Within Google's global cloud infrastructure, there are many data center groups. Each data center group is called a **GCP region**. These regions are located worldwide, in Asia, Australia, Europe, North America, and South America. These regions are connected by Google's global backbone network for performance optimization and resiliency. Each GCP region is a collection of **zones** that are isolated from each other. Each zone has one or more data centers and is identified by a name that combines a letter identifier with the region's name. For example, zone *US-Central1-a* is a zone in the *US-Central1* region, which is physically located in Council Bluffs, Iowa, the United State of America. In the GCP global infrastructure, there are also many **edge locations** or **points of presence** (**POPs**) where Google's global networks connect to the internet. More details about GCP regions, zones, and edge locations can be found at `https://cloud.google.com/about/locations`.

GCP provides on-demand cloud resources at a global scale. These resources can be used together to build solutions that help meet business goals and satisfy technology requirements. For example, if a company needs 1,000 TB of storage in Tokyo, its IT professional can log into their GCP account console and provision the storage in the *Asia-northeast1* region at any time. Similarly, a 3,000 TB database can be provisioned in Sydney and a 4,000-node cluster in Frankfurt at any time, with just a few clicks. And finally, if a company wants to set up a global website, such as `zeebestbuy.com`, with the lowest latencies for their global users, they can build three web servers in the global regions of London, Virginia, and Singapore, and utilize Google's global DNS service to distribute the web traffic along these three web servers. Depending on the user's web browser location, DNS will route the traffic to the nearest web server.

Getting started with GCP

Now that we have learned about Google's global cloud infrastructure and the on-demand resource provisioning concept of cloud computing, we can't wait to dive into Google Cloud and provision resources in the cloud!

In this section, we will build cloud resources by doing the following:

- Creating a free-tier GCP account
- Provisioning a virtual computer instance in Google Cloud
- Provisioning our first storage in Google Cloud

Let's go through each of these steps in detail.

Creating a free-tier GCP account

Google provides a free-tier account type for us to get started on GCP. More details can be found at `https://cloud.google.com/free/docs/gcp-free-tier`.

Once you have signed up for a GCP free-tier account, it's time to plan our first resources in Google Cloud – a computer and a storage folder in the cloud. We will provision them as needed. How exciting!

Provisioning our first computer in Google Cloud

We will start with the simplest idea: provisioning a computer in the cloud. Think about a home computer for a moment. It has a **Central Processing Unit (CPU)**, **Random Access Memory (RAM)**, **hard disk drives (HDDs)**, and a **network interface card (NIC)** for connecting to the relevant **Internet Service Provider (ISP)** equipment (such as cable modems and routers). It also has an operating system (Windows or Linux), and it may have a database such as MySQL for some family data management, or Microsoft Office for home office usage.

To provision a computer in Google Cloud, we will need to do the same planning for its hardware, such as the number of CPUs, RAM, and the size of HDDs, as well as for its software, such as the operating system (Linux or Windows) and database (**MySQL**). We may also need to plan the network for the computer, such as an external IP address, and whether the IP address needs to be static or dynamic. For example, if we plan to provision a web server, then our computer will need a static external IP address. And from a security point of view, we will need to set up the network firewalls so that only specific computers at home or work may access our computer in the cloud.

GCP offers a cloud service for consumers to provision a computer in the cloud: **Google Compute Engine (GCE)**. With the GCE service, we can build flexible, self-managed **virtual machines (VMs)** in the Google Cloud. GCE offers different hardware and software options based on consumers' needs, so you can use customized VM types and select the appropriate operating system for the VM instances.

Following the instructions at `https://cloud.google.com/compute/docs/instances/create-start-instance`, you can create a VM in GCP. Let's pause here and go to the GCP console to provision our first computer.

How do we access the computer? If the VM has a Windows operating system, you can use **Remote Desktop** to access it. For a Linux VM, you can use **Secure Shell (SSH)** to log in. More details are available at `https://cloud.google.com/compute`.

Provisioning our first storage in Google Cloud

When we open the computer case and look inside our home computer, we can see its hardware components – that is, its CPU, RAM, HDD, and NIC. The hard disks within a PC are limited in size and performance. *EMC*, a company founded in 1979 by Richard Egan and Roger Marino, expanded PC hard disks outside of the PC case to a separate computer network storage platform called *Symmetrix* in 1990. Symmetrix has its own CPU/RAM and provides huge storage capacities. It is connected to the computer through fiber cables and serves as the **storage array** of the computer. On the other hand, *SanDisk*, founded in 1988 by Eli Harari, Sanjay Mehrotra, and Jack Yuan, produced the first Flash-based **solid-state drive** (**SSD**) in a 2.5-inch hard drive, called *Cruzer*, in 2000. Cruzer provides portable storage via a USB connection to a computer. By thinking out of the box and extending either to Symmetrix or Cruzer, EMC and Sandisk extended the hard disk concept out of the box. These are great examples of start-up ideas!

And then comes the great idea of cloud computing – the concept of storage is further extended to cloud-block storage, cloud **network-attached storage** (**NAS**), and cloud object storage. Let's look at these in more detail:

- **Cloud block storage** is a form of software-based storage that can be attached to a VM in the cloud, just like a hard disk is attached to our PC at home. In Google Cloud, cloud block storage is called **persistent disks** (**PD**). Instead of buying a physical hard disk and installing it on the PC to use it, PDs can be created instantly and attached to a VM in the cloud, with only a couple of clicks.

- **Cloud network-attached storage** (**Cloud NAS**) is a form of software-based storage that can be shared among many cloud VMs through a virtual cloud network. In GCP, cloud NAS is called **Filestore**. Instead of buying a physical file server, installing it on a network, and sharing it with multiple PCs at home, a Filestore instance can be created instantly and shared by many cloud VMs, with only a couple of clicks.

- **Cloud object storage** is a form of software-based storage that can be used to store objects (files, images, and so on) in the cloud. In GCP, cloud object storage is called **Google Cloud Storage** (**GCS**). Different from PD, which is a cloud block storage type that's used by a VM (it can be shared in read-only mode among multiple VMs), and Filestore, which is a cloud NAS type shared by many VMs, GCS is a cloud object type used for storing immutable objects. Objects are stored in GCS buckets. In GCP, bucket creation and deletion, object uploading, downloading, and deletion can all be done from the GCP console, with just a couple of clicks!

GCS provides different storage classes based on the object accessing patterns. More details can be found at `https://cloud.google.com/storage`.

Following the instructions at `https://cloud.google.com/storage/docs/creating-buckets`, you can create a storage folder/bucket and upload objects into it. Let's pause here and go to the GCP console to provision our first storage bucket and upload some objects into it.

Managing resources using GCP Cloud Shell

So far, we have discussed provisioning VMs and buckets/objects in the cloud from the GCP console. There is another tool that can help us create, manage, and delete resources: GCP Cloud Shell. Cloud Shell is a command-line interface that can easily be accessed from your console browser. After you click the **Cloud Shell** button on the GCP console, you will get a Cloud Shell – a command-line user interface on a VM, in your web browser, with all the cloud resource management commands already installed.

The following tools are provided by Google for customers to create and manage cloud resources using the command line:

- The `gcloud` tool is the main command-line interface for GCP products and services such as GCE.

- The `gsutil` tool is for GCS services.

- The `bq` tool is for BigQuery services.

- The `kubectl` tool is for Kubernetes services.

Please refer to `https://cloud.google.com/shell/docs/using-cloudshell-command` for more information about GCP Cloud Shell and commands, as well as how to create a VM and a storage bucket using Cloud Shell commands.

GCP networking – virtual private clouds

Think about home computers again – they are all connected via a network, wired or wireless, so that they can connect to the internet. Without networking, a computer is almost useless. Within GCP, a cloud network unit is called a **virtual private cloud** (**VPC**). A VPC is a software-based logical network resource. Within a GCP project, a limited number of VPCs can be provisioned. After launching VMs in the cloud, you can connect them within a VPC, or isolate them from each other in separate VPCs. Since GCP VPCs are global and can span multiple regions in the world, you can provision a VPC, as well as the resources within it, anywhere in the world. Within a VPC, a public subnet has VMs with external IP addresses that are accessible from the internet and can access the internet; a private subnet contains VMs that do not have external IP addresses. VPCs can be peered with each other, within a GCP project, or outside a GCP project.

VPCs can be provisioned using the GCP console or GCP Cloud Shell. Please refer to `https://cloud.google.com/vpc/` for details. Let's pause here and go to the GCP console to provision our VPC and subnets, and then launch some VMs into those subnets.

GCP organization structure

Before we discuss the GCP cloud services further, we need to spend some time talking about the GCP organization structure, which is quite different from that of the **Amazon Web Services** (**AWS**) cloud and the Microsoft Azure cloud.

The GCP resource hierarchy

As shown in the following diagram, within a GCP cloud domain, at the top is the GCP organization, followed by folders, then projects. As a common practice, we can map a company's organizational hierarchy to a GCP structure: a company maps to a GCP organization, its departments (sales, engineering, and more) are mapped to folders, and the functional projects from the departments are mapped to projects under the folders. Cloud resources such as VMs, **databases (DBs)**, and so on are under the projects.

In a GCP organization hierarchy, *each project is a separate compartment, and each resource belongs to exactly one project*. Projects can have multiple owners and users. They are managed and billed separately, although multiple projects may be associated with the same billing account:

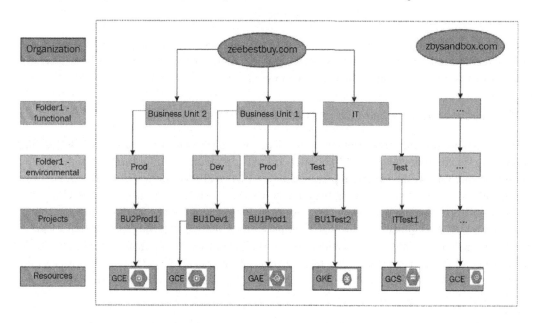

Figure 1.1 – Sample GCP organization structure

In the preceding diagram, there are two organizations: one for production and one for testing (sandbox). Under each organization, there are multiple layers of folders (note that the number of folder layers and the number of folders at each layer may be limited), and under each folder, there are multiple projects, each of which contains multiple resources.

GCP projects

GCP projects are the logical separations of GCP resources. Projects are used to fully isolate resources based on Google Cloud's **Identity and Access Management (IAM)** permissions:

- **Billing isolation**: Use different projects to separate spending units
- **Quotas and limits**: Set at the project level and separated by workloads
- **Administrative complexity**: Set at the project level for access separation
- **Blast radius**: Misconfiguration issues are limited within a project
- **Separation of duties**: Business units and data sensitivity are separate

In summary, the GCP organization structure provides a hierarchy for managing Google Cloud resources, with projects being the logical isolation and separation. In the next section, we will discuss resource permissions within the GCP organization by looking at IAM.

GCP Identity and Access Management

Once we have reviewed the GCP organization structure and the GCP resources of VMs, storage, and network, we must look at the access management of these resources within the GCP organization: IAM. GCP IAM manages cloud identities using the **AAA** model: **authentication**, **authorization**, and **auditing** (or **accounting**).

Authentication

The first *A* in the *AAA* model is **authentication**, which involves verifying the cloud identity that is trying to access the cloud. Instead of the traditional way of just asking for a username and password, **multi-factor authentication (MFA)** is used, an authentication method that requires users to verify their identity using multiple independent methods. For security reasons, all user authentications, including GCP console access and any other **single sign-on (SSO)** implementations, must be done while enforcing MFA. Usernames and passwords are simply ineffective in protecting user access these days.

Authorization

Authorization is represented by the second *A* in the *AAA* model. It is the process of granting or denying a user access to cloud resources once the user has been authenticated into the cloud account. The amount of information and the number of services the user can access depend on the user's authorization level. Once a user's identity has been verified and the user has been authenticated into GCP, the user must pass the authorization rules to access the cloud resources and data. Authorization determines the resources that the user can and cannot access.

Authorization defines *who can do what on which resource*. The following diagram shows the **authorization** concept in GCP. As you can see, there are three parties in the authorization process: the first layer in the figure is identity – this specifies *who* can be a user account, a group of users, or an application (**Service Account**). The third layer specifies *which* cloud resources, such as GCS buckets, GCE VMs, VPCs, service accounts, or other GCP resources. A **Service Account** can be an identity as well as a resource:

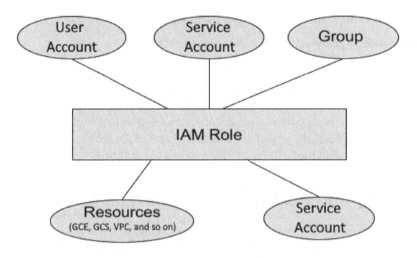

Figure 1.2 – GCP IAM authentication

The middle layer is **IAM Role**, also known as the *what*, which refers to specific privileges or actions that the identity has against the resources. For example, when a group is provided the privilege of a compute viewer, then the group will have read-only access to get and list GCE resources, without being able to write/change them. GCP supports three types of IAM roles: **primitive** (**basic**), **predefined**, and **custom**. Let's take a look:

- **Primitive (basic) roles**, include the Owner, Editor, and Viewer roles, which existed in GCP before the introduction of IAM. These roles have thousands of permissions across all Google Cloud services and confer significant privileges. Therefore, in production environments, it is recommended to not grant basic roles unless there is no alternative. Instead, grant the most limited predefined roles or custom roles that meet your needs.

- **Predefined roles** provide granular access to specific services following role-based permission needs. Predefined roles are created and maintained by Google. Google automatically updates its permissions as necessary, such as when Google Cloud adds new features or services.

- **Custom roles** provide granular access according to the user-specified list of permissions. These roles should be used sparingly as the user is responsible for maintaining the associated permissions.

In GCP, authentication is implemented using IAM policies, which bind identities to IAM roles. Here is a sample IAM policy:

```
{
  "bindings": [
    {
      "members": [
        "user:jack@example.com"
      ],
      "role": "roles/resourcemanager.organizationAdmin"
    },
    {
      "members": [
        "user:jack@example.com",
        "user:joe@example.com"
      ],
      "role": "roles/resourcemanager.projectCreator"
    }
  ],
  "etag": "BwUjMhCsNvY=",
  "version": 1
}
```

In the preceding example, Jack (`jack@example.com`) is granted the Organization Admin predefined role (`roles/resourcemanager.organizationAdmin`) and thus has permissions for organizations, folders, and limited project operations. Both Jack and Joe (`joe@example.com`) can create projects since they have been granted the Project Creator role (`roles/resourcemanager.projectCreator`). Together, these two role bindings provide fine-grained GCP resource access to Jack and Joe, though Jack has more privileges.

Auditing or accounting

The third *A* in the *AAA* model refers to **auditing** or **accounting**, which is the process of keeping track of a user's activity while accessing GCP resources, including the amount of time spent in the network, the services they've accessed, and the amount of data transferred during their login session. Auditing data is used for trend analysis, access recording, compliance auditing, breach detection, forensics and investigations, accounts billing, cost allocations, and capacity planning. With the Google Cloud Audit Logs service, you can keep track of users/groups and their activities and ensure the activity records are genuine. Auditing logs are very helpful for cloud security. For example, tracing back to events of a cybersecurity incident can be very valuable to forensics analyses and case investigations.

Service account

In GCP, a service account is a specialized account that can be used by GCP services and other applications running on GCE instances or elsewhere to interact with GCP **application programming interfaces** (**APIs**). They are like *programmatic access users* by which you can give access to GCP services. Service accounts exist in GCP projects but can be given permissions at the organization and folder levels, as well as to different projects. By leveraging service account credentials, applications can authorize themselves to a set of APIs and perform actions within the permissions that have been granted to the service account. For example, an application running on a GCE instance can use the instance's service account to interact with other Google services (such as a Cloud SQL Database instance) and their underlying APIs.

When we created our first VM, a default service account was created for that VM at the same time. You can define the permissions for this VM's service account by defining its **access scopes**. Once defined, all the applications running on this VM will have the same permission to access other GCP resources, such as a GCS bucket. When the number of VMs has increased significantly, this will generate a lot of service accounts. That's why we often create a service account and assign it to a VM or other resources that need to have the same GCP permissions.

GCP compute services

Previously, we looked at the GCE service and created our VM instances in the cloud. Now, let's look at the whole GCP compute spectrum, which includes **Google Compute Engine (GCE)**, **Google Kubernetes Engine (GKE)**, Cloud Run, **Google App Engine (GAE)**, and Cloud Functions, as shown in the following diagram:

| Compute | Kubernetes | Cloud | App | Cloud |
| Engine | Engine | Run | Engine | Functions |

Figure 1.3 – GCP compute services

The GCP compute spectrum provides a broad range of business use cases. Based on the business model, we can choose GCE, GKE, GAE, Cloud Run, or Cloud Functions to match the requirements. We will discuss each of them briefly in the next few sections.

GCE virtual machines

We discussed the concepts surrounding GCE and provisioned VMs using the cloud console and Cloud Shell. In this section, we will discuss GCP GCE VM images and the pricing model.

Compute Engine images provide the base operating environment for applications that run in **Compute Engines** (that is, VMs), and they are critical to ensuring that your application deploys and scales quickly and reliably. You can also use golden/trusted images to archive application versions for disaster recovery or rollback scenarios. GCE images are also crucial in security since they can be used to deploy all the VMs in a company.

GCE offers different pricing models for VMs: pay-as-you-go, preemptive, committed usage, and sole-tenant host.

Pay-as-you-go is for business cases that need to provision VMs on the fly. If the workload is foreseeable, we want to use committed usage for the discounted price. If the workload can be restarted, we want to further leverage the *preemptive* model and bid for the VM prices. If licenses tied to the host exist, the *sole-tenant host* type fits our needs. For more details about GCE VM pricing, check out `https://cloud.google.com/compute/vm-instance-pricing`.

Load balancers and managed instance groups

A single computer may be down due to hardware or software failures, and it also does not provide any scaling when computing power demands are changed along the timeline. To ensure high availability and scalability, GCP provides **load balancers (LBs)** and **managed instance groups (MIGs)**. LBs and MIGs allow you to create homogeneous groups of instances so that load balancers can direct traffic to more than one VM instance. MIG also offers features such as auto-scaling and auto-healing. Auto-scaling lets you deal with spikes in traffic by configuring the appropriate minimum and maximum instances in the autoscaling policy and scaling the number of VM instances up or down based on specific signals, while auto-healing performs health checking and, if necessary, automatically recreates unhealthy instances.

Let's look at an example to explain this idea:

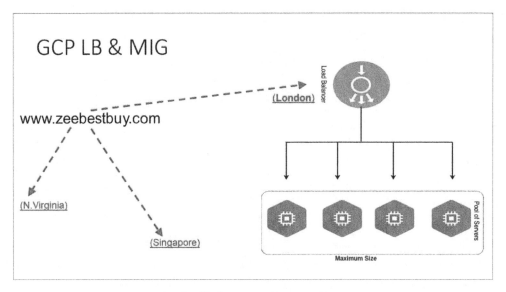

Figure 1.4 – GCP load balancers and managed instance groups

As shown in the preceding diagram, www.zeebestbuy.com is a global e-commerce company. Every year, when *Black Friday* comes, their website is so heavily loaded that a single computer cannot accommodate the traffic – many more web servers (running on VM instances) are needed to distribute the traffic load. After *Black Friday*, the traffic goes back to normal, and not that many instances are needed. On the GCP platform, we use LBs and MIGs to solve this problem. As shown in the preceding diagram, we build three web servers globally (N. Virginia in the US, Singapore, and London in the UK), and GCP DNS can distribute the user traffic to these three locations based on the user's browser location and the latency to the three sites. At each site, we set up an LB and a MIG: the desired capacity, as well as the minimum and maximum capacities, can be set appropriately based on the normal and peak traffic. When *Black Friday* comes, the LB and MIG work together to elastically launch new VM instances (web servers) to handle the increased traffic. After the *Black Friday* sale ends, they will stop/delete the VM instances to reflect the decreased traffic.

MIG uses a launch template, which is like a launch configuration, and specifies instance configuration information, including the ID of the VM image, the instance type, the scaling thresholds, and other parameters that are used to launch VM instances. LB uses health checks to monitor the instances. If an instance is not responding within the configured threshed times, new instances will be launched based on the launch template.

Containers and Google Kubernetes Engine

Just like the transformation from physical machines into VMs, the transformation from VMs into containers is revolutionary. Instead of launching a VM to run an application, we package the application into a standard unit that contains everything to run the application or service in the same way on different VMs. We build the package into a Docker image; a container is a running instance of a Docker image. While a hypervisor virtualizes the hardware into VMs, a Docker image virtualizes an operating system into application containers.

Due to loose coupling and modular portability, more and more applications are being containerized. Quickly, a question arose: how can all these containers/Docker images be managed? There is where **Google Kubernetes Engine (GKE)** comes in, a container management system developed by Google. A GKE cluster usually consists of at least one control plane and multiple worker machines called nodes, which work together to manage/orchestrate the containers. A Kubernetes Pod is a group of containers that are deployed together and work together to complete a task. For example, an app server pod contains three separate containers: the app server itself, a monitoring container, and a logging container. Working together, they form the application or service of a business use case.

Following the instructions at `https://cloud.google.com/kubernetes-engine/docs/how-to/creating-a-zonal-cluster`, you can create a GKE zonal cluster. Let's pause here and use GCP Cloud Shell to create a GKE cluster.

GCP Cloud Run

GCP Cloud Run is a managed compute platform that enables you to run stateless containers that can be invoked via HTTP requests on either a fully managed environment or in your GKE cluster. Cloud Run is serverless, which means that all infrastructure management tasks are the responsibility of Google, leaving the user to focus on application development. With Cloud Run, you can build your applications in any language using whatever frameworks and tools you want, and then deploy them in seconds without having to manage the server infrastructure.

GCP Cloud Functions

Different from the GCE and GKE services, which deploy VMs or containers to run applications, respectively, Cloud Functions is a serverless compute service that allows you to submit your code (written in JavaScript, Python, Go, and so on). Google Cloud will run the code in the backend and deliver the results to you. You do not know and do not care about where the code was run – you are only charged for the time your code runs on GCP.

Leveraging Cloud Functions, a piece of code can be triggered within a few milliseconds based on certain events. For example, after an object is uploaded to a GCS bucket, a message can be generated and sent to GCP Pub/Sub, which will cause Cloud Functions to process the object. Cloud Functions can also be triggered based on HTTP endpoints you define or by events in Firebase mobile applications.

With Cloud Functions, Google takes care of the backend infrastructure for running the code and lets you focus on the code development only.

GCP storage and database service spectrum

Previously, we examined the GCS service and created our storage bucket in the cloud, as well as the persistent disks and Filestore instances for our cloud VM instances. Now, let's look at the whole GCP storage and database service spectrum, which includes Cloud Storage, Cloud SQL, Cloud Spanner, Cloud Firestore, Bigtable, and BigQuery, as shown in the following diagram:

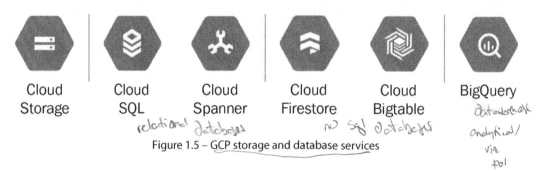

Figure 1.5 – GCP storage and database services

Here, Cloud Storage stores objects, Cloud SQL and Cloud Spanner are the relational databases, Cloud Firestore and Bigtable are NoSQL databases.BigQuery is a data warehouse as well as a bigdata analytical/visualization tool. We will discuss BigQuery in the *GCP big data and analytics services* section.

GCP storage

We have already discussed GCP storage, including **Google Cloud Storage (GCS)**, persistent disks, and Filestore. GCS is a common choice for GCP ML jobs to store their training data, models, checkpoints, and logs. In the next few sections, we will discuss more GCP storage databases and services.

Google Cloud SQL

Cloud SQL is a fully managed GCP relational database service for MySQL, PostgreSQL, and SQL Server. With Cloud SQL, you run the same relational databases you are familiar with on-premises, without the hassle of self-management, such as backup and restore, high availability, and more. As a managed service, it is the responsibility of Google to manage the database backups, export and import, ensure high availability and failover, perform patch maintenance and updates, and perform monitoring and logging.

Google Cloud Spanner

Google Cloud Spanner is a GCP fully managed relational database with unlimited global scale, strong consistency, and up to 99.999% availability. Like a relational database, Cloud Spanner has schemas, SQL, and strong consistency. Also, like a non-relational database, Cloud Spanner offers high availability, horizontal scalability, and configurable replications. Cloud Spanner has been used for mission-critical business use cases, such as online trading systems for transactions and financial management.

Cloud Firestore

Cloud Firestore is a fast, fully managed, serverless, cloud-native NoSQL document database. Cloud Firestore supports ACID transactions and allows you to run sophisticated queries against NoSQL data without performance degradation. It stores, syncs and query data for mobile apps and web apps at global scale. Firestore integrates with Firebase and other GCP services seamlessly and thus accelerates serverless application development.

Google Cloud Bigtable

Cloud Bigtable is Google's fully managed NoSQL big data database service. Bigtable stores data in tables that are sorted using key/value maps. Bigtable can store trillions of rows and millions of columns, enabling applications to store petabytes of data. Bigtable provides extreme scalability and automatically handles database tasks such as restarts, upgrades, and replication. Bigtable is ideal for storing very large amounts of semi-structured or non-structured data, with sub-10 milliseconds latency and extremely high read and write throughput. Many of Google's core products such as Search, Analytics, Maps, and Gmail use Cloud Bigtable.

[Handwritten margin note: nosql databases - store & modeling structured, semi-structured unstructured data in same database]

GCP big data and analytics services

Distinguished from storage and database services, the big data and analytics services focus on the big data processing pipeline: from data ingestion, storing, and processing to visualization, it helps you create a complete cloud-based big data infrastructure:

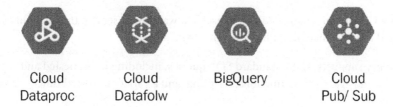

Cloud Dataproc   Cloud Datafolw   BigQuery   Cloud Pub/ Sub

Figure 1.6 – GCP big data and analytics services

As shown in the preceding diagram, the GCP big data and analytics services include Cloud Dataproc, Cloud Dataflow, BigQuery, and Cloud Pub/Sub.

Let's examine each of them briefly.

Google Cloud Dataproc

Based on the concept of Map-Reduce and the architecture of Hadoop systems, **Google Cloud Dataproc** is a managed GCP service for processing large datasets. **Dataproc** provides organizations with the flexibility to provision and configure data processing clusters of varying sizes on demand. Dataproc integrates well with other GCP services. It can operate directly on Cloud Storage files or use Bigtable to analyze data, and it can be integrated with **Vertex AI**, **BigQuery**, **Dataplex**, and other **GCP** services.

Dataproc helps users process, transform, and understand vast quantities of data. You can use Dataproc to run Apache Spark, Apache Flink, Presto, and 30+ open source tools and frameworks. You can also use Dataproc for data lake modernization, ETL processes, and more.

Google Cloud Dataflow

Cloud Dataflow is a GCP-managed service for developing and executing a wide variety of data processing patterns, including **Extract, Transform, Load** (**ETL**), batch, and streaming jobs. Cloud Dataflow is a serverless data processing service that runs jobs written with Apache Beam libraries. Cloud Dataflow executes jobs that consist of a pipeline – a sequence of steps that reads data, transforms it into different formats, and writes it out. A dataflow pipeline consists of a series of pipes, which is a way to connect components, where data moves from one component to the next via a pipe. When jobs are executed on Cloud Dataflow, the service spins up a cluster of VMs, distributes the job tasks to the VMs, and dynamically scales the cluster based on job loads and their performance.

Google Cloud BigQuery

BigQuery is a Google fully managed enterprise data warehouse service that is highly scalable, fast, and optimized for data analytics. It has the following features:

- BigQuery supports ANSI-standard SQL queries, including joins, nested and repeated fields, analytic and aggregation functions, scripting, and a variety of spatial functions via geospatial analytics.

- With BigQuery, you do not physically manage the infrastructure assets. BigQuery's serverless architecture lets you use SQL queries to answer big business questions with zero infrastructure overhead. With BigQuery's scalable, distributed analysis engine, you can query petabytes of data in minutes.

- BigQuery integrates seamlessly with other GCP data services. You can query data stored in BigQuery or run queries on data where it lives using external tables or federated queries, including GCS, Bigtable, Spanner, or Google Sheets stored in Google Drive.

- BigQuery helps you manage and analyze your data with built-in features such as ML, geospatial analysis, and business intelligence. We will discuss BigQuery ML later in this book.

Google BigQuery is used in many business cases due to it being SQL-friendly, having a serverless structure, and having built-in integration with other GCP services.

Google Cloud Pub/Sub

GCP Pub/Sub is a widely used cloud service for decoupling many GCP services – it implements an event/message queue pipe to integrate services and parallelize tasks. With the Pub/Sub service, you can create event producers, called publishers, and event consumers, called subscribers. Using Pub/Sub, the publishers communicate with subscribers asynchronously by broadcasting events – a publisher can have multiple subscribers and a subscriber can subscribe to multiple publishers:

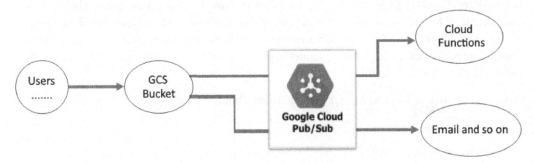

Figure 1.7 – Google Cloud Pub/Sub services

The preceding diagram shows the example we discussed in the *GCP Cloud Functions* section: after an object is uploaded to a GCS bucket, a request/message can be generated and sent to GCP Pub/Sub, which can trigger an email notification and a cloud function to process the object. When the number of parallel object uploads is huge, Cloud Pub/Sub will help buffer/queue the requests/messages and decouple the GCS service from other cloud services such as Cloud Functions.

So far, we have covered various GCP services, including compute, storage, databases, and data analytics (big data). Now, let's take a look at various GCP **artificial intelligence** (**AI**) services.

GCP artificial intelligence services

The AI services in Google Cloud are some of its best services. Google Cloud's AI services include the following:

- **BigQuery ML (BQML)**
- TensorFlow and Keras
- Google Vertex AI
- Google ML API

Google BQML is built from Google Cloud BQ, which serves as a serverless big data warehouse and analytical platform. BQML trains ML models from the datasets already stored in BQ, using SQL-based languages. TensorFlow introduces the concepts of tensors and provides a framework for ML development, whereas Keras provides a high-level structure using TensorFlow. We will discuss BQML, TensorFlow, and Keras in more detail in part three of this book, along with Google Cloud Vertex AI and the Google Cloud ML API, which we will briefly introduce next.

Google Vertex AI

Google Vertex AI (`https://cloud.google.com/vertex-ai/docs/start/introduction-unified-platform`) aims to provide a fully managed, scalable, secure, enterprise-level ML development infrastructure. Within the Vertex AI environment, data scientists can complete all of their ML projects from end to end: data preparation and feature engineering; model training, validation, and tuning; model deployment and monitoring, and so on. It provides a unified API, client library, and user interface.

Vertex AI provides end-to-end ML services, including, but not limited to, the following:

- Vertex AI data labeling and dataset
- Vertex AI Feature Store
- Vertex AI Workbench and notebooks
- Vertex AI training
- Vertex AI models and endpoints
- Vertex AI Pipelines
- Vertex AI Metadata
- Vertex AI Experiments and TensorBoard

We will examine each of these in detail in the third part of this book.

Google Cloud ML APIs

Google Cloud ML APIs provide application interfaces to customers with Google's pre-trained ML models, which are trained with Google's data. The following are a few AI APIs:

- **Google Cloud sight APIs**, which include the Google Cloud Vision API and Cloud Video API. The pre-trained models of the sight APIs use ML to understand your images with industry-leading prediction accuracy. They can be used to detect objects/faces/scenes, read handwriting, and build valuable image/video metadata.

- **Google Cloud language APIs**, which includes the Natural Language Processing API and Translation API. These powerful pre-trained models of the Language API empower developers to easily apply **natural language understanding** (**NLU**) to their applications, alongside features such as sentiment analysis, entity analysis, entity sentiment analysis, content classification, and syntax analysis. The Translation API allows you to detect a language and translate it into the target language.

- **Google Cloud conversation APIs**, which include the Speech-to-Text, Text-to-Speech, and Dialogflow APIs. The pre-trained models of the Conversation APIs accurately convert speech into text, text into speech, and enable developers to develop business applications for call centers, online voice ordering systems, and so on using Google's cutting-edge AI technologies.

AI is the ability of a computer (or a robot controlled by a computer) to perform tasks that are usually done by humans because they require human intelligence. In the history of human beings, from vision development (related to the Cambrian explosion) to language development, to tool development, a fundamental question is, how did we humans evolve and how can we teach a computer to learn to see, speak, and use tools? The GCP AI service spectrum includes vision services(image recognition, detection, segmentation, and so on), language services(text, speech, translation, and so on), and many more. We will learn more about these services later in this book. We are certain that many more AI services, including hand detection tools, will be added to the spectrum in the future.

Summary

In this chapter, we started by creating a GCP free-tier account and provisioning our VM and storage bucket in the cloud. Then, we looked at the GCP organization's structure, resource hierarchy, and IAM. Finally, we looked at the GCP services that are related to ML, including compute, storage, big data and analytics, and AI, to have a solid understanding of each GCP service.

To help you with your hands-on GCP skills, we have provided examples in *Appendix 1*, *Practicing with Basic GCP Services*, where we have provided labs for provisioning basic GCP resources, step by step.

In the next chapter, we will build another foundation: Python programming. We will focus on Python basic skill development and Python data library usage.

Further reading

To learn more about the topics that were covered in this chapter, take a look at the following resources:

- `https://cloud.google.com/compute/`

- `https://cloud.google.com/storage/`

- `https://cloud.google.com/vpc`

- `https://cloud.google.com/products/databases`
- `https://cloud.google.com/products/security-and-identity`
- `https://cloud.google.com/solutions/smart-analytics`
- `https://cloud.google.com/products/ai`
- *Appendix 1, Practicing with Basic GCP Services*

2
Mastering Python Programming

Before we train a machine to learn, we need to teach it a language. Computers are very good at binary code since they were created to operate in zeros and ones. Human beings have invented a language compiler to compile a high-level language (such as Python) program into binary code so that a computer can run it. Python is a high-level language that is intuitive – it has a simplified syntax very similar to natural language. Python is widely used in solving problems using computer programming, especially in **machine learning** (**ML**).

In this chapter, we will start with a simple mathematical problem and show how Python can solve it directly and concisely. Understanding the solution will help us understand the Python basics, including variables, data structures, conditions, and controls. Then, we will cover Python's data processing packages, including NumPy and Pandas for data manipulation and Matplotlib and Seaborn for data visualization.

Python is a programming language and practicing is a big portion of mastering the language. In *Appendix 1* of this book, we have provided a step-by-step guide to using Python data processing packages. Practicing these steps is essential to mastering Python skills.

In the chapter, we will cover the following topics:

- The basics of Python
- Python data libraries and packages

Before we begin, let's take a look at the prerequisites for this chapter.

Technical requirements

To follow the instructions in this chapter, make sure that you have set up Google Colab, a product from Google Research that allows programmers to write and execute Python code through a browser (https://colab.research.google.com). Colab is well suited to ML and data analysis, and we will use it to run basic Python code in this chapter. Let's get started!

The basics of Python

We will cover the basics of Python programming by starting with a simple egg-counting problem.

There are less than 2,000 eggs in a big basket. Let's say that we take the eggs out in groups of two each time so that one egg is left in the basket at the end. Here, we have the following:

- If a group of 3 is used, 0 are left.
- If a group of 4 is used, 1 is left.
- If a group of 5 is used, 4 are left.
- If a group of 6 is used, 3 are left.
- If a group of 7 is used, 0 are left.
- If a group of 8 is used, 1 is left.
- If a group of 9 is used, 0 are left.

So, how many eggs are in the bucket?

Let's look at a solution to this problem using Python programming:

```
for i in range (1, 2001, 2):
    if ( ((i % 3) == 0) and ((i % 4) == 1) and ((i % 5) == 4)
and ((i % 6) == 3) and ((i % 7) == 0) and ((i % 8) == 1) and
((i % 9) == 0) ):
    print("Total number of eggs in the bucket can be %d" %i)
```

As you can see, we tell the computer to try each odd number (why?) between 1 and 2,000 and test it against all the conditions specified in the problem. If, for a certain number, all the conditions are met, then we print out the number. When all the odd numbers are examined, the numbers that meet the conditions are printed out. That's neat!

Executing the preceding program on Colab yields the following output:

```
Total number of eggs in the bucket can be 1449
```

If we examine the Python program more closely, we can observe the following: we use i as a variable that is assigned an odd number at a time, between 1 and 2000, and we use a for clause to construct a loop that repeatedly checks if the value of i satisfies the conditions (the if clause) and print the value if it does. The variables and their operations, the if clause, and the for clause are the basics of Python. Next, we will examine these basic concepts in Python.

Basic Python variables and operations

Programming languages use variables. A Python variable is a reserved memory location in a computer that stores values – that is, a variable in a Python program gives data to the computer for processing. Every value in Python has a data type. The action of placing data in a variable is called **assignment**. The action of calling a variable after it is created is called **using the variable**.

For example, the following actions are *assignments*:

Python Statement	Action
X=5	Assigns an integer, 5, to the X variable
Y=5.0	Assigns a real number, 5.0, to the Y variable
a="hello"	Assigns a string, "hello", to the a variable
b=True	Assigns a Boolean value, True, to the b variable

Table 2.1 – Python variable assignments

The following actions are *using variables*:

Python Statement	Action
c=x+y	Uses the x and y variables to assign the c variable
d=c ** x	Uses the x and c variables to assign the d variable

Table 2.2 – Python using variables

To further understand the variables' data types and their operations, let's run some small Python code snippets using Colab:

```
x = int(2.8)
print(x)
2

z = str(3.0)
```

```
z = float(z)
z = int(z/2)
z = z * 4.5
print(z)
4.5

z = z ** x
print (z)
20.25

y = float("3")
a = (x==y)
print (a)
False

b = ((z==z) and (a != x))
print (b)
True
```

Please take a moment here and make sure you understand how the preceding code snippet was executed to get the results.

For Python variables, we can operate on them using mathematical operations. The following table lists the arithmetic operations for Python variables:

Arithmetic Operation	Syntax	Examples
Addition	+	A=x+y
Subtraction	-	B=x-y
Multiplication	*	C=x*y
Division	/	C=x/y
Exponentiation	**	E=x**3

Table 2.3 – Python arithmetic operations

The following table lists the Boolean operations for Python variables:

Boolean Operation	Syntax	Examples
Equal	= =	x==y
Not equal	! =	x!=y
Less than	<	x<y
More than	>	x>y
Less than or equal to	<=	x<=y
More than or equal to	>=	x>=y

Table 2.4 – Python Boolean operations

The following table lists the logical operations for Python variables:

Logical Operation	Syntax	Examples
and	True if both operands are true	(x==y) and (a<b)
or	True if either operand is true	(x==y) or (a<b)
not	True if the operand is false	not (x==y)

Table 2.5 – Python logical operations

Now that we've introduced Python variables and their basic operations, let's look at Python's basic data structures and control operations.

Basic Python data structure

Python has five basic data types:

- Numbers
- Strings
- Lists
- Tuples
- Dictionaries

Since we've already covered numbers and strings, we will cover **lists**, **tuples**, and **dictionaries** here:

- A **list** is an ordered collection of values. The values in the list are called elements, or items. A list can contain zero or more items and is a collection that maintains the order of its items. Lists are written in brackets, [ ]. The following is an example:

```
ints = [10, 20, 30, 40]
words = ["flower", "soil", "water"]
mix = ["flower", -3.2, True, 6]
empty_list = []
floats = [4.7, -6.0, 0.22, 1.6]
```

The basic operations of lists are shown in the following table:

Operation	Definition	Example
len(list)	Returns the length of the list	len(floats)
list.append(elem)	Adds an element to the end of the list	floats.append(2.0)
list.pop()	Removes the element from the end of the list	floats.pop()

Table 2.6 – Python list operations

- A **tuple** is a collection of Python objects separated by commas. Like a list, a tuple has an index and allows nested objects. Unlike a list, which is mutable, a tuple is immutable. Tuples are written in round brackets, (). The following is an example:

```
coordinates = (1, 2, 3)
```

- A **dictionary** is a Python container that stores mappings of unique keys to their values. Unlike a set, a dictionary is unordered. Like a list, a dictionary is mutable. Dictionaries are written with curly brackets, {}, and the key-value pairs inside a dictionary are separated by commas (,). Each key is separated from its value by a colon (:). The following is an example:

```
person = {'name': 'Lini', 'year': 1989, 'expertise':
'data analytics'}
```

Python conditions and loops

Python programs need to make decisions based on conditions, such as the following:

- **if** (condition) **else** (action)
- **while** (condition) **do** (action loop)
- **for** (condition) **do** (action loop)

As you saw in the egg-counting program, it contains a `for` loop and `if` statements:

```
for i in range (1, 2001, 2):
    if ( ((i %for  3) == 0) and ((i % 4) == 1) and ((i % 5) ==
4) and ((i % 6) == 3) and ((i % 7) == 0) and ((i % 8) == 1) and
((i % 9) == 0) ):
    print («Total number of eggs is %d» %i)
```

With the `for` loop and `if` statements, the problem was solved. These control statements manage how the logic flows in Python programs.

Python functions

Python functions have two parts in a program: the **function definition** and the **function call**. First, a function is defined, and then the function that was defined is called. Let's look at an example to explain function definition and calling:

- **Problem**: Find all the prime numbers between 1 and 100
- **Solution**: Use Python functions

Here is how function definition and calling are used to solve the given problem:

1. *Function 1* takes in a number and checks if it's a prime number:

```
def Prime(Number):
for i in range(2, (int(math.sqrt(Number))+1)):
        if(Number % i == 0):
                return 0
        else:
                continue
        return 1
```

2. *Function 2* finds and returns all the prime numbers between the a and b integers. For each integer between a and b, it checks if it's a prime number by calling *Function 1*. If it is, then it adds it to a list. In the end, the list is returned:

```python
def PNlist(a,b):
        list=[]
        for Number in range (a, b):
            if (Prime(Number)==1):
                list.append(Number)
        return list
```

3. The main() program finds and returns all the prime numbers between 1 and 100:

```python
list1=PNlist(1,100)
print(list1)
```

As you can see, when the computer executes the main program, it will call *Function 2*, PNlist(1,100), to examine the numbers between 1 and 100: for each number, it will call *Function 1*, Prime(number), to see if it is a prime number or not – if it is, it's put into the list. Finally, the main() program prints the list of prime numbers.

Opening and closing files in Python

The following Python code opens an input file and reads it from user inputs:

1. Open a file named "lifeguards.in" for reading only.

2. Read a line in the file.

3. Convert the text read into integers:

```python
f1=open("lifeguards.in", "r")
n1=f1.readline()
n=int(n1)
f1.close
```

The following Python code block calculates the answer, writes it to the output file, and closes the file:

```python
answer=n*(n+1)/2
f2=open("lifeguards.out", "w")
f2.write(str(answer))
f2.close
```

Now that we have gone over the basics of Python, let's solve an interesting problem using the knowledge and skills we have learned so far.

An interesting problem

In this section, we'll use the basic Python knowledge and skills we have learned so far to solve the USA Computer Olympiad problem (source: http://www.usaco.org/index.php?page=viewproblem2&cpid=784).

Farmer John has opened a swimming pool and hired N cows as lifeguards, each of which has a shift that covers some contiguous interval of time during the day. For simplicity, the pool is open from time $t=0$ until time $t=1000$ daily, and each shift can be described by two integers – the starting and ending time. For example, a lifeguard starting at time $t=4$ and ending at time $t=7$ covers three time units. Unfortunately, John is over budgeted and must fire exactly one lifeguard. What is the maximum amount of time that can still be covered by the shifts of the remaining lifeguards? An interval of time is covered if at least one lifeguard is present. Let's take a look:

- **Input**

  The first line of input contains N *(1≤N≤100)*. Each of the next N lines describes a lifeguard in terms of two integers between 0 and 1000 to provide the start/end point of a lifeguard's shift. All such endpoints are distinct. The shifts of different lifeguards may overlap.

- **Output**

  Write a single number that specifies the maximum amount of time that can still be covered if Farmer John fires 1 lifeguard:

  ```
  SAMPLE INPUT:
  3
  5 9
  1 4
  3 7
  SAMPLE OUTPUT:
  7
  ```

Let's look at the following diagram to understand the problem:

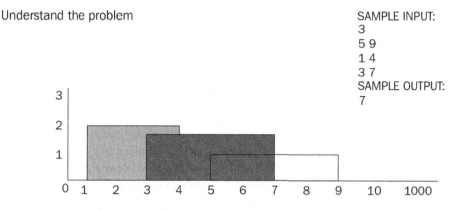

Figure 2.7 – Understanding the sample inputs and output

The preceding diagram shows the sample inputs and output. Here, we can see that there are three guards and that their time coverages are 5-9, 1-4, and 3-7, respectively. If we remove the first guard, the remaining coverage will be 1-7, which is 6. If we remove the second guard, the remaining coverage will be 3-9, which equals 6. If we remove the third guard, the remaining coverage will be 1-4 and 5-9, which equals 7. So, the maximum coverage when removing one guard at a time is $max(6,6,7)=7$.

Understanding this sample helps us think about the solution. We need to find out what the largest coverage is by comparing the remaining coverage after removing one guard at a time. The simplest way to do this is by using brute-force and Python lists. The following is a solution using Python:

1. Claim/initialize the variable and arrays:

    ```python
    start=[0 for i in range(1001)]
    end=[0 for i in range(1001)]
    cover=[0 for i in range(1001)]
    cover1=[0 for i in range(1001)]
    ```

2. Open the input file and read the input data:

    ```python
    f1 = open("lifeguards.in", "r")
    n=f1.readline()
    n=int(n)
    ```

3. Read the data and assign it to variables (`start[i]` and `end[i]` are the start/end time for guard `i`):

    ```python
    for i in range(1, n+1):
        a,b=f1.readline().split()
    ```

```
a=int(a)
b=int(b)
start[i]=a
end[i]=b
```

4. Use a new list to record the total guard coverage at time j:

```
for j in range (a, b):
    cover[j] += 1
f1.close()
```

5. Remove one guard at a time, compare the maximum coverages, and get the maximum:

```
answer=0
for i in range (1, n+1):
    for j in range (1, 1000):
    cover1[j]=cover[j]
    max = 0
    for j in range (int(start[i]), int(end[i])):
     cover1[j] -= 1
 for k in range (1, 1000):
        if (cover1[k] > 0): max=max+1
    if (answer < max):
    answer = max
```

6. Open the output file, write the output data in it, and close the file:

```
f2 = open("lifeguards.out", "w")
f2.write(str(answer))
F2.close()
```

While there are many solutions to this problem, this solution shows a simple and logical way to tackle the problem. It helps Python beginners follow and learn the problem-solving logic and skills that are required.

Python data libraries and packages

As we mentioned earlier, Python has five standard data types: numbers, strings, lists, tuples, and dictionaries. Using these data structures, Python can handle many tasks. To extend its ability for data manipulation and visualization, Python libraries and packages are created. We will briefly introduce four libraries: **NumPy**, **Pandas**, **Matplotlib**, and **Seaborn**.

NumPy

NumPy is short for **Numerical Python**. It is a fundamental library in Python and is a general-purpose array-processing package. NumPy is very good at basic and advanced array operations. It is used to process arrays that store values of the same data type.

Pandas

Pandas is considered the most powerful and flexible open source data analysis and manipulation tool available. It is a Python library that's been optimized for data manipulation and analysis. In particular, it offers data structures and operations for manipulating multidimensional arrays of data. Pandas contains the Series and DataFrame data structures. The Series data structure is for storing a 1D array (or vector) of data elements, whereas a DataFrame is a Pandas data structure for storing and manipulating 2D arrays. In practice, we often think of it as an Excel spreadsheet. Pandas also has a robust set of plotting functions that we will also use for dataset visualizing. The plotting features of Pandas can be found in the plotting module.

Matplotlib

Matplotlib is a graphics package for data visualization in Python. It is a plotting library for the Python programming language and its numerical mathematics extension, NumPy, and it is well integrated with NumPy and Pandas.

Seaborn

On top of Matplotlib, Seaborn is an open source Python library that is used for data visualization and exploratory data analysis. Seaborn works with Pandas DataFrames and supports built-in Python types such as lists and dictionaries. Most Seaborn functions support objects from the Pandas and NumPy libraries.

Summary

In this chapter, we reviewed the Python basics, including variables, data structures, condition and loop clauses, and various Python data libraries. It is essential to understand the Python code snippets in this chapter and go through the examples in *Appendix 2, Practicing with Python Data Libraries*, where we have provided examples to help you practice using Python data libraries, step by step. By doing so, you can develop Python code with Google Colab.

Now we have built up the foundation of GCP and Python, it is time to conclude *Part 1* of this book. In *Part 2*, we will explore the ML process, including problem framing, data preparation and feature engineering, ML model development, neural networks, and deep learning. In this next chapter, we will look at ML problem framing.

Further reading

To learn more about the topics that were covered in this chapter, take a look at the following resources:

- `https://colab.research.google.com/?utm_source=scs-index`
- `https://colab.research.google.com/github/cs231n/cs231n.github.io/blob/master/python-colab.ipynb`
- `https://www.geeksforgeeks.org/python-programming-language/`
- `https://www.geeksforgeeks.org/top-10-python-libraries-for-data-science-in-2021/`
- *Appendix 2, Practicing with Python Data Libraries*

Part 2:
Introducing
Machine Learning

This part introduces machine learning (ML) concepts. We start with the preparations for the machine learning process, including ML problem definition and data preparations. We dive into the ML process, including platform preparation, dataset splitting, model training, validation, testing, and deployment. We then introduce the modern ML concepts such as neural networks, deep learning, cost function, optimizer algorithm, activation function, and so on. We further discuss several neural network models and their business use cases.

This part comprises the following chapters:

- Chapter 3, Preparing for ML Development
- Chapter 4, Developing and Deploying ML Models
- Chapter 5, Understanding Neural Networks and Deep Learning

3

Preparing for ML Development

In *Part 2* of the book, we will examine the ML process. We will start from the preparation work, which includes ML problem framing to define an ML problem; data preparation and feature engineering to get the data ready; followed by the ML model development phases, which include model training, model validation, model testing, and model deployment. We will end *Part 2* with neural networks and DL.

In this chapter, will discuss the two ML preparation tasks: ML problem framing and data preparation. We will address the following questions for the problem we are solving:

- What are the business requirements?
- Is ML the best way to solve the problem?
- What are the inputs and outputs for the problem?
- Where is my data?
- How do I measure the success of the ML solution?
- Is the data ready?
- How do I collect my data?
- How do I transform and construct my data?
- How do I select features for the ML model?

It is very important that we identify the business requirements, understand the problem and its inputs/outputs, establish the business success measurements, and collect, transform, and construct high-quality datasets before model training and deployment. Through this process, we will learn and develop the following skills:

- Defining and understanding a business problem
- Translating it to an ML problem
- Defining and measuring the success of the business problem

- Defining high-quality datasets

- Collecting data

- Transforming and constructing data

- Feature engineering

Let's keep these questions and skills in mind as we go through this chapter.

Starting from business requirements

A typical ML process starts by defining business requirements. Follow the following steps to define the business requirements of the problem:

1. Clearly define the business outcome that your ML solution is supposed to achieve, among all the stakeholders. For example, for a prediction ML problem, we need to define a range of accuracy that is acceptable by the business and agreed upon by all the stakeholders.

2. Clearly define the data source of the ML problem. All ML projects are based on loads of data. You need to clearly define what the reliable data sources are, including training data, evaluation data, testing data, and a feed of regularly updated data.

3. Clearly define the frequency of ML model updating (since data distributions drift over time), and the strategies for maintaining production during the model updating times.

4. Clearly define the financial indications of the ML product or project. Understand any limitations such as resource availability and budget planning, and so on.

5. Clearly define the rules, policies, and regulations for the problem.

Let us look at an example of the problem and the business requirements:

- **Example 1**: A real estate company called Zeellow does great business buying and selling properties in the United States. Due to the nature of the business, accurately predicting house prices is critical for Zeellow. Over the past few years, they have accumulated a large amount of historical data for US houses.

Here, the business outcome is accurately predicting house prices in the United States. It is agreed by business stakeholders that more than 2% prediction error is not acceptable. The data source is defined as the in-house historical property database. Due to database updates, the model needs to be updated every month. There are two data scientists and two data engineers working full-time on the project, and enough funding has been provided. There are no regulations about the house data and the ML problem.

Defining ML problems

After we have identified the business requirements, we need to define the problem by identifying the features and target of the problem. For *Example 1*, the house price is the target, and features are the house attributes that affect the house price, such as the location, the house size (total square footage), the age of the house, the number of bedrooms and bathrooms of the house, and so on. *Table 3.1* shows a small sample dataset:

House No	Square Foot	Age	# of Bedrooms	# of Bathrooms	Longitude	Latitude	Sale Price
1	1500	5	2	1	-96.6988856	33.0198431	250
2	2000	10	3	2	-96.6988856	33.0198431	300
5	3000	40	3	2	-96.6988856	33.0198431	350
10	5500	50	4	3	-96.6988856	33.0198431	450

Table 3.1 – Example 1 dataset

The problem is then defined as building a model among the features and the target and discovering their relationships. During the problem definition process, we will understand the problem better, decide whether ML is the best solution for the problem, and to what category the problem belongs.

Is ML the best solution?

When facing a problem, the first thing we need to do is choose the best modeling/solution for the problem. For example, given the initial position and speed of a physical object, its mass, and the forces acting on it, how can we precisely predict its position at any time t? For this problem, a traditional mathematical model, based on Newton's laws in the classic mechanical world, works much better than any ML models!

While scientific modeling provides the mathematical relationship between the prediction target and features, there are many problems that are very hard or even impossible to build a mathematical model for, and ML may be the best way to solve these problems. How do we know whether ML is the best way to solve a given problem? There are several conditions that need to be checked when judging whether ML is a potentially good solution for a problem:

- There is a pattern among the features and the predicting target. For *Example 1*, we know the house price will be related to house features such as location, the total square footage, age, and so on, and there are patterns between the house price and its features.

- The existing pattern or relationship cannot be modeled using mathematics or science. For *Example 1*, the relationships between the price of the house and the features cannot be mathematically formulated.

- There is plenty of quality data available. For *Example 1*, Zeellow has accumulated a large amount of historical data for US houses, including prices and their features.

- In *Example 1*, Zeellow needs to predict house prices. Apparently, there are relationships between the house price and the features of the house, but it is very difficult to build a mathematical model to describe the relationships. Since we have enough historical data, ML is potentially a good way to solve the problem.

Let's look at more examples and see whether ML is the best solution for them:

- **Example 2**: Zeellow Mortgage is a subsidiary of Zeellow and is a mortgage business in the States. They have also accumulated a large amount of historical data on mortgage applicants and are trying to automate the decision process of approval or denial for new applications.

- **Example 3**: Zeellow Appraisal is a subsidiary of Zeellow and they evaluate the prices of existing houses when they are under contract. One good approximation for that is to see how similar properties are priced, and this leads to the grouping of properties.

After we examine these two problems and check their conditions, we can decide whether ML is the way to solve the problems. Further, we will look at the categories of ML problems and what types our three examples belong to.

ML problem categories

ML problems can be divided into several categories. For *Example 1*, Zeellow needs to predict house prices, which is a continuous value, compared to *Example 2* where ML needs to predict an approval (yes) or denial (no) for a mortgage application. An ML problem that outputs a continuous value is called **Regression**, while a problem that outputs discrete values (two or more) is called **Classification**. If there are two outputs (yes and no), then it's called **Binary classification**. If there are more than two outputs, then it's called **Multiclass classification**.

In both *Example 1* and *Example 2*, we let the machine learn from the existing dataset that is labeled with results. *Example 1*'s datasets are for houses that have been sold in the past few years and thus include house location, the number of bedrooms and bathrooms, the age of the house and the sale price. *Example 2*'s datasets include the mortgage applicant's gender, age, income, marital status, and so on, and whether the application was approved or denied. Since the inputs for both examples are labeled, they are called **supervised learning**. Input data such as the house's location, the number of bedrooms and bathrooms, and the age of the house in *Example 1*, and the applicant's gender, age, income, and marital status in *Example 2*, are called **features** since they reflect the datasets attributes (features).

Unsupervised learning problems, on the other hand, have inputs that are not labeled. For *Example 3*, Zeellow Appraisal needs to divide houses into different groups, and each group has similar features. The focus here is not on the house prices but to identify meaningful patterns in the data and split the houses into groups. Since we do not label the datasets, it is an unsupervised learning problem.

Another type of machine learning problem is **reinforcement learning** (**RL**). In RL, you don't collect examples with labels. You set up the model (agent) and a reward function to reward the agent when it performs a task. With reinforcement learning, the agent can learn very quickly how to outperform humans. More details can be found on the Wikipedia page (`https://en.wikipedia.org/wiki/Reinforcement_learning`).

ML model inputs and outputs

In an ML problem, the inputs are usually datasets, including all kinds of data formats/media such as numerical data, images, audio, and so on. Input datasets are extremely important and will decide how good the ML model will be.

For supervised learning, labeled data is used to train the model, which is a piece of software representing what a machine has learned from the training data. Inputs to supervised learning are marked datasets of features and targets, and the model learns by comparing the labeled target values with the model outputs to find errors. The error is what we want to optimize. Note we refer to the optimization of the error, not the minimization of the error. In other words, minimizing the error to zero may not generate the best model.

Within supervised learning, the output for a regression model is a continuous numerical value, and for a classification model, the output is a discrete value indicating a category (yes/no for binary classifications).

For unsupervised learning, input data is not labeled, and usually, the objective is to find the input data patterns and group them into different categories, called **clustering** or **grouping**.

For reinforcement learning, the input is a state, and the output is the action performed by ML. Between input and output, we have a function that takes a state as input and returns an action as output.

Measuring ML solutions and data readiness

After we define the problem and conclude that ML is a potentially good solution to the problem, we need to set up a way of measuring the problem solution and whether it's ready for production deployment. For *Example 1*, we need to have a consensus as to what range is acceptable for the house prediction errors and we can use the ML model in production.

ML model performance measurement

To evaluate the performance of ML solutions, we use ML metrics. For regression models, there are three metrics: mean square error, mean absolute error, and r-square. For classification models, we use the confusion matrix. We will discuss that more in the following chapters.

Is the ML solution ready to be deployed? We need to circle back to the model's original business goals in the ML problem framing:

- For Zeellow, is predicting a house price with 95% accuracy good enough?

- For Zeellow Mortgage, are we allowed to make a decision with 95% confidence?

- For Zeellow Appraisal, can we categorize a house into the proper group with 95% accuracy?

After we have evaluated the ML model with the testing datasets and confirmed that the model reaches the business requirements, we will be ready to deploy it into production.

Data readiness

Data plays such a significant role in the machine learning process that the quality of data has a huge impact on the model performance, the so-called *garbage in, garbage out*. An ML model's accuracy relies on many factors, including the size and quality of the dataset. The perception that *The more data, the more model accuracy* is not always true. In real time, it is a big challenge to obtain a big amount of clean, high-quality data. Often in an ML project, we spend a big portion of time collecting and preparing the datasets. Depending on the ML problem we need to solve, there are several ways to collect data and sources to collect it from. For example, we can go with the following:

- Historical data collected by companies, such as user data and media data

- Publicly available data from research institutes and government agencies

How much data is enough for my ML model, and how do we measure the quality of our data? It depends on the type of machine learning problem you want to solve. As part of the problem framing process, we need to check and make sure we have enough high-quality data to go with building an ML solution. Next, we will discuss more details about data preparation and feature engineering.

Collecting data

Data collection is collecting the source data and storing it in a central safe location. In the data collection phase, we try to answer the following questions:

- What is the nature of the problem and do we have the right data for it?

- Where is the data and do we have access to the data?

- What can we do to ingest all the data into one central repository?

- How do we safeguard the central data repository?

These questions are crucial in any ML project because, in a real business, data is typically spread across many different heterogeneous source systems, and bringing all the source data together to form a dataset may involve huge challenges.

A common data collection and consolidation process called **Extract, Transform, and Load** (ETL) has the following steps:

1. **Extract**: Pull the data from the various sources to a single location.

2. **Transform**: During data extraction and consolidation, we may need to change the data format, modify some data, remove duplicates, and so on.

3. **Load**: Data is loaded into a single repository, such as Google Cloud Storage or Google BigQuery.

During this ETL process, we also need to address the data size, quality, and security:

- **Data size**: How much data do we need to get useful ML results? While the answer is dependent on the ML problem, the rule of thumb is that the training datasets will be several times more than the model's trainable parameters. For example, a typical regression problem may need ten times as many observations as features. A typical image classification problem may require tens of thousands of images to create a high-accuracy image classifier. Generally speaking, simple models trained with large datasets perform better than complex models with small datasets.

- **Data quality**: This can include the following:

  - **Reliability**: Are the data sources reliable? Is the dataset labeled correctly? Is the dataset filtered properly? Are there duplicates or missing values?

  - **Feature representation**: Does the dataset represent the useful ML features? Are there any outliers?

  - **Consistency between training and production data**: Are there any skews that exist between the datasets for training and for production?

- **Data security**: Is the data secure? Do we need to encrypt the data? Is there any **Personally Identifiable Information** (**PII**) in the dataset? Are there any laws or regulatory requirements for accessing the dataset?

After the data is collected and stored in a central safe repository, we need to construct and transform it into the right format so that it can be used for ML model training. We will discuss this in the next section.

Data engineering

The objectives of data engineering are to make sure that the datasets represent the real ML problem and have the right format for ML model training. Often, we use statistical techniques to sample, balance, and scale datasets, and handle missing values and outliers in the datasets. This section covers the following:

- Sampling data with sub-datasets
- Balancing dataset classes
- Transforming data

Let us start with data sampling and balancing.

Data sampling and balancing

Data sampling is a statistical analysis technique used to select, manipulate, and analyze a representative subset in a larger dataset. Sampling data plays an important role in data construction. When sampling data, you need to be very careful not to introduce biased factors. For more details, please refer to `https://developers.google.com/machine-learning/data-prep/construct/sampling-splitting/sampling`.

A classification dataset has more than two dataset classes. We call the classes that make up a large proportion of the set **majority classes**, and those that make up a small proposition **minority classes**. When the dataset has skewed class proportions – meaning the proportion of the minority classes is significantly less than that of the majority classes, it is an imbalanced dataset, and we need to balance it using statistical techniques called **downsampling** and **upweighting**. Let's consider a fraud detection dataset with 1 positive and 200 negatives. The model training process will not reflect the real problem since the positive proportion is so small. In this case, we will need to process the dataset in two steps:

- **Downsampling**: Extract data examples from the dominant class to balance the classes. With a factor of 50 downsampling, the proportion will be 40:1 after downsampling.
- **Upweighting**: Increase the dominant class weight by the same factor of 50 (the same as the downsampling factor) during ML model training.

Some ML libraries have provided built-in features to facilitate the process. For more details about the techniques and why we perform the previous steps, refer to `https://developers.google.com/machine-learning/data-prep/construct/sampling-splitting/imbalanced-data`.

Numerical value transformation

For a dataset that has numeric features covering distinctly different ranges (for example, the age feature in a mortgage application approval ML model), it is strongly recommended to normalize the dataset since it will help algorithms such as gradient descent to converge. Common ways to normalize data are the following:

- Scaling to a range
- Clipping
- Log scaling
- Bucketing/binning

Scaling to a range

Scaling to a range normalization is converting floating-point feature values from their natural range (for example, the age range of 0-90) into a standard range (for example, 0 to 1, or -1 to +1). When you know the approximate range (upper and lower bounds) of your data, and the data is approximately uniformly distributed across that range, then it is a good normalization practice. For example, most age values fall between 0 and 90, and every part of the range has a substantial number of people, thus normalizing age values is a common practice.

Feature clipping

Feature clipping caps all feature values above (or below) a certain value to a fixed value. If your dataset contains extreme outliers, feature clipping may be a good practice. For example, you could clip all temperature values above 80 to be exactly 80. Feature clipping can be applied before or after other normalizations.

Log scaling

Log scaling computes the log of your feature values, thus compressing a wide data range to a narrow range. When a handful of the data values have many points and most of the other values have few points, *log scaling* becomes a good transformation method. For example, movie ratings are good business use cases for *log scaling*, since most movies have very few ratings, while a few movies have lots of ratings.

Bucketing

Bucketing is also called binning. It transforms numeric features into categorical features, using a set of thresholds. A good example is transforming house prices into low, medium, and high categories, for better modeling.

Categorical value transformation

Categorical values are discrete values that aren't in an ordered relationship, with each value marking a category. If categorical data doesn't have any order to it, for example, a *color* feature that has values such as red, green, and blue, and there is no preference among the categories, if you assign values of *1*, *2*, and *3* to represent *red*, *green*, and *blue*, respectively, the model might interpret blue as more important than red, since it has a higher numeric value. We often encode non-ordinal data into multiple columns or features, called **one-hot encoding**. *Figure 3.2* shows the one-hot encoding transformation for the color feature – red is 100, blue is 010, and green is 001:

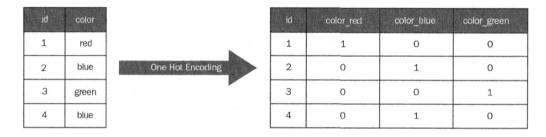

Figure 3.2 – One-hot encoding for the "color" feature

One-hot encoding transforms the non-ordinal categorical values into numerical values without introducing any ordinal bias. It is used widely in ML data transformations.

Missing value handling

When preparing the dataset, we often see missing data. For example, some columns in your dataset might be missing because of a data collection error, or data wasn't collected on a particular feature. Missing data can make it difficult to accurately interpret the relationship between the feature and the target variable and dealing with missing data is an important step in data preparation.

Based on what has caused the missing data, the total dataset size, and the proportion of missing values, we can either drop the whole feature or impute the missing values. For example, if a row or column has a large percentage of missing values, *dropping* the entire row or column may be a viable option. If the missing values are randomly spread throughout the dataset and it's only a small portion of its rows or columns, then *imputation* may be a better option. For categorical variables, we can usually replace missing values with mean, median, or most frequent values. For numerical or continuous variables, we typically use the mean or median to impute. Sometimes, we also encounter nulls or zeros, but those should be approached with care as zero can be a value in a column while an ETL pipeline will replace all missing values with zero.

Outlier processing

Often, we also see outliers – data points that lie at an abnormal distance from other values in the dataset. Outliers can make it harder for models to predict accurately because they skew values away from the other more normal values that are related to that feature. Depending on the causes of the outliers, you want to clean them up, or transform them to add richness to your dataset (some algorithms have built-in functions to handle outliers):

- **Deleting the outlier or imputing the outlier**: If your outlier is based on an artificial error, such as incorrectly entered data
- **Transforming the outlier**: Taking the natural log of a value to reduce the outlier's influence on the overall dataset

Through the previously shown process of data construction and transformation, the dataset is ready. And now it's time to go to the next step: checking and selecting the features (the variables that affect the model target) – the process called feature engineering.

Feature engineering

Feature engineering is the process of selecting and transforming the most relevant features in ML modeling. It is one of the most important steps in the ML learning process. Feature engineering includes **feature selection** and **feature synthesis** (transformation).

Feature selection

For an ML problem that has a lot of features extracted during the initial phase, feature selection is used to reduce the number of those features (input variables), so that we can focus on the features that are most useful to a model to predict the target variable. After you extract features for the problem, you need to use feature selection methods to choose the most appropriate features for model training. Depending on whether ML training is needed, there are two main types of feature selection methods you can use – filter methods and wrapper methods:

- **Filter methods** use statistical techniques to evaluate and score the relationship between each input variable and the target variable. The scores are used to compare the features and decide the input variables that will be used in the model.
- **Wrapper methods** create many models with different subsets of input features and perform model training and compare their performances. The feature subsets fitting the best-performing model according to a performance metric will be selected. Wrapper methods need ML training on different subsets.

Feature synthesis

A synthetic feature is created algorithmically, usually with a combination of the real features using arithmetic operations such as addition, subtraction, multiplication, and division to train machine learning models. **Feature synthesis** provides great insights into data patterns and helps model training for some ML problems.

After data collection, construction and transformation, and feature engineering, our data is ready for the next stage – modeling development.

Summary

In this chapter, we discussed preparations for an ML process. Starting from business requirements, you need to understand the problem and see if ML is the best solution for it. You then define the ML problem, set up performance measurement, and identify the data to be used for ML modeling to make sure we have a high-quality dataset.

Data plays such an important role! We have also discussed data preparation and feature engineering in this chapter. From data collection and construction to data transformation, feature selection, and feature synthesis, data pipelines prepare the dataset for ML model training. Mastering these data preparation and feature engineering skills will provide us with insights into the data and help us in model development. In the next chapter, we will discuss the ML model development process, from model training and validation to model testing and deployment.

Further reading

For further insights into what you've learned in this chapter, you can refer to the following links:

- `https://developers.google.com/machine-learning/problem-framing`
- `https://developers.google.com/machine-learning/data-prep`

4

Developing and Deploying ML Models

In the previous chapter, we discussed the preparation stage for the ML process, including problem framing and data preparation. After we have framed the problem and have a clean dataset, it's time to develop and deploy the ML model. In this chapter, we will discuss the model development process. We will start from model data input and hardware/software platform setup, then focus on the model development pipeline, including model training, validation, testing, and finally deploying to production. Our emphasis is on understanding the basic concepts and the thought processes behind them and strengthening the knowledge and skills by practicing. The following topics are covered in this chapter:

- Splitting the dataset
- Building the platform
- Training the model
- Validating the model
- Tuning the model
- Testing and deploying the model
- Practicing with scikit-learn

In *Appendix 3*, we provide practice examples of ML model development using the Python data science package scikit-learn.

Splitting the dataset

Through the data preparation process, we have gained a dataset that is ready to be used for model development. To avoid model underfitting and overfitting, it is a best practice to split the dataset randomly yet proportionally, into independent subsets based on the model development process: a training dataset, a validation dataset, and a testing dataset:

- **Training dataset**: The subset of data used to train the model. The model will learn from the training dataset.

- **Validation dataset**: The subset of data used to validate the trained model. Model hyperparameters will be tuned for optimization based on validation.

- **Testing dataset**: The subset of data used to evaluate a final model before its deployment to production.

A common practice is to use 80 percent of the data for the training subset, 10 percent for validation, and 10 percent for testing. When you have a large amount of data, you can split it into 70 percent training, 15 percent validation, and 15 percent testing.

Preparing the platform

While data input has a big impact on model quality, the hardware/software platform where we train/validate/test the model will also impact the model and the development process. Choosing the right platform is very important to the ML process.

While certainly, you can choose to use a desktop or laptop for ML model development, it is a recommended practice to use cloud platforms, thanks to the great advantages that cloud computing provides: self-provisioning, on-demand, resilience, and scalability, at a global scale. Many tools are provided in cloud computing to assist data scientists in data preparation and model development.

Among the cloud service providers, Google Cloud Platform provides great ML platforms to data scientists: flexible, resilient, and performant, from end to end. We will discuss more details of the Google Cloud ML platform in the third part of the book.

Now that we have prepared the datasets and ML platform, let's dive right into the ML model development process, starting with model training.

Training the model

Using the training data subset, on the platform, we train ML models to learn the relationships between the target and the features. ML model training is an iterative process: it starts from an assumed model with initial parameters and continues the learning process until it fits the training dataset. *Figure 4.1* shows a sample ML model training process, where we have selected a linear regression model ($z=wx+b$)

and chosen the initial parameters (*w* and *b*). We calculate the model predict-error – the gap between the model output and the actual data label – this step is called forward propagation. If the error is not optimized (the accuracy is not within the specified range), we will need to move back and adjust the model's parameters (*w* and *b*) – this step is called backward propagation. We will then go forward to recalculate the error again. This model training process repeats the steps of *forward propagation*, *backward propagation*, and *forward propagation* until we get a model that yields the predict-error within the expected range, that is, meeting the accuracy defined by the business objectives. The model training process is then complete.

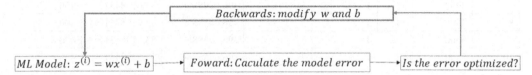

Figure 4.1 – ML model training process

As you may have noticed, we chose a linear model (*z=wx+b*) in the previous example. In real life, we often use domain knowledge and certain assumptions when selecting an ML model. It could be linear, polynomial, or even something that can only be expressed by neural networks.

Next, we will look at the sample ML problems framed in the previous chapter (*examples 1, 2*, and *3*), discuss linear regression and binary classification, and then extend them to advanced models and algorithms.

Linear regression

In *Chapter 3, Preparing for ML Development*, we talked about *example 1*: Zeellow needs to accurately predict house prices from their historical dataset. Since the inputs for the problem are labeled, it is a supervised learning problem, and since the output is a continuous value, it is a regression problem.

From a mathematical point of view, this is a typical problem of finding the function (relationship) between the target and the features, and the only things we have are the sample datasets. So, how do we figure out the function? Let's inspect a simple dataset of *example 1*: the sale prices for 10 houses for a certain time period, at a certain location. The sample dataset is shown in *Table 4.2*.

House No	Square Foot (x)	Age	BedRoom	BathRoom	Longitude	Latitude	Sale Price (y, $k)
1	1500	5	2	1	-96.6988856	33.0198431	250
2	2000	10	3	2	-96.6988856	33.0198431	300
3	2500	20	3	2	-96.6988856	33.0198431	300
4	2750	10	3	2	-96.6988856	33.0198431	400
5	3000	40	3	2	-96.6988856	33.0198431	350
6	3500	30	3	2	-96.6988856	33.0198431	375
7	4000	5	4	3	-96.6988856	33.0198431	450
8	4500	30	4	3	-96.6988856	33.0198431	400
9	5000	10	4	3	-96.6988856	33.0198431	450
10	5500	50	4	3	-96.6988856	33.0198431	450

Table 4.2 – Example 1 housing dataset

There are multiple features related to the target (house price). We will start by examining the relationship between the house price and one feature of the house. Let us look at the house sale price (target, denoted by y) and the house square footage (feature, denoted by x), leading to the topic of one variable regression.

One variable regression

As you can see from *Table 4.2*, there are 10 rows from the sample training dataset, and we need to find a function $y=f(x)$ that will best describe the relationship between target y and feature x. Naturally, we will use a diagram to visualize their relationship. If we put the 10 items in the dataset into a coordinate system, we get *Figure 4.3*. As you can see, there are 10 points distributed in the first quadrant and we need to make an assumption about the relationship between the house price (y) and the house square footage (x). Is it a linear function (as shown by lines l_1 and l_2) or a quadratic function (curve shown as d1) that represents the relationship of y and x? Evidently, d1 does not work since intuitively we know that y will increase when x increases. Now, among line l_1 and l_2, which one do we choose? This becomes a one-variable linear regression problem: find the best line $y=w^*x+b^*$ (with parameters w^* and b^*) that best fits the training dataset.

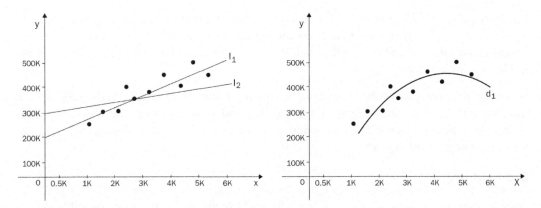

Figure 4.3 – Linear regression

Our objective here is to find the function that best fits the existing data and will predict the best target value (closest to the actual value) for new data. How do you define a *best fit*? To answer this question, we came up with the mathematical concept of a *cost function* to measure a model's performance: the difference or distance between the predicted values and the actual values.

There are several ways to measure the difference between predicted values and actual values. Denote (x_i, y_i) using the coordinate of the ith data point; that is, y_i is the actual value for x_i, and $\hat{y}$ is the predicted value for x_i. The cost function can then be defined as one of the following (here N is the number of samples, $N=10$ for our *example 1*):

- The **Mean Absolute Error (MAE)** is the sum of the absolute differences between the prediction and true values:

$$MAE = \frac{1}{N}\sum_{i=1}^{N} |y_i - \hat{y}_i|$$

- The **Mean Squared Error (MSE)** is the sum of the squared differences between the prediction and true values:

$$MSE = \frac{1}{N}\sum_{i=1}^{N} (y_i - \hat{y}_i)^2$$

While the MSE and MAE can be both used as cost functions, there are some differences between them: minimizing the MAE tends to decrease the gap at each point and can lead some to zeros (thus removing some features and making the model scarce). Minimizing the MSE will avoid big gaps but will not lead to zero gaps.

Now the problem becomes: how do we choose the right parameter (w, b) such that the MSE or MAE is minimized? We will use the MSE as the cost function, and our focus is to find the right parameters (w, b) so that the cost function MSE is minimized for the training dataset. To that end, we introduce the concept of **gradient descent**.

Gradient descent

From a mathematical point of view, if we simplify the MSE function with just one variable w, then the diagram will be something similar to *Figure 4.4*. Mathematically we can find the value w^* that minimizes $f(w)$ by using derivatives, since the derivative of $f(w)$ is zero at w^*.

From a computer programming point of view, we will need to use an algorithm called gradient descent to find the best point w^*. With one variable, a gradient is the derivative of the cost function. Starting from an initial point (w_0, f_0), we want to find the next point at (w_1, f_1) where $f_1 = f(w_1)$ is smaller than $f_0 = f(w_0)$. Since the derivative of $f(w)$ at w_0 is negative and we want to minimize f, the moving direction from w_0 to w_1 will be increasing, and the moving magnitude (also called step-size or learning rate) needs to be tweaked, such that it will neither be too small to cause many steps to reach w^* nor be too big and cause divergence away from w^*.

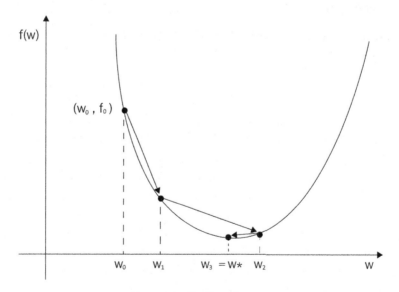

Figure 4.4 – Gradient descent

Figure 4.4 also shows the steps for the gradient descent algorithm: moving from the initial point *(w₀, f₀)* to *(w₁, f₁)*, to *(w₂, f₂)*, till it reaches the optimized point *(w₃, f₃) = (w*, f*)*. Note that the starting point is important for non-convex cost functions where multiple minimum values existed for *w*, as shown in *Figure 4.5*.

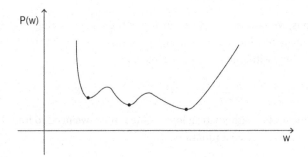

Figure 4.5 – Non-convex cost functions

The gradient descendent algorithm lets us find the minimum *f* value by repeatedly moving from *(wᵢ, fᵢ)* to *(wᵢ₊₁, fᵢ₊₁)*, in the direction as depicted by the gradient at the point *(wᵢ, fᵢ)*: if gradient *(wᵢ)* is negative, move toward the direction of increasing *w*; otherwise, move toward decreasing *w*. After certain moves, if we can find the minimum *f** at point *(w* f*)*, we call the model converges at weight *w**, and we have found the parameter *w**. Otherwise, the model is non-convergent. After we find the converged *w**, finding parameter *b** is relatively easy, and we have found the best fit line: *f(x) = w*x + b**, which can be used to predict the house price for new values of *x*.

Extending to multiple features (variables)

With the gradient descendent algorithm, we are able to find the best model that fits the sample dataset. We will use it to predict the sale price (target *y*) from new data. In real life, there are many features affecting a house's sale price, such as its age, the number of bedrooms and bathrooms, and of course the house's location. So, we need to extend our model to multiple features (variables).

When extending to multiple features, we use a vector $X=(x_1, x_2, x_3, ..., x_n)^T$ to represent the multiple feature values $x_1, x_2, x_3, ..., x_n$, and the linear function will become this:

```
Y=WX+B
```

where *W* is a matrix and *B* is a vector.

Then, the cost function can be written as follows:

```
F (W) =WᵀAW/2
```

where *A* is a matrix constructed from the dataset.

Mathematically, we can find the value W that minimizes $F(W)$ by using partial derivatives with multiple variables. Accordingly, we can also extend the gradient descendent algorithm from one dimension to multiple dimensions, to find a matrix W that best fits the datasets by minimizing the cost function $F(W)$.

Extending to non-linear regression

In previous discussions, we assumed the relationship of the sale price (target y) and the house square footage x is linear. In many real-life ML models, there always exist non-linear relationships, for example, a polynomial relationship (with one feature/variable x here):

$$y = w_1x + w_2x^2 + w_3x^3 + \dots + w_nx^n$$

From linear to non-linear, the mathematical logic is the same – we need to find the model parameters $(w_1, w_2, \dots w_n)$ by minimizing the cost function.

By extending from the linear one-variable solution to non-linear and multi-variables, the regression model solves the type of ML problems that predict continuous values. Due to the mathematical complexity of the problem, we will not discuss it further here. In the next section, we will look at another type of ML problem, **classification**, and we will start with the simplest case of binary classification.

Binary classification

In the previous chapter, we also talked about another sample ML problem (*example 2*) – Zeellow Lender is trying to automate the decision process of approval or denial for new loan applications. Since the model output is *yes* or *no*, this is a binary classification problem. Another type of classification problem is multi-category classification. For example, given an image, we need to tell whether it is a dog, a cat, or a cow.

For classification problems, we always use the concept of *probability*. For *example 2*, the ML model will output *yes* or *no*, based on the customer's loan default probabilities: if the default probability is higher than a threshold value, we will deny the application. For the image classification example, we will say how probable it is that the image is of a cat, a dog, or a cow. Let us start with the binary problem of *example 2*.

Logistic regression

From a mathematical point of view, *example 2* is a problem of finding the function (relationship) between the target (*yes/no*) and the application features, and the only thing we have are the sample datasets. So, how do we figure out the function? Let's inspect a simple dataset we have with *example 2*: the loan application decisions for 10 applications for a certain time period at a certain location. The sample dataset is shown in *Table 4.6*.

No	Applicant Credit Score	Loan amount($k)	Annual Income (x, $k)	Age	Marriage status	Approval or not (1 for yes, 0 for no)
1	730	300	150	45	1	1
2	670	200	100	20	0	1
3	700	300	50	20	0	0
4	780	150	80	32	0	1
5	400	300	20	29	0	0
6	500	120	70	38	0	1
7	690	200	140	25	1	1
8	823	300	150	30	1	1
9	450	100	30	49	1	0
10	650	200	120	27	1	1

Table 4.6 – Example 2 loan dataset

From *Table 4.6*, we can see that there are many features of an applicant that affect their loan application's approval or denial. To simplify, we choose the applicant's income x as the single feature/variable and use z as a linear function of x:

$z = wx + b$

Since the final output target is a yes (*1*) or no (*0*), we will need a function that maps the above z value to a probability p that has a value between *0* and *1*: the probability of approving the loan (target variable $y=1$).

From statistics, we have the following:

```
p=eᶻ/(1+eᶻ)=1/(1+e⁻ᶻ)
```

And this is the so-called **sigmoid function** *(Figure 4.7)*, which maps the probability of loan approval p with the value of z.

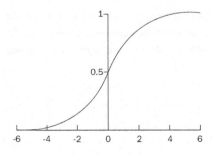

Figure 4.7 – Sigmoid function

With the sigmoid function, the output transforms a real value z to a probability value p, which is between 0 and 1. This brings in the concept of *logistic regression*, a classification algorithm used to predict the probability of a target value of yes (*1*). Simply put, logistic regression can be thought of as a linear regression with the output as the probability of target is *1*, ranging in $(0,1)$.

The threshold for binary classification

As we see from the preceding binary classification model, logistic regression returns a probability value between 0 and 1. To convert a probability value to a classification, we need to determine the threshold value – when the probability is above the threshold, the class is *1* (yes); otherwise, it is *0* (no). For *Example 2*, if you set the threshold as *0.9*, then you will approve the loan application when the probability is higher than 90%; otherwise, you will reject the application. But how do we define the threshold? The answer is related to the business case and a model measurement metric called a **confusion matrix**. We will discuss them more in the model validation section.

Extending to multi-class classification

We can extend binary classification problems to multi-class classification problems. There are different ways to go from binary to multi-class. Given a multi-classification model, we can decompose it into multiple binary classification problems. Please refer to the following link for more details:

```
https://svivek.com/teaching/lectures/slides/multiclass/multiclass-full.pdf
```

So far, we have discussed regression and classification problems and introduced the gradient descent algorithm. Now let's look at some advanced algorithms.

Support vector machine

One popular advanced ML algorithm is called **support vector machine**, or **SVM**. It is a model commonly used for classification problems. The idea of SVM is simple: the algorithm finds a line (two dimensions) or a hyperplane (three or more dimensions) that separates the data into different classes.

Let's use a two-dimension separation problem to illustrate SVM. As shown in *Figure 4.8*, we are trying to find a line that separates the points into two groups: a group of circles and a group of squares. There are three lines separating the points. Out of the three lines, which one is the best choice?

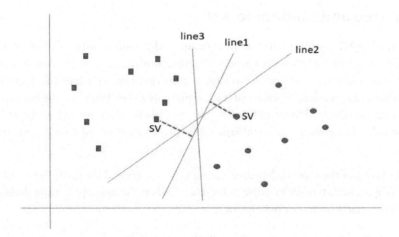

Figure 4.8 – SVM illustration

Let's take a closer look at the diagram. For each line, there are points that are closest to the line from both classes – we call these points **support vectors**, and we call the distance between the line and its support vectors the **margin**. The objective of SVM is to maximize the margin. Out of the three lines in *Figure 4.8*, you can see that line 1 is our choice since it has the greatest margin out of the three.

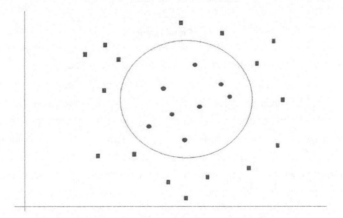

Figure 4.9 – Non-linear curve separating the data

If we extend this two-dimensional problem to three dimensions, then a hyperplane for which the margin is maximum is the optimal hyperplane. Nevertheless, both are still linear models. However, in real life, the separation is often not linear. *Figure 4.9* shows an example where the separation is a circle (non-linear).

Decision tree and random forest

For a classification ML problem with multiple features, the natural thing to think of doing would be to classify the feature values – do a binary classification at each feature. Another popular ML algorithm, the decision tree model, uses this logic to construct a decision tree, in which each internal node represents a test on a feature, each leaf node represents a class label, and the branches represent feature combinations that lead to the leaf nodes – the class labels. From root to leaf, the paths represent classification rules. Decision trees are constructed to split a dataset based on different conditions for each feature.

Decision tree is one of the most widely used methods for supervised learning. *Figure 4.10* illustrates a logic flow of a decision tree for *example 2* discussed earlier: the loan application decision process. The decision tree starts from the credit history:

- If the credit history (score) is good, it will check the applicant's income and the loan amount – if the income is low and the loan amount is big, it will reject the application. Otherwise, the loan application will be approved.

- If the credit history is bad, it will check the applicant's income and loan amount – if the income is high and the loan amount is small, it will approve the application. Otherwise, the loan application will be rejected:

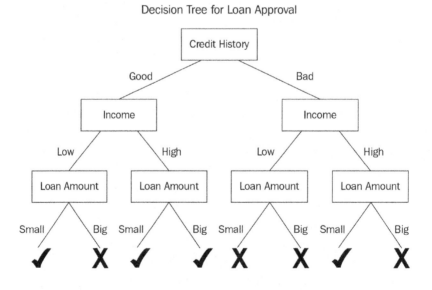

Figure 4.10 – Decision tree for example 2

With the decision-tree model, you can predict results based on new feature data, such as a new application's feature values. However, in a situation where the dataset size is large, then a decision tree can be complex and may lead to overfitting. To tackle the problem, we often use random forest, which consists of many decision trees. Random forest gets the predictions from these individual decision trees and does a final optimization by combining the decision tree prediction values with a voting or averaging process. Random forest is usually better than a single decision tree because it avoids overfitting using the averaging or voting mechanism.

In this section, we discussed various ML model training algorithms: from one-variable linear regressions to multi-variable non-linear regressions; from binary classifications to multi-class classifications; from support vector machine to decision trees and random forest. The result of ML training is a model that fits the training dataset well. Will such a model make good predictions on new production data? The answer is that we need to validate the model using the validation dataset before deploying the model to test and predict production data.

Validating the model

After you train your model, you will need to determine whether it will perform well in predicting the target on future new data, and that is the validation process: you must validate the model performance on a labeled dataset that was not used in training – the validation dataset that was built during the dataset splitting phase.

Model validation

Recall what we have discussed in *Chapter 3*: in the ML problem framing phase, you define the business problem and craft a business metric to measure model success. Now, in this model validation phase, the model validation metric needs to be linked to that business metric as closely as possible.

Earlier in this chapter, we have defined the cost function, which is used to find the optimized model. The cost function is also used for ML model validation. For regression problems, the cost function (the gap between the model value and the actual value) is usually the MSE, which was discussed in the previous section. For binary classification, the cost function is usually expressed in a metric called a confusion matrix. Let's take a closer look at the confusion matrix, as well as the impact of changing the classification threshold on the confusion matrix.

Confusion matrix

A confusion matrix is used to measure a binary classification model's predictions, as shown in *Figure 4.11*.

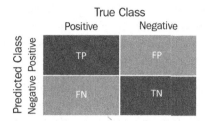

Figure 4.11 – Confusion matrix

Based on whether the model predicts the actual classes, there are four situations:

- **True Positive (TP)** is where the model *correctly* predicts the *positive* class.

- **True Negative (TN)** is where the model *correctly* predicts the *negative* class.

- **False Positive (FP)** is where the model *incorrectly* predicts the *positive* class.

- **False Negative (FN)** is where the model *incorrectly* predicts the *negative* class.

Let's look at a computer vision ML problem: you trained two models for image recognition – to classify an image as being of a cat or not. You have run the two models on the validation dataset and compared the results with the labels, and *Figure 4.12* shows the confusion matrices for the two ML models. How do we measure which model performs better?

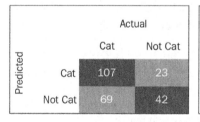 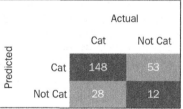

Figure 4.12 – Confusion matrices for two ML models

To help us compare the classification model performances, we need to define more metrics:

- `Recall` (`sensitivity`) measures the proportion of actual positives that were identified correctly:

    `Recall =TP/(TP+FN)`

- `Specificity` measures the proportion of actual negatives that were identified correctly:

  `Specificity =TN/(FP+TN)`

Applying the preceding metrics to the two models, we have come up with the following table:

Recall	Specificity
Model 1: 107/(107+69)=60%	Model 1: 42/(42+23)=64%
Model 2: 148/(148+28)=84%	Model 2: 12/(12+53)=18%

Table 4.13 – Recall and specificity for two ML models

Depending on the business goal, these two models' performance can be measured and interpreted from different points of view. If the goal is to identify as many cats as possible and the amount of false positives does not matter, then model two is better performed since it has a high recall metric. However, if your goal is to identify the not-cats, then model one may be a better choice since it has a high specificity metric.

You can use more metrics to help with your decision making. Next, we introduce the concepts of the receiver operating characteristic curve and the area under the curve.

ROC curve and AUC

In previous chapters, we discussed the cutoff for converting a probability into a class. The threshold will impact the confusion matrix.

An **Receiver Operating Characteristic (ROC)** curve is a graph showing the **True Positive Rate (TPR)** and **False Positive Rate (FPR)**, as two dimensions, under all threshold values.

The TPR is a synonym for recall and is therefore defined as follows:

`TPR =TP/(TP+FN) (Of all the positive cases, the proportion of cases identified as positive)`

The FPR is defined as follows:

`FPR =FP/(FP+TN) (Of all the native cases, the proportion of cases identified as positive)`

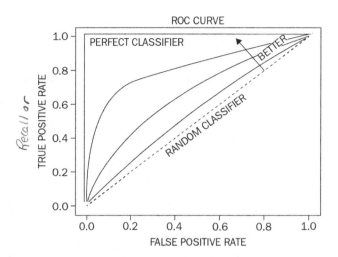

Figure 4.14 – ROC curves

To build an ROC curve, you calculate the TPR (or recall) against the FPR for each threshold and plot it on a graph. *Figure 4.14* shows a sample ROC. If we take a close look at the graph, we will see that the point at *(0,0)* represents zero true positives and zero false positives. The point at *(1,1)* means that all the positives are correctly identified but all the negatives also incorrectly identified. The dotted line from *(0,0)* to *(1,1)*, called a **random classifier**, represents *TPR=FPR*. In the diagram, the ideal line is the *perfect classifier*, which represents *TPR=1* with no *false positives*:

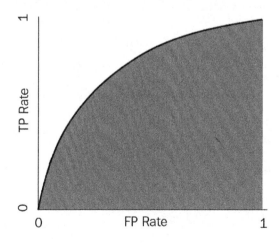

Figure 4.15 – AUC: the area under the curve

Since the goal for a classification problem is a model that has a high TPR and a low FPR – as close as possible to the *perfect classifier* – we often use the **Area Under the Curve (AUC)**-ROC as a measurement of classification model performance: the greater the AUC-ROC, the better. A sample AUC-ROC is shown in *Figure 4.15*.

More classification metrics

As you can see, with the four numbers from the confusion matrix, you can calculate a model's recall and specificity, and here we introduce accuracy, precision, and F1-score:

- `Accuracy` measures the proportion of correct predictions among the total number of cases:

  `Accuracy=(TP+TN)/(TP+TN+FP+FN)`

- `Precision` measures the proportion of positive identifications that are actually correct:

  `Precision=TP/(TP+FP)`

- `F1-score` combines precision and sensitivity and measures the overall performance:

  `F1-score =2 X Precision X Recall/(Precision + Recall)`

So far, we have introduced many classification metrics – which one should you choose? It really depends on the business context and goals. For a classification model that identifies emails as spam or not spam, while precision is good to identify the spam, you also want to avoid labeling a legitimate email as spam. For a classification model that identifies whether a patient has a terminal illness or not, it is vitally important to identify the illness for a patient who actually has that illness. In this situation, sensitivity is a better metric than precision to use.

The F1 score combines precision and recall to give you one number that quantifies the overall performance. You might want to use the F1 score when you have a class imbalance but you want to preserve the equality between precision and sensitivity.

Tuning the model

During the model validation process, we evaluate the model performances, and there are situations where the model does not fit the validation dataset. Let's examine the different cases.

Overfitting and underfitting

While underfitting describes the situation where prediction error is not minimized, overfitting is the case where the model fits the training dataset very well but does not fit the validation dataset. An overfitting model gets a very low cost function value during training but poorly predicts on new data. *Figure 4.16* depicts the situations for underfitting, robust, and overfitting.

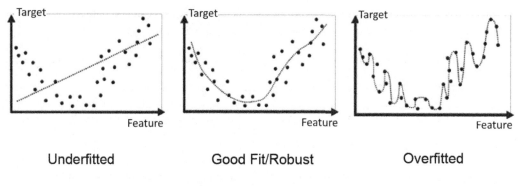

Figure 4.16 – Model fittings

When we try to minimize the cost function and avoid underfitting, we need to make sure our model is generalized and not prone to overfitting. From our ML practice, we know that overfitting is often caused by making a model more complex than necessary. As you can see in *Figure 4.16*, overfitting makes a training model memorize data. The ML's fundamental principle is making the model fit well on the data without losing generality. To avoid overfitting, we introduce regularization to decrease model complexity.

Regularization

To avoid overfitting, we need to reduce model complexity. Model complexity can be thought of in two ways:

- Model complexity as a function of the *total number of features* with nonzero weights
- Model complexity as a function of the *weights* of all the features in the model

The idea of regularization is introduced to add a factor to penalize the model complexity and enhance model generalization. Corresponding to the preceding two complexities, we have two kinds of regularization/generalization:

- Quantify complexity with the *L2 regularization* formula, which defines the regularization term as the sum of the squares of all the feature weights – weights close to zero have little effect on model complexity, while outlier weights can have a huge impact. *Ridge regression* uses L2 regularization: the cost function is altered by adding a penalty equivalent to the square of the weights. Let p be the number of features, and the coefficient (weight) of the ith feature is w_i; then, the cost function is written as follows:

$$Loss = Error\,(y, \hat{y}) + \lambda \sum_{i=1}^{N} w_1^2$$

- Quantify complexity with the *L1 regularization* formula, which defines the regularization term as the sum of the absolute of all the feature weights – weights close to zero have a large effect on model complexity, while outlier weights have less impact. Lasso regression uses L1 regularization: the cost function is altered by adding a penalty equivalent to the absolute of the weights:

$$Loss = Error\,(y, \hat{y}) + \lambda \sum_{i=1}^{N} |w_i|$$

How should you choose the parameter lambda for the preceding formulas? If the lambda value is too high, the model will be simple and carry a risk of underfitting the data. If the lambda value is too low, the model will be more complex, with the risk of overfitting your data and leading to generalization issues with new data. The ideal value of lambda produces a model that fits the training data and generalizes well to new data. One objective of model tuning is to balance the model complexity and generalization.

Other than regularization, we can use early stopping to avoid overfitting. Early stopping is a form of regularization used to avoid overfitting when training a learner with an iterative method, such as gradient descent. This means ending the training when the training results are good enough, and before the model fully reaches convergence.

Hyperparameter tuning

Hyperparameter tuning is the process of finding the best version of a model by running many training jobs on your dataset. It uses the algorithm and ranges of hyperparameters that you specify, then chooses the hyperparameter values that result in a model that performs the best, as measured by a metric that you choose.

There are two basic types of hyperparameters. The first kind is model hyperparameters. They are directly linked to the model that is selected and thus have a direct impact on the performance of that model. They help define the model itself, for example, the number of layers in a neural network model and the activation functions that are used.

The second kind is algorithm hyperparameters. They do not affect the performance of the algorithm directly but affect the efficiency and the rate of model training. For example, the learning rate for a gradient descent algorithm may affect how quickly an ML model converges.

The process of tuning hyperparameters involves changing the hyperparameter values and attempting to find those that yield the best results. The common hyperparameters that are often tuned include the following:

- **The batch size**: The number of samples that are processed during training, before the model is updated

- **The number of training epochs**: The number of times that we run through the full set of training data during model training

- **The learning rate**: The distance we travel when trying to find the optimal value for a parameter

Through the ML model training, validation, and hyperparameter tuning, we have come up with a model that can be deployed for testing.

Testing and deploying the model

To test and get performance metrics from your model, you must make inferences or predictions from the model—which typically requires deployment. The goal of the deployment phase is to provide a managed environment to host models for inference both securely and with low latency. You can deploy your model in one of two ways:

- **Single predictions**: Deploy your model online with a permanent endpoint. For example, we can deploy the housing model (price prediction) with an online endpoint.

- **Batch transform**: Spin up your model and perform the predictions for the entire dataset that you provide. For example, with a `.csv` file or multiple sets of records to be sent at a time, the model will return a batch of predictions.

After deploying a model into testing, you evaluate the model to see whether it meets the performance requirements and the business requirements, which is the ultimate goal for any ML problem. All the stakeholders will need to evaluate the ML solution's benefits and approve the model's deployment to production. Keep in mind that the most accurate model may not be the best solution to an ML problem.

After all the stakeholders approve the model, we then deploy the model to production. Otherwise, we need to go back to the process of model training, validation and tuning, re-testing, and re-evaluation.

After deploying a model to production, you still need to monitor the production data, since new data accumulates over time, and alternative or new outcomes can potentially be identified. Therefore, deploying a model is a continuous process, not a one-time exercise.

Practicing model development with scikit-learn

Scikit-learn is one of the most useful libraries for ML in Python. The scikit-learn library contains a lot of tools for ML, including ones for classification and regression.

In *Appendix 3* of the book, we have provided a step-by-step practice exercise for using scikit-learn to develop ML models. Practicing these steps is essential to master scikit-learn skills. Please refer to *Appendix 3*, *Practicing with Scikit-Learn*, to learn and practice with examples of ML model training, validation, and testing using scikit-learn.

Summary

In this chapter, we have discussed the basic concepts of the ML model development process: data splitting, platform setup, ML model training, validation, testing, and deployment.

Since the concept of AI emerged in the 1950s, there were no big breakthroughs until 2012, when **deep learning** (**DL**) was invented using neural networks. DL has greatly improved ML model performance and opened up a huge avenue for applying ML to many business use cases. In the next chapter, we will discuss neural networks and DL.

Further reading

For further insights into the topics of the chapter, you can refer to the following:

- `https://scikit-learn.org/stable/tutorial/basic/tutorial.html`
- `https://scikit-learn.org/stable/tutorial/index.html`
- *Appendix 3, Practicing with ScikitLearn*

5

Understanding Neural Networks and Deep Learning

Since its debut in 2012, **Deep Learning** (**DL**) has made a huge breakthrough and has been applied in many research and industrial areas including computer vision, **Natural Language Processing** (**NLP**), and so on. In this chapter, we will introduce basic concepts, including the following:

- Neural networks and DL

- The cost function

- The optimizer algorithm

- The activation functions

After we master the concepts, we will discuss several neural network models and their business use cases, including the following:

- **Convolutional Neural Networks (CNNs)**

- **Recurrent Neural Networks (RNNs)**

- **Long Short-Term Memory (LSTM)** networks

- **Generative Adversarial Networks (GANs)**

Understanding neural networks and DL concepts, common models, and business use cases is extremely important in our cloud ML journey. Let's get started.

Neural networks and DL

In the history of us human beings, there are many interesting milestones, from vision development and language development to making and using tools. How did humans evolve and how can we train a computer to *see*, *speak*, and *use* tools? Looking for answers to these questions has led us to the modern AI arena.

How do our brains work? Modern science reveals that in the brain, there is a layered neural network consisting of a set of neurons. A typical neuron collects electrical signals from others through a fine structure called **dendrites** and sends out spikes of signals through a conducting structure called an **axon**, which splits into many branches. At the end of each branch, a synapse converts the signals from the axon into electrical effects to excite activity on the target neuron. *Figure 5.1* shows the working mechanism of a biological neuron:

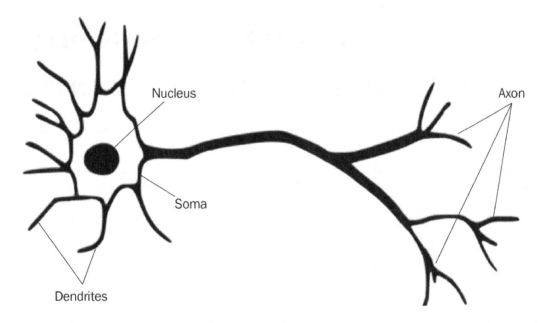

Figure 5.1 – How a biological neuron works

Inspired by the biological neural network model, an **Artificial Neural Network (ANN)** model consists of artificial neurons called **perceptrons**. A perceptron receives weighted inputs from the other perceptrons, applies the transfer function, which is the sum of the weighted inputs, and the activation function, which adds nonlinear activation to the sum, and outputs to excite the next perceptron. *Figure 5.2* shows the working mechanism of an artificial neuron (perceptron):

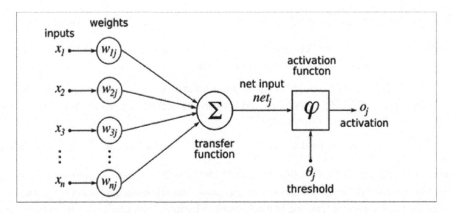

Figure 5.2 – How an artificial neuron (perceptron) works

ANNs consist of perceptrons working together via layers. *Figure 5.3* shows the structure of a multilayer ANN where each circular node represents a perceptron, and a line represents the connection from the output of one perceptron to the input of another. There are three types of layers in a neural network: an input layer, one or more hidden layers, and an output layer. The neural network in *Figure 5.3* has one input layer, two hidden layers, and an output layer:

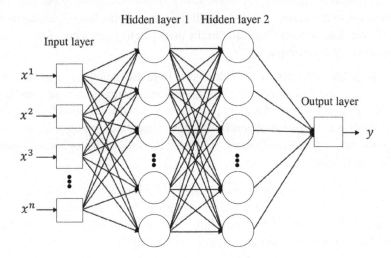

Figure 5.3 – A multilayer ANN

Using neural networks to perform ML model training, the data flows in the network as follows:

1. A dataset (x^1, x^2, x^3, ..., x^n) is prepared and sent to the input layer, which has the same amount of perceptrons as the number of features of the dataset.

2. The data then moves through to the hidden layers. At each hidden layer, the perceptron processes the weighted inputs (sum and activate, as described earlier), and sends the output to the neurons at the next hidden layer.

3. After the hidden layers, the data finally moves to the output layer, which provides the outputs.

The objective of the neural network is to determine the weights that minimize the cost function (average prediction error for the dataset). Similar to the regression model training process we discussed in the previous chapters, DL model training is implemented by iterations of a two-part process, forward propagation and backpropagation, as follows:

- **Forward propagation** is the path that information flows from the input layer to the output layer, through the hidden layers. At the beginning of the training process, data arrives at the input layer where they are multiplied with the weights randomly initialized, then passed to the first hidden layer. Since the input layer has multiple nodes, each one is connected to each node in the first hidden layer; a node in the hidden layer sums up the weighted values to it and applies an activation function (adds nonlinearity). It then sends the output to the nodes of the next layer, where the nodes do the same, till the output of the last hidden layer is multiplied by the weights and becomes the input to the final output layer, where further functions are applied to generate the output.

- **Backpropagation** is the path information flows from the output layer all the way back to the input layer. During this process, the neural network compares the predicted output to the actual output as the first step of backpropagation and calculates the cost function or prediction error. If the cost function is not good enough, it moves back to adjust the weights based on algorithms such as **Gradient Descent (GD)** and then starts the forward propagation again with the new weights.

Forward propagation and backpropagation are repeated multiple times—each time the network adjusts the weights, trying to get a better cost function value—until the network gets a good cost function (an acceptable accuracy) at the output layer. At this time, the model training is completed and we have got the optimized weights, which are the results of the training.

DL is training ML models with neural networks. If you compare the preceding DL model training process using neural networks with the ML model training process we discussed in the *Training the model* section in *Chapter 4, Developing and Deploying ML Models*, you will find that the concepts of ML and DL are very similar. Via iterative forward propagation and backward propagation, both are trying to minimize the cost function of the model—ML is more about computers learning from data with traditional algorithms, while DL is more about computers learning from data mimicking the human brain and neural networks. Relatively speaking, ML requires less computing power and DL needs less human intervention. In the following sections, we will take a close look at the cost function, the optimizer algorithm, and the activation function for DL with neural networks.

The cost function

We introduced the concept of the cost function in the *Linear regression* section in *Chapter 4*. The cost function gives us a mathematical way of determining how much error the current model has—it assigns a cost for making an incorrect prediction and provides a way to measure the model performance. The cost function is a key metric in ML model training—choosing the right cost function can improve model performance dramatically.

The common cost functions for regression models are MAE and MSE. As we have discussed in previous chapters, MAE defines a summation of the absolute differences between the prediction values and the label values. MSE defines the summation of squares of the differences between the prediction values and the label values.

The cost functions for classification models are quite different. Conceptually, the cost function for a classification model is the difference between the probability distributions for different classes. For binary classification models where the model outputs are binary, 1 for yes or 0 for no, we use **binary cross entropy**. For multi-class classification models, depending on the dataset labels, we use **categorical cross entropy** and **sparse categorical cross entropy** as follows:

- If the labels are integers, for example, to classify an image of a dog, a cat, or a cow, then we use sparse categorical cross entropy since the output is one exclusive class.

- Otherwise, if the labels are encoded as a series of zeros and ones for each class (same for the one-hot-encoding format that we have discussed in the previous chapters), we'll use categorical cross entropy. For example, given an image, you need to detect whether there exists a driver's license, a passport, or a social security card, we will use categorical cross entropy as cost functions since the output has a combination of classes.

The cost function is a way of measuring our models so we can adjust the model parameters to minimize them—the model optimization process. In the following section, we'll talk about the optimizer algorithms that minimize the cost function.

The optimizer algorithm

In the *Linear regression* section in *Chapter 4*, we discussed the **GD** algorithm, which optimizes the linear regression cost function. In neural networks, the optimizer is an algorithm used to minimize the cost function in model training. The commonly used optimizers are **Stochastic Gradient Descent (SGD)**, **RMSprop**, and **Adam** as follows:

- **SGD** is useful for very large datasets. Instead of GD, which runs through all of the samples in your training dataset to update parameters, SGD uses one or a subset of training samples.

- **RMSprop** improves SGD by introducing variable learning rates. The learning rate, as we discussed in *Chapter 4*, impacts model performances—larger learning rates can reduce training time but may lead to model oscillation and may miss the optimal model parameter values. Lower learning rates can make the training process longer. In SGD, the learning rate is fixed. RMSprop adapts the learning rate as training progresses, and thus it allows you to start with big learning rates when the model has a high cost function, but it gradually reduces the learning rate when the cost function decreases.

- **Adam** stands for **Adaptive Moment Estimation** and is one of the most widely used optimizers. Adam adds momentum to the adaptive learning rate from RMSprop, and thus it allows changes to the model to accelerate while moving in the same direction during training, making the model training process quicker and better.

Choosing the right cost function and optimizer algorithms is very important for model performance and training speed. Google's TensorFlow framework provides many optimizer algorithms. For further details, please refer to `https://www.tensorflow.org/api_docs/python/tf/keras/optimizers`.

Other important features for neural networks are non-linearity and output normalization, which are provided by the activation functions. We will examine them in the following section.

The activation functions

As you can see from the preceding section, the activation function is part of the training process. The purpose of the activation function is to transform the weighted-sum input to the nodes: non-linearize and change the output range. There are many activation functions in neural networks. We will discuss some of the most used ones: the sigmoid function, the tanh activation function, the ReLu function, and the LeakyReLU function. *Figure 5.4* shows the curves of these functions:

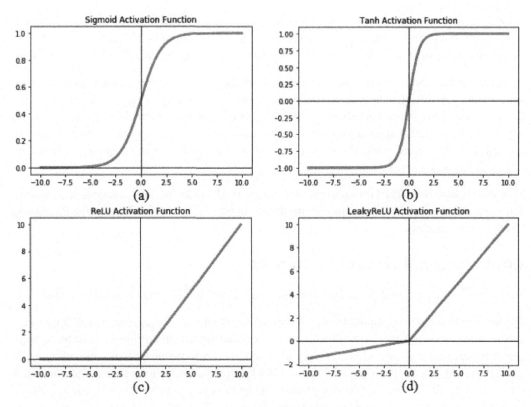

Figure 5.4 – Activation functions

Let's inspect each of the preceding activation functions as follows:

- The sigmoid activation function was discussed earlier ithe T*he cost function* section. We use the sigmoid function to change continuous values to a range between 0 and 1, which fits the models to predict the probability as an output.

- The tanh activation function is very similar to sigmoid, but the output is from -1 to +1 and thus it is preferred to sigmoid due to the output being zero-centered.

- The ReLU activation function stands for Rectified Linear Unit. It is widely used since it converts the negative values to 0 and keeps the positive values as such. Its range is between 0 and infinity. Because the gradient value is 0 in the negative area, the weights and biases for some neurons may not be updated during the training process, causing dead neurons that never get activated.

- The LeakyReLU is an improved version of the ReLU function to solve the dying ReLU problem as it has a small positive slope in the negative area. The advantages of LeakyReLU are the same as that of the ReLU, in addition to the fact that it enables training even for negative input values.

Another activation function is the *softmax* function, which is often used in the output layer for multi-class classifications. The softmax activation function converts the output layer values into probabilities summing up to 1 and thus outputs probabilities for each class in multi-class classification problems.

Among all of these activation functions, which shall we choose? The answer depends on factors such as the type of predictions, the architecture of the network, the number of layers, the current layer in the network, and so on. For example, sigmoid is more used for binary classification use cases, whereas softmax is often applied for multi-classifications, and regression problems may or may not use activation functions. While there will be trial and error involved at the beginning, experience will build up good practices.

Now that we have introduced the concepts of neural networks and activation functions, let's examine some neural networks that are commonly used in computer vision, **Natural Language Processing (NLP)**, and other areas.

Convolutional Neural Networks

Now that we have learned about neural networks and DL, let's look at some business use cases.

The first case is image recognition. How can we teach a computer to recognize an image? It is an easy task for a human being but a very difficult one for a computer. The first thing we need to do, since computers are only good at working with 1s and 0s, is to transform the image into a numerical matrix using pixels. As an example, *Figure 5.5* shows a black and white image for a single digit number, *8*, represented by a 28x28 pixel matrix. While human beings can easily recognize the image as a number *8* by some *magic sensors* in our eyes, a computer needs to input all of the 28x28=784 pixels, each having a **pixel value—a** single number representing the brightness of the pixel. The pixel value has possible values from 0 to 255, with 0 as black and 255 as white. Values in between make up the different shades of gray. If we have a color image, the pixel will have three numerical RGB values (red, green, and blue) to represent its color instead of one black value.

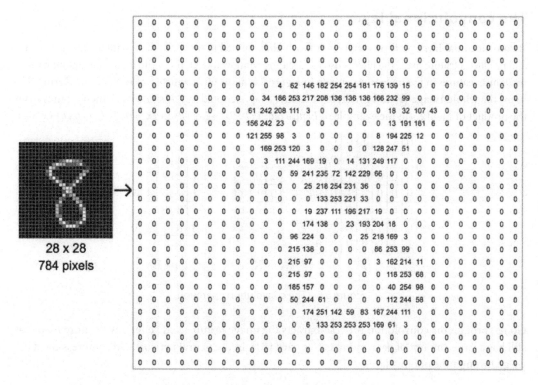

Figure 5.5 – Representing the number 8 with pixel values

After we have a pixel matrix representation of the image, we can start developing a **Multi-Layer Perceptron** (**MLP**) network for training. We will construct the input layer with 784 nodes and input 784 pixel values, one for each. Each node from the input layer will then output to each node in the next layer (a hidden layer), and so on. When the number of layers increases, the total number of calculations will be huge for the entire network. To decrease the total calculations, the idea of feature filtering comes into play and leads to the concept of a **CNN**.

CNNs are widely used in computer vision, especially in image recognition and processing. A CNN consists of three layers: the convolutional layer, the pooling layer, and the fully connected layer. The convolutional layer convolutes the inputs and filters the image features, the pooling layer compresses the filtered features, and the fully connected layer, which is basically an MLP, does the model training. Let's examine each of these layers in detail.

The convolutional layer

A **convolutional layer** performs convolution, which is applied to the input data to filter the information and produce a feature map. The filter is used as a sliding window to scan the entire image and autonomously recognize features in the images. As shown in *Figure 5.6*, a 3x3 filter, which is also called the **Kernel (K)**, scans the whole **Image (I)** and generates a feature map, denoted as *I*K* since its element comes from the product of *I* and *K* (in the example of *Figure 5.6*: *1x1+0x0+1x0+0x1+1x1+0x0+1x1+0x1+1x1=4*).

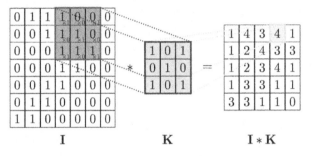

Figure 5.6 – The convolution operation

Going through the convolution process extracts the image features and generates a feature map that still has a large amount of data and makes it hard to train the neural network. To compress the data, we go through the pooling layer.

The pooling layer

A **pooling layer** receives the results from a convolutional layer, the feature map, and compresses it using a filter. Depending on the function used for calculation, it can either be maximum pooling or average pooling. As shown in *Figure 5.7*, a 2x2 filter patch scans the feature map and compresses it. With max pooling, it takes the maximum value from the scanning windows, *max(15,8,20,9) = 20*, and so on. With average pooling, it takes the average value, *average(15,8,20,9) = 13*. As you can see, the filter of a pooling layer is always smaller than a feature map.

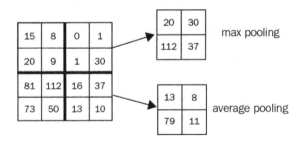

Figure 5.7 – The pooling layer

From the input image, the process of convolution and pooling iterates, and the final result is input to a fully connected layer (MLP) to process.

The fully connected layer

After the convolution and pooling layers, we need to flatten the result and pass it to an MLP, a fully connected neural network, for classification. The final result will then be activated with the softmax activation function to yield the final output – an understanding of the image.

Recurrent Neural Networks

The second type of neural network is an RNN. RNNs are widely used in time series analysis, such as NLP. The concept of an RNN came about in the 1980s, but it's not until recently that it gained its momentum in DL.

As we can see, in traditional feedforward neural networks such as CNNs, a node in the neural network only counts the current input and does not memorize the precious inputs. Therefore, it cannot handle time series data, which needs the previous inputs. For example, to predict the next word of a sentence, the previous words will be required to do the inference. By introducing a hidden state, which remembers some information about the sequence, RNNs solved this issue.

Different from feedforward networks, RNNs are a type of neural network where the output from the previous step is fed as the input to the current step; using a loop structure to keep the information allows the neural network to take the sequence of input. As shown in *Figure 5.8*, a loop for node A is unfolded to explain its process; first, node A takes X_0 from the sequence of input, and then it outputs h_0, which, together with X_1, is the input for the next step. Similarly, h_1 and X_2 are inputs for the next step, and so on and so forth. Using the loop, the network keeps remembering the context while training:

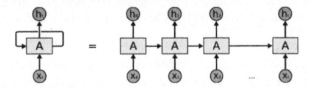

Figure 5.8 – The RNN unrolled loop (source: https://colah.github.io/posts/2015-08-Understanding-LSTMs/)

The drawback for a simple RNN model is the vanishing gradient problem, which is caused by the fact that the same weights are used to calculate a node's output at each time step during training and also done during backpropagation. When we move backward further, the error signal becomes bigger or smaller, thus causing difficulty in memorizing the contexts that are further away in the sequence. To overcome this drawback, the **LSTM** neural network was developed.

Long Short-Term Memory Networks

An LSTM network was designed to overcome the vanishing gradient problem. LSTMs have feedback connections, and the key to LSTMs is the cell state—a horizontal line running through the entire chain with only minor linear interactions, which persists the context information. LSTM adds or removes information to the cell state by gates, which are composed of activation functions, such as sigmoid or tanh, and a pointwise multiplication operation.

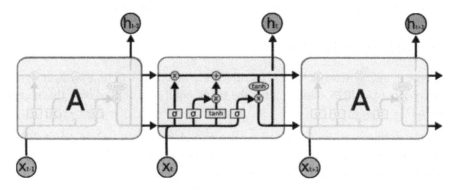

Figure 5.9 – An LSTM model (source: https://colah.github.io/posts/2015-08-Understanding-LSTMs/)

Figure 5.9 shows an LSTM that has the gates to protect and control the cell state. Using the cell state, LSTM solves the issue of vanishing gradients and thus is particularly good at processing time series sequences of data, such as text and speech inference.

Generative Adversarial networks

GANs are algorithmic architectures that are used to generate new synthetic instances of data that can pass for real data. As shown in *Figure 5.10*, GAN is a generative model that trains the following two models simultaneously:

- A **Generative (G)** model that captures the data distribution to generate plausible data. The latent space input and random noise can be sampled and fed into the generator network to generate samples that become the negative training examples for the discriminator.

- A **Discriminative (D)** model that compares the generated image with a real image and tries to identify whether the given image is fake or real. It estimates the probability that a sample came from the training data rather than the real data to distinguish the generator's fake data from real data. The discriminator penalizes the generator for producing implausible results.

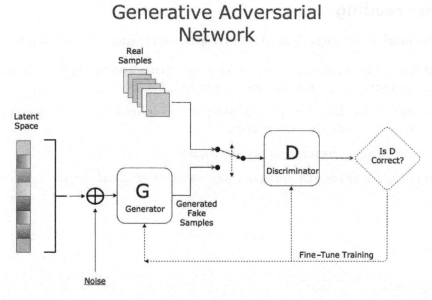

Figure 5.10 – The GAN (source: https://developers.google.com/machine-learning/recommendation)

The model training starts with the generator generating fake data and the discriminator learns to tell that it's false by comparing it with real samples. The GAN then sends the results to the generator and the discriminator to update the model. This fine tuning training process iterates and finally produces some extremely real-looking data. GANs can be used to generate text, images, and video, and color or denoise images.

Summary

Neural networks and DL have added the modern color to the traditional ML spectrum. In this chapter, we started by learning the concepts of neural networks and DL by examining the cost functions, optimizer algorithms, and activation functions. Then, we introduced advanced neural networks, including CNN, RNN, LSTM, and GAN. As we can see, by introducing neural networks, DL extended ML concepts and made a breakthrough in many applications such as computer vision, NLP, and others.

This chapter concludes part two of the book: *Machine Learning and Deep Learning*. In part three, we will focus on *Machine Learning the Google Way*, where we will talk about how Google does ML and DL in Google Cloud. We will start part three with learning about BQML, Google TensorFlow, and Keras in the following chapter.

Further reading

For further insights on the topics learned in this chapter, you can refer to the following links:

- `https://developers.google.com/machine-learning/crash-course/introduction-to-neural-networks/anatomy`
- `https://www.ibm.com/cloud/blog/ai-vs-machine-learning-vs-deep-learning-vs-neural-networks`
- `https://aws.amazon.com/what-is/neural-network/`
- `https://developers.google.com/machine-learning/gan`

Part 3: Mastering ML in GCP

In this part, we learn how Google does ML in the Google Cloud Platform. First, we discover Google's BigQuery ML for structured data, and then we look at Google's ML frameworks, TensorFlow and Keras. We examine Google's end-to-end ML suite, Vertex AI, and the ML services it provides. We then look at the Google pre-trained model APIs for ML development: GCP ML APIs. We end this part with a summary of the ML implementation best practices in Google Cloud.

This part comprises the following chapters:

- Chapter 6, Learning BQML, TensorFlow, and Keras
- Chapter 7, Exploring Google Cloud Vertex AI
- Chapter 8, Discovering Google Cloud ML API
- Chapter 9, Using Google Cloud ML Best Practices

6

Learning BQ/BQML, TensorFlow, and Keras

After building the GCP and Python foundations in part one and understanding the ML concepts and development process in part two, we are now entering part three of the book: *Mastering ML in GCP*. We will start by learning how Google does ML for structured data and the Google ML frameworks TensorFlow and Keras. In this chapter, we will cover the following topics:

- GCP BQ
- GCP BQML
- Introduction to TensorFlow
- Introduction to Keras

In recent years, relational databases have been widely used in many enterprises, and thus structural data is a big portion of the big data available for many businesses. Google's BQ and BQML play a big role in relational/structural data processing and analytics.

GCP BQ

As we mentioned in the *Google Cloud BigQuery* section in *Chapter 1, Comprehending Google Cloud Services*, BigQuery is a petabyte cloud enterprise data warehouse. BigQuery has the following features:

- **Fully managed GCP service** – you do not concern yourself with the underlying backend data processing infrastructure, including compute, network storage, and other resources.
- **Serverless** – you do not manage any servers in BigQuery. All of the data processing engines are taken care of by Google, including the invisible BigQuery BI Engine and ML Engine.
- **Highly scalable** – it is incredibly elastic and can scale to any size, quickly and seamlessly.
- **Cost-effective** – you are only charged for the BigQuery resources you consume.

In the Google Cloud big data processing pipeline, BigQuery is a key service for data ingestion, storing, analyzing, and visualization, as follows:

- BigQuery ingests data from data sources in three ways: archive, batch, and real-time streaming. With archived data, you can create a dataset with tables generated from data sources such as your computer, GCS, other GCP databases such as Bigtable, and Amazon **Simple Storage Services** (**S3**). With batch processing, you can load data into BigQuery from cloud storage or local storage, and the source data can be in the format of Avro, CSV, ORC, JSON, Parquet, or Firestore exports stored in GCS. Real-time events can be streamed into BigQuery. A common pattern is to push the events to GCP Pub/Sub, process them using a dataflow job, and ingest the outputs to BigQuery.

- BigQuery stores data with scalable storage, which is ACID compliant and cost-effective. The separation of storage and compute in BigQuery provides high performance and service decoupling.

- BigQuery processes data with an in-memory business intelligence engine – BigQuery BI Engine. Because BigQuery supports standard SQL, which is compliant with the ANSI SQL 2011 standard, it opens an avenue for the traditional relational databases and professionals to transform to BQ and BQML platforms. With SQL, BigQuery allows you to run queries, create reports and dashboards quickly, and export the results to Google Sheets or GCS.

- With BigQuery, you can visualize your data with its integrated Google Data Studio tool. Leveraging the BigQuery connector in Data Studio, you can create a data source, a report, and charts that visualize data in BigQuery data warehouses. You can leverage other tools such as Google Datalab, Looker, and Tableau.

You can launch the BigQuery service from the GCP web console, or the command-line tools from Cloud Shell – bq is a Python-based command-line tool. There are also a number of client libraries for programmatic access to BigQuery, using C#, Go, Java, Node.js, PHP, Python, Ruby, and so on.

GCP BQML

BQML enables data scientists to create and train ML models directly in BigQuery using standard SQL queries. BQML improves the ML model development speed by eliminating the need to move data and directly using BigQuery datasets as training and testing datasets. BQML-trained models can be exported directly to Vertex AI (to be discussed in later chapters) or other cloud serving layers.

BQML can be accessed and used in the following ways:

- The GCP console via a web browser

- The bq command-line tool via Google Cloud Shell or a VM shell

- The BigQuery REST API

- External tools such as Jupyter Notebook

As we discussed in *Chapter 3*, *Preparing for ML Development*, and *Chapter 4*, *ML Model Developing and Deploying*, the ML process includes data preparation, model creation and training, model validation/evaluation, and model deployment/prediction. Let's go over this process with BQML.

The *first step* is data preparation. With BQML, you can prepare the training dataset by loading CSV files in the BigQuery console and directly running SQL statements after data is imported to BigQuery.

The *second step* is model creation and training. BigQuery ML supports the following ML models:

- **Linear regression** – where we have a number of data points, and we basically fit a line to those data points to minimize the error.

- **Binary logistic regression** – where we have two classes and we assign each example to one of the classes.

- **Multiclass logistic regression** – where we have more than two classes and we assign each example to one of the classes.

- **K-means clustering** – where we have a number of points and we are able to separate them into different clusters.

- Other models are supported by BQML. For more details, please refer to https://cloud.google.com/bigquery-ml/docs/introduction#supported_models_in.

BQML implements the model creation and training in a single step using the BQML `create model` statement. Using *example 2* that we discussed in the previous chapters, *Table 6.1* shows two samples for the loan application processing model where the target is a binary value, *approval or not*, and the features include the application date, applicant credit score, loan amount, annual income, age, and so on.

Date	Applicant Credit Score	Loan amount($k)	Annual Income (x, $k)	Age	Marriage status	Approval (1 for yes, 0 for no)
20160801	730	300	150	45	1	1
20191207	670	200	100	20	0	1

Table 6.1 – Sample table structure

The following is sample code for creating a model with logistic regression using the dataset from a sample table `t`:

```
CREATE OR REPLACE MODEL m
 OPTIONS(MODEL_TYPE='LOGISTIC_REG' DEL_TYPE='LOGISTIC_REG')
AS
```

```
SELECT * FROM t
WHERE t.date BETWEEN '20160801' AND '20190731'
```

When the preceding code is run, BQML will execute the SELECT statement to filter all of the samples ranging from August 01, 2016 to July 31, 2019, and then use the results as the dataset input to train the logistic regression model.

The *third step* is model validation/evaluation to determine how good the model is. With BQML, model evaluation is done using the ML.EVALUATE function as follows:

```
SELECT *
FROM
  ML.EVALUATE(MODEL `m`, (
SELECT * FROM t
WHERE t.date BETWEEN '20190801' AND '20200731'))
```

When the preceding code is run, BQML will execute the SELECT statement to filter all of the samples ranging from August 01, 2019 to July 31, 2020, and then use the results as the dataset input to evaluate the performance of the classifier (the logistic regression model). When the code is completed, you can view the results.

precision	recall	accuracy	f1_score	log_loss	roc_auc
0.4451901	0.0887996	0.9716829	0.1480654	0.0792178	0.970706

Table 6.2 – Sample BQML model evaluation result

Table 6.2 shows the sample metrics for our binary classification model as follows:

- Precision – a metric that identifies the frequency with which a model was correct when predicting the positive class.

- recall – a metric that answers the following question: out of all the possible positive labels, how many did the model correctly identify?

- accuracy – the fraction of predictions that a classification model got right.

- f1_score – the harmonic average of the precision and recall.

- log_loss – the loss function used in a logistic regression.

- roc_auc – the area under the ROC curve.

Depending on the business use case, we can review the evaluation results, measure the model performance, and find the business indications. During the model evaluation process, we can tune model perimeters using the `model create` statement. More details are at `https://cloud.google.com/bigquery-ml/docs/reference/standard-sql/bigqueryml-hyperparameter-tuning`.

In the *fourth step*, we can use the model to predict production outcomes. A sample query to predict the outcome is as follows:

```
SELECT *
FROM
ML.PREDICT(MODEL `m`, (
SELECT * FROM t
WHERE t.date BETWEEN '20200801' AND '20210731'))
```

As you can see from the preceding four steps, BQML completes the full process of ML development within the BigQuery cloud service. For structured data, BQML has many advantages for our data scientists to train and develop ML models.

Google Cloud BQ and BQML provide services for structured data processing and learning, and they are widely used in many business use cases. In the following section, we will introduce Google's ML frameworks, TensorFlow and Keras.

Introduction to TensorFlow

pytorch is main competitor

TensorFlow is an end-to-end open source platform for ML, developed by Google Brain, and it is one of the most widely used ML frameworks by data scientists.

TensorFlow flow tensors – TensorFlow's name is directly derived from its core framework components: tensors. Let's start by understanding **tensors**.

Understanding the concept of tensors

A tensor is a container that holds data of various sizes and shapes in an N-dimensional space. A tensor can be originated from the input data or a computation of the input data. In ML, we call the tensor components **features**. A tensor has three main characters to describe itself, called a tensor's **rank**, **shape**, and **dtype** as follows:

- Rank is the number of directions
- Shape is the number of elements in each direction
- Dtype is the data type

The rank of a tensor specifies the number of directions being measured for a tensor. From the number of ranks, a tensor can be categorized as follows:

- **Rank 0**: A tensor that only has a magnitude and 0 directions.
- **Rank 1**: A tensor that has one direction and a magnitude.
- **Rank 2**: A tensor that has two directions (rows and columns), with each element having a magnitude.
- **Rank 3**: A tensor that has three directions.
- **Rank 4**: A tensor with four directions.
- **High-rank tensors**.

Figure 6.3 illustrates the ranks of the tensors using the basic geometrical objects as follows:

- A rank 0 tensor is a scalar with a magnitude but no directions.
- A rank 1 tensor is a vector with one direction and a magnitude.
- A rank 2 tensor is a matrix with two directions – its elements have magnitudes.
- A rank 3 tensor has three directions – its elements have two-dimensional magnitudes.
- A rank 4 tensor is a list of rank 3 sensors.

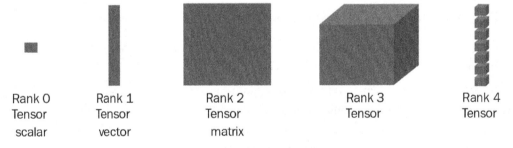

Rank 0	Rank 1	Rank 2	Rank 3	Rank 4
Tensor	Tensor	Tensor	Tensor	Tensor
scalar	vector	matrix		

Figure 6.3 – Ranks of tensors

If we use the `list` data type, which we discussed in The *Python Basic Data Structure* section in *Chapter 2, Mastering Python Programming*, to define the rank of a tensor, then *each rank of tensors gives us a list of the objects from the previous rank of sensors* as follows:

- Rank 1 tensors (vectors) gave us a list of rank 0 tensors (scalars).
- Rank 2 tensors (matrixes) gave us a list of rank 1 tensors (vectors).
- Rank 3 tensors (tensors) gave us a list of rank 2 tensors (matrixes).
- Rank 4 tensors gave us a list of rank 3 tensors (tensors).

Let's use a color image as an example to illustrate the concept of *rank* for a tensor. For a color image, we can use three channels to describe each pixel: a red channel, a green channel, and a blue channel. Each channel measures the magnitude of the pixel within that color channel. The red channel is a *rank 2* tensor since it uses a matrix to represent the image pixel map in red light (0 means zero light and 255 means maximum light), and so are the green channel and the blue channel. Combining these three channels, we have a *rank 3* tensor. If we add a time axis for the order of the color frames/images to form a video, then it becomes a *rank 4* tensor. If we then batch the videos, it will then come up with a list of *rank 4* tensors – a *rank 5* tensor.

After we have examined the tensor ranks, let's check out the shape and dtype of a tensor – shape is the number of elements of a tensor and dtype is the element's data type. With the tensors of ranks 0, 1, 2, 3, and n, we have the following:

- The shape for the *rank 0* tensor (scalar) is empty *()*.

- The shape for a *rank 1* tensor, for example, a vector ([3, 5, 7]), is *(3)* since it has three elements.

- The shape for a *rank 2* tensor, for example, a matrix ([3, 5, 7], [4, 6, 8]) is *(2,3)* since it has two elements in one direction (rows) and three elements in the other direction (columns).

Now that we have a good understanding of the tensor concept, let's look at the second part of the name *TensorFlow*, flow, and see how tensors flow.

How tensors flow

To describe the flowing of tensors in the **TensorFlow** (**TF**) framework, we adopt a computational graph with nodes and edges called a **Directed Acyclic Graph** (**DAG**). Directed means that the tensor (data) moves in a given order along a path in the graph. Acyclic means that the moving path does not form any cycles. So, tensors flow in no-loop DAGs to transform data.

Using DAGs, a tensor has a node and an edge. The nodes represent the operations we perform on the tensor/data, and the edges represent the path that the tensor/data flows along. Let's use a DAG to describe a sample algorithm. As shown in *Figure 6.4*, we input two numbers, multiply them to get their product, and add the numbers to get their sum. Then, we divide the product by the sum and print the result. If we replace the constant values with variables and add more complex mathematical operations, we can see that this tensor flowing process is really an ML model – we can change the variables or the weights to produce the expected output from the inputs.

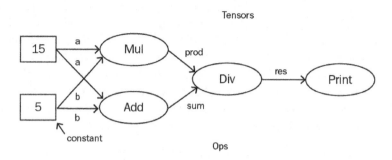

Figure 6.4 – A sample algorithm with DAG

Since DAGs are mono-directional and have an order of execution, we can parallelize the operations when tensors flow in the diagram. For example, If you want to add 1,000 tensors and multiply the same 1,000 tensors, the addition and multiplication operations can be performed in parallel by distributing the operations to multiple computing resources by utilizing many CPU, **Graphics Processing Unit (GPU)**, or **Tensor Processing Unit (TPU)** cores, or even **Quantum Processors (QU)**. Since DAG allows the execution of parallel operations on different physical machines or platforms, we can further execute these operations in parallel on distributed server farms or edge devices. As we know, cloud computing is featured as on-demand, globally distributed, auto-scalable, and pay-as-you-go and thus it provides a perfect environment to parallelize TensorFlow operations and train ML models. As we have also discussed in the previous chapters, Google Colab has preinstalled TensorFlow packages, and you can practice TensorFlow in Colab, with GPU and TPU free of cost.

Now that we have grasped the concepts of tensors and understand how tensors flow in the TF frame, it's time to introduce Keras—a high-level API that is designed for us to develop ML models with TensorFlow very easily.

Introduction to Keras

Keras is a Google platform and a high-level interface to build ML/DL models with TensorFlow. Keras provides a high-level API that encapsulates data transformations and operations using logic units, called **layers**, as the building blocks to create neural networks. A layer performs data manipulation operations such as taking an average, calculating the minimum, and so on.

With Keras, ML models are built from layers. During the ML model training process, the variables in the layers are adjusted, via backpropagation, to optimize the model cost function. Behind the scenes, TensorFlow and Keras complete detailed data operations, such as linear algebra and calculus calculations, in the background. Keras provides the following two APIs:

- The **sequential API** provides the simplest interface and least complexity. With the sequential API, we can create the model layer by layer and thus build an ML/DL model as a simple list of layers.

- The **functional API** is more flexible and powerful than the sequential API since it allows thebranching or sharing of layers. With the functional API, we can have multiple inputs and outputs for ML models.

The following snippet shows an ML model training with the sequential API:

```
##Import the tensorflow libraries
from tensorflow.keras.models import Sequential
from tensorflow.keras.layers import Dense, Activation
from tensorflow.keras.optimizers import Adam
## Creating the model
model = Sequential()
model.add(Dense(4,activation='relu'))
model.add(Dense(4,activation='relu'))
model.add(Dense(1))
## defining the optimizer and loss function
model.compile(optimizer='adam',loss='mse')
## training the model
model.fit(x=X_train,y=y_train,
          validation_data=(X_test,y_test),
          batch_size=128,epochs=400)
```

The following snippet shows an ML model training with the functional API:

```
##Import the tensorflow libraries
from tensorflow.keras.models import Model
from tensorflow.keras.layers import Input,Dense
## Creating the layers
input_layer = Input(shape=(3,))
Layer_1 = Dense(4, activation="relu")(input_layer)
Layer_2 = Dense(4, activation="relu")(Layer_1)
output_layer= Dense(1, activation="linear")(Layer_2)
##Defining the model by specifying the input and output layers
model = Model(inputs=input_layer, outputs=output_layer)
## defining the optimizer and loss function
model.compile(optimizer='adam',loss='mse')
## training the model
```

```
model.fit(X_train, y_train,epochs=400, batch_
size=128,validation_data=(X_test,y_test))
```

As we can see, the preceding two Keras APIs have their own pros and cons. The sequential API is simple and straightforward, and the functional API can be used to build complex models.

Summary

In this chapter, we discussed Google Cloud BQ and BQML and introduced some examples of using BQ/BQML for data processing and ML model development. We also learned about the concepts of TensorFlow and Keras – Google's frameworks for building ML models and projects.

In the following chapter, we will focus on Vertex AI, which provides an end-to-end platform for ML in the Google Cloud.

Further reading

For further insights on the learning of the chapter, you can refer to the following links:

- https://cloud.google.com/bigquery/docs/
- https://cloud.google.com/bigquery-ml/docs/
- https://www.tensorflow.org/
- https://keras.io/about/

7
Exploring Google Cloud Vertex AI

In the last chapter, we discussed Google Cloud BQML, which is used to develop ML models from structured data, and Google's TensorFlow and Keras frameworks, which provide a high-level API interface for ML model development. In this chapter, we will discuss Cloud Vertex AI, which is Google's integrated cloud service suite for ML model development. We will examine the Vertex AI suite and all its products and services.

Google Vertex AI is an integrated set of Google Cloud products, features, and a management interface that simplifies the management of ML services. It offers users a complete platform to build, train, and deploy ML applications in Google Cloud, from end to end. Vertex AI provides a single stop for data scientists to build machine learning applications.

In this chapter, we will discuss the following Vertex AI products and services:

- Vertex AI data labeling and datasets
- Vertex AI Feature Store
- Vertex AI Workbench and notebooks
- Vertex AI training
- Vertex AI models and predictions
- Vertex AI Pipelines
- Vertex AI metadata
- Vertex AI experiments and TensorBoard

Let's start with data labeling and datasets in the Vertex AI suite.

Vertex AI data labeling and datasets

Datasets play such a significant role in the machine learning process that the quality of datasets has a huge impact on the ML model performance. As we discussed in *Chapter 4, Developing and Deploying ML Models*, data preparation is the first and most important step in any machine learning process.

Vertex AI Data labeling is a Google Cloud service that lets end users work with human workers to review and label datasets uploaded by users. After the datasets are labeled, they can be used to train machine learning models. The human workers are employed by Google, and the users will need to provide the dataset, the labels, and instructions to the human workers for labeling.

End users can also upload labeled datasets directly. **Vertex AI datasets** are part of a Google Cloud service that provides users with the ability to upload data of varying types for the purpose of building, training, and validating machine learning models. Currently, Vertex AI supports four types of datasets (image, tabular, text, and videos):

- **Image datasets**: You can create image datasets within Vertex AI, and use them to train models for image classification, image segmentation, and object detection. With Vertex AI, you can either upload the image datasets directly or use the images stored in Google Cloud Storage buckets.

- **Tabular datasets**: You can directly upload a CSV file from your local computer, use one from Google Cloud Storage, or select a table from the BigQuery service. Once the tabular dataset is generated, the data is available in Vertex AI datasets for model training.

- **Video datasets**: Vertex AI allows you to directly upload videos from your local computers or use videos from Google Cloud buckets. Once you have the video datasets, you can use them for video classifications or action recognitions.

- **Text datasets**: In Vertex AI, you create a text dataset, and import the CSVs from a Google Cloud Storage bucket into the dataset. Then, you can use the dataset for text document classification, custom text entity identification, sentiment analysis, and so on.

Vertex AI datasets allow you to create and manage datasets directly within the Vertex AI suite, and the datasets uploaded through Vertex AI are automatically stored in the Cloud Storage bucket, which is created and managed by Vertex AI.

Vertex AI Feature Store

In ML/DL model training, features are the attributes to build a model and make future inferences. Google Vertex AI Feature Store is a fully managed cloud service that provides a centralized repository to store, organize, and serve ML features. You can create and manage a **Vertex AI Feature Store** that contains all the model features and their values. With a central feature store, users in a Google Cloud organization can share and reuse these features for model training or serving tasks in different ML/DL projects to speed up machine learning application development and model deployment.

Vertex AI Feature Store enables users to manage features in ML models. A feature store can serve real-time, online predictions, or batch predictions for the new data. For example, after loading information about movie-watching habits, the Feature Store can serve to predict what movie a new user may watch based on their characteristics.

In traditional ML frameworks, you may have computed feature values and saved them in various locations including Cloud Storage buckets or BQ tables, and you may have separate solutions for storing and managing the feature values. With Vertex AI Feature Store, you are provided with a unified solution, consistent across the organization, to store and serve features that can be shared among different teams for different projects or use cases.

Vertex AI Workbench and notebooks

The **Vertex AI Workbench** service provides a single development platform for the entire data science workflow; you can use it to launch Cloud VM instances/notebooks to query and explore data and to develop and train a model for deployment.

As we explained earlier in the *Preparing the platform* section, Jupyter Notebook is a widely used platform for ML model development. Vertex AI Workbench provides two Jupyter-Notebook-based options for your data scientists, managed notebooks and user-managed notebooks:

- **Managed notebooks** are Google-managed, Jupyter-based, scalable, enterprise-ready compute instances that help you set up and work in an end-to-end ML production environment.
- **User-managed notebooks** are heavily customizable instances and are thus fitting for users who need a lot of control over their environment. With a user-managed notebook instance, you have a suite of deep learning packages pre-installed, including TensorFlow and PyTorch frameworks.

Vertex AI Workbench provides flexible notebook options. It offers a great ML model training platform for data scientists to train and develop models.

Vertex AI Training

In an ML model development process, training jobs are discrete tasks that generate ML models. In Vertex AI, you can choose different training methods based on the source of model and data; **Vertex AI AutoML**, which is managed by Google, uses Google's model and your data to train, and the **Vertex AI platform**, with user-defined code or custom containers, utilizes your model and your data to perform model training.

Vertex AI AutoML

Vertex AI AutoML is a managed Google Cloud service that enables users to build models across a wide variety of use cases without writing any code. The objective is to enable ML model development for various levels of AI expertise.

The types of models supported by Vertex AutoML are shown in *Table 7.1*:

Image data	Tabular data	Text data	Video data
Classification	Regression	Classification	Action recognition
Object detection	Classification	Entity extraction	Video classification
	Forecasting	Sentiment analysis	Video object tracking

Table 7.1 – Vertex AI AutoML models

When creating an AutoML training pipeline job, you have the following options:

- **Dataset**: Managed by Vertex AI and uploaded by a user

- **Model type**: Selected from the supported models (as described above)

- **Data split** (Optional): Split dataset between training, validation, and testing data using custom parameters

- **Encryption** (Optional): Option to select a **customer-managed encryption key** (**CMEK**) for in-process encryption

Vertex AI AutoML helps you to build a code-free model based on your training data. With Vertex AI AutoML, you customize Google's models using your own data.

The Vertex AI platform

The **Vertex AI platform**, with custom containers, enables you to build your own models from scratch, with your own data. **Custom containers** are user-created Docker images that are selected while creating a pipeline. A typical workflow for a custom container environment is shown in *Figure 7.2*, and it has the following steps:

1. **Code development**: You can build an application in the programming language of your choice, locally or within a notebook, and dependencies can be sourced from any internet location by default.

2. **Build**: You can build code into a packaged artifact or write a configuration to automatically package code and various dependencies into a container runtime artifact.

3. **Artifact storage**: You can push newly built customized artifacts into Cloud Storage or a container registry.

4. **Start training pipeline**: You can select a *custom container* when creating a training pipeline to build an ML model.

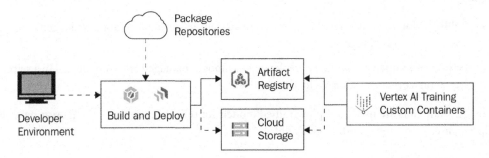

Figure 7.1 – Vertex AI platform custom container

After the models are trained in Vertex AI, you can use either AutoML or custom containers, accessed/managed in Vertex AI Models, and be deployed in Vertex AI Endpoints for individual predictions or batch predictions.

Vertex AI Models and Predictions

Vertex AI Models provides a platform for managing ML models. With Vertex AI Models, you can develop and manage ML models in many ways:

- **Create model**: Users can choose to create a new model and be redirected to the **training Pipelines** screen.

- **Upload model**: Users can upload a model that's been trained elsewhere for use within their Vertex AI project.

- **Deploy model**: Users can deploy a selected model to an endpoint, making it available through a REST API.

- **Export model**: Users can export a trained model to a GCS bucket, where it can be stored or used in another project.

After the models are trained, they can be exported or deployed publicly or privately to predict production cases. When you deploy a model to an endpoint resource for online predictions, or when you request batch predictions, you can always customize the VM types that the prediction service uses, and you can also configure prediction nodes to use GPUs. We will discuss model deployment in the next sections.

Vertex AI endpoint prediction

Vertex AI Endpoints allow users to create REST API endpoints based on Vertex AI models, to predict results for new data. With Vertex AI, a model can be deployed into either public endpoints or private endpoints:

- **Public endpoints**: The model is deployed to an internet-routable, Google-managed endpoint hosted in a selected region.

- **Private endpoints**: The model is deployed to a Google-managed endpoint hosted in a selected region on a private IP address in a selected VPC.

Vertex AI Endpoints are used to deploy trained models for online prediction. When creating a new endpoint, users can configure the following:

- **Endpoint Name**
- **GCP Region**
- **Private or Public Access**
- **Encryption (Optional)**
- **Model(s)**: One or more models to be served by the new endpoint.

Integrating with Vertex AI training and Vertex AI Models, Vertex AI Endpoints allow users to predict individual results interactively.

Vertex AI batch prediction

Different from Vertex AI Endpoints, **Vertex AI batch prediction** jobs are discrete tasks that run batch sets of input data against a prediction model. As shown in *Figure 7.3*, it can input files in Google Cloud Storage, and outputs the results to a specified GCS location.

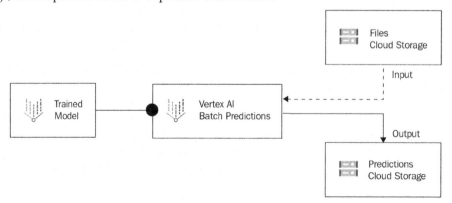

Figure 7.2 – Vertex AI batch prediction

When creating a batch prediction job, you have the following options:

- **Region**: Where the model is stored
- **Model**: Points to the ML model
- **Input data**: Cloud Storage bucket where input data is stored
- **Output directory**: Cloud Storage bucket to store predictions
- Compute-related information including machine type and number of nodes

As we can see from the preceding services, Vertex AI provides an ML development and management suite for you to create and manage datasets, create and manage notebooks to conduct model training, and develop and manage models for the endpoint of batch prediction. With Vertex AI, you can perform all the tasks in an ML workflow, from end to end. And that leads us to the Vertex AI Pipelines discussion: automating the ML workflow.

Vertex AI Pipelines

Vertex AI Pipelines allow you to automatically orchestrate your ML workflow in a serverless manner using **TensorFlow Extended** (**TFX**) or **Kubeflow**. Each Vertex AI pipeline job is generated from a configuration file that outlines a list of steps. A typical Vertex AI pipeline imports data into a dataset, trains a model using a **training pipeline**, and deploys the model to a new endpoint for prediction. Pipeline jobs are run using compute resources, with the following options:

- You can write custom configurations for pipeline jobs using the **Kubeflow DSL**.
- You can create, run, and schedule pipeline jobs.
- You can specify **Service Account** or use **Compute Default Service Account** if not specified.

Google Vertex AI Pipelines orchestrates your ML workflow, based on your descriptions of the workflow as a pipeline. ML pipelines are portable and scalable ML workflows that are based on containers. ML pipelines are composed of a set of input parameters and a list of steps – each step is an instance of the pipeline.

Vertex AI Metadata

Vertex AI Metadata is a repository of metadata that is generated across a variety of Vertex AI components. When models are developed in the ML workflow pipelines, metadata is generated and stored, and you can consolidate this metadata into a single metadata store, which allows users to query and answer questions such as the following:

- Which version of a trained model has achieved a certain quality threshold?
- Which pipeline runs/uses a certain dataset?

Within a Vertex AI pipeline, users can also configure data objects that are written to the metadata store. And from there, users can create *Context* objects that organize these data objects into logical groupings and obtain more insights.

Using the Vertex AI metadata API, users can build schemas, organize data objects, or query data that's been stored within Vertex AI metadata.

Vertex AI experiments and TensorBoard

TensorBoard is a Google open source project for machine learning experiment visualization. Vertex AI experiments are an implementation of TensorBoard. With Vertex AI experiments, users can create TensorBoard instances and upload TensorBoard logs generated from Vertex AI Models to run experiments – visual representations of a variety of metrics, such as loss function and accuracy over different model parameters at different running times. *Figure 7.4* shows a sample workflow for Vertex AI experiments and TensorBoard:

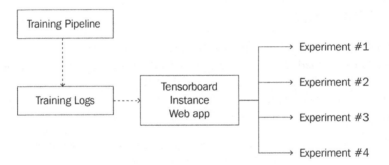

Figure 7.3 – Vertex AI experiments and TensorBoard

These TensorBoard visualizations are available via a web application that can be shared with other users by setting up GCP IAM permissions. With Vertex AI experiments, you can configure the following options:

- **Manage TensorBoard Instances**: Users can create, update, or delete TensorBoard instances; instances are used for experiments.

- **Create Experiments**: By uploading pipeline log data, users can generate experiments and visualizations.

- **View TensorBoard Web Application**: Users can view TensorBoard via a web application generated for each TensorBoard instance.

- **Export Data**: Users can export pipeline metadata and TensorBoard data points using the API.

Vertex AI experiments provide users with a platform to experiment and tune model parameters. With Vertex AI experiments, we can interact on the TensorBoard web and check the results. It is an important and integral part of the Google Vertex AI suite.

Summary

In this chapter, we have introduced the Google Vertex AI suite, including its services, platforms, and tools for ML model development and deployment. With Vertex AI, you can manage the datasets, models, and pipelines easily and flexibly. Without a doubt, mastering Vertex AI needs hands-on practice for each service in the suite, and we have provided sample hands-on practice steps in *Appendix 4, Practicing with Google Vertex AI*. Please follow these practices and understand the steps in the appendix. In the next chapter, we will discuss another Google Cloud ML service: Google Cloud ML APIs.

Further reading

For further insights on the learning of the chapter, you can refer to the following links:

- *Vertex AI documentation*

  https://cloud.google.com/vertex-ai/docs

- *All dataset documentation | Vertex AI*

  https://cloud.google.com/vertex-ai/docs/datasets/datasets

- *Introduction to Vertex AI Feature Store*

  https://cloud.google.com/vertex-ai/docs/featurestore/overview

- *Introduction to Vertex AI Workbench*

  https://cloud.google.com/vertex-ai/docs/workbench/introduction

- *Choose a notebook solution | Vertex AI Workbench*

  https://cloud.google.com/vertex-ai/docs/workbench/notebook-solution

- *Introduction to Vertex AI Model Monitoring*

  https://cloud.google.com/vertex-ai/docs/model-monitoring/overview

- *Introduction to Vertex AI Pipelines*

  https://cloud.google.com/vertex-ai/docs/pipelines/introduction

- *Vertex Explainable AI | Vertex AI*

  `https://cloud.google.com/vertex-ai/docs/explainable-ai`

- *Deploy a model using the Cloud console | Vertex AI*

  `https://cloud.google.com/vertex-ai/docs/predictions/deploy-model-console`

- *Appendix 4, Practicing with Google Vertex AI*

8
Discovering Google Cloud ML API

Application programming interfaces (**APIs**) allow one computer program to make its data and functionality available for other programs to use. In other words, through the APIs of a program or a service, users can send a request to and get a response back from the program/service. ML APIs are cloud-based AI services that help you build ML intelligence into your applications, by leveraging APIs from the **Cloud Service Provider** (**CSP**). They are available as REST APIs, client library SDKs, and user interfaces.

Google Cloud ML APIs provide an interface to leverage Google's ML services in the cloud. In this chapter, we will discuss the Google Cloud ML API spectrum, which includes the following cloud services:

- Google Cloud sight APIs, including the Cloud Vision API and Cloud Video API
- Google Cloud language APIs, including **Natural Language Processing** (**NLP**) and Translation
- Google Cloud conversation APIs, including Speech-to-Text, Text-to-Speech, and Dialogflow

Let's start with Google's Cloud Sight API.

Google Cloud Sight API

The **Google Cloud Sight API** offer powerful Google pre-trained machine learning models for vision processing and video processing. We will examine the concepts for both the Cloud Vision API and the Cloud Video API.

The Cloud Vision API

The **Cloud Vision API** is a tool to decipher images through Google's pre-trained advanced ML models. It can interpret images and classify them into lots of categories. It can extract and detect text, whether the text is within pictures or document photos.

Google Cloud Vision allows developers to easily integrate vision detection features within applications, including image labeling, landmark detection, logo detection, and content detection:

- Image label detection can detect, identify, and label objects, locations, activities, animal species, products, and many other things that exist within an image.

- Landmark detection can identify landmarks, such as popular landmarks and natural or man-made structures, within an image. It provides the name of the landmark, the bounding polygon vertices, and the location of the landmark (latitude and longitude).

- Logo detection detects popular product logos, such as popular company logos, product logos, and so on, within an image.

- Content detection detects explicit content, such as adult content, violent content, racy content, and so on, within an image. It provides a likelihood that such content is present within the image.

Some of the use cases for the Google Cloud Vision API are listed as follows:

- **Text digitization**: The Cloud Vision API can detect text in images, especially in scanned images. The best part of it is that you can customize your own models and train them for a specific scenario on top of the core built-in feature. For example, you can put specific doctors' prescriptions in a customized model and train it on top of the models that Google already provides, to make it more robust.

- **Security and surveillance**: Google Cloud Vision provides very precise facial recognition, facial comparison, and facial tracking.

- **Brand research with the Logo API**: Google Cloud Vision offers a separate logo detection API where you can look up a logo in banner ads to tell the brand name.

- **In-store sentiment analysis**: Real-time marketing and customer support can leap forward if we detect the opinions and emotions of a customer who's inside a store in real time. Google Cloud Vision catches customers' sentiments through the facial expressions of a user in a store.

- **Robotics**: Enabling robots to understand their environment is a huge challenge and requires precise object detection by Google Vision APIs.

One of the major areas in Cloud Vision is Google's Cloud Vision **optical character recognition (OCR)**, a method of converting handwritten texts or printed texts into machine-encoded text. With OCR, the Google Vision API can identify and extract text from images, with two annotations: **Text Detection** identifies and extracts text from images, and **Document Text Detection** extracts text from images with a format that is optimized for dense text and documents. The JSON extraction response from Text Detection contains the extracted text together with all the individual words that occurred in that text, and the JSON extraction response from Document Text Detection includes page information, blocks, paragraphs, and words, as well as page break information. Google Cloud Vision OCR has the following benefits:

- **Multi-language support**: Google Cloud Vision OCR supports many languages.

- **Ease of use**: The OCR model itself is part of the built-in Google Vision `librarysur.` and can be used very easily.

- **Fast speed**: The Google Cloud Storage platform integrates with the OCR API service. Utilizing GCS, the OCR API can be very fast.

- **Scalability**: It can scale, and Google's OCR pricing strategy encourages users to scale up the usage of the API, as more usage leads to a cheaper average price.

With Google's pre-trained models, the Cloud Vision API provides many ML features that enable developers to integrate them into various application developments. OCR has many business use cases: banks use OCR to compare statements, hospitals use OCR to convert handwritten forms to standard-text-filled forms, and governments use OCR for survey feedback collections, among others.

The Cloud Video API

The **Google Cloud Video API** enables powerful content discovery within videos. It supports common video formats, including `.MOVIE`, `.MPEG4`, `.MP4`, and `.AVI`. The Google Cloud Video API provides the following features:

- **Label detection**: It can detect the entities within a video, and provide a list of video segment annotations, a list of frame annotations, or a list of shot annotations upon request.

- **Shot change detection**: It can annotate a video by a shot or scene, and label objects that are relative to the video scene.

- **Text detection**: It can provide the actual text as well as the location of the text within the video.

- **Explicit content detection**: It can annotate explicit content and place a timestamp within the video.

- **Object tracking**: It can track multiple objects within a video and provide the location of each object within the various frames.

- **Speech transcription:** It can capture the spoken words/sentences within a video and transcribe them into text.

Through the Google Cloud Video API, developers can annotate videos stored locally or in Cloud Storage, or live-streamed, with contextual information at the level of the entire video, per segment, per shot, and per frame, and develop related intelligent applications.

The Google Cloud Language API

Google's **Cloud Language API** includes language translation and NLP. The Cloud Translation API allows you to detect a language and translate it to another one, thus you only need to specify a target language since it detects the source language automatically. NLP allows you to uncover the structure and the meaning of the input text. It provides an interface for developers or computer programs to send requests and get responses.

Google's NLP API has several methods to perform text analysis and annotations:

- **Sentiment analysis:** Inspects the given text and attempts to determine the overall attitude expressed within the text, such as positive, negative, or neutral. Sentiment analysis is performed through the `analyzeSentiment` method. The sentiment analysis response fields consist of the following:

  - **Document sentiment** contains the overall sentiment of the document, which consists of a score of the sentiment ranging between `-1.0` (negative) and `1.0` (positive), based on the overall emotional leaning of the text, and a magnitude of the sentiment, which indicates the overall strength of emotion (both positive and negative) within the given text, between `0.0` and `+inf`. The score of a document's sentiment indicates the overall emotion of a document. The magnitude of a document's sentiment indicates how much emotional content is present within the document.

  - **Language** contains the language of the document, either passed in the initial request or automatically detected if absent.

  - **Sentences** contain a list of the sentences extracted from the original document, and the sentence-level sentiment values attached to each sentence, which contain score and magnitude values as described previously.

  Sentiment analysis indicates the differences between positive and negative emotions in a document but it does not identify the specific positive and negative emotions. For example, when detecting something that is considered *angry*, or text that is considered *sad*, the analysis response only indicates that the sentiment is negative, not *sad* or *angry*.

- **Entity analysis**: Inspects the given text for known entities, such as proper nouns that map to unique entities (specific people, places, and so on) or common nouns (also called **nominals**, such as restaurants, stadiums, and so on). Entity analysis returns a set of detected entities and parameters associated with those entities, such as the entity's type, the relevance of the entity to the overall text, and locations in the text that refer to the same entity. Entities are returned in the order (highest to lowest) of their salience scores, which reflect their relevance to the overall text.

- **Entity sentiment analysis**: Combines both entity analysis and sentiment analysis and attempts to determine the sentiment (positive or negative) expressed about entities within the text. Entity sentiment is represented by numerical score and magnitude values for each detected entity. Those scores are then aggregated into an overall sentiment score and magnitude for an entity.

- **Syntactic analysis**: Extracts linguistic information, breaks up the given text into a series of sentences and tokens, and provides further analysis on those tokens. Syntactic analysis is performed with the `analyzeSyntax` method. Syntactic analysis consists of the following operations:

  - Sentence extraction breaks up the stream of text into a series of sentences.

  - Tokenization breaks the stream of text up into a series of tokens, with each token usually corresponding to a single word.

  - The Natural Language API then processes the tokens and, using their locations within sentences, adds syntactic information to the tokens.

- **Content classification**: Analyzes the input text content and returns a content category for the content. Content classification is performed by using the `classifyText` method. For an input text, Google's Natural Language API filters the categories returned by the `classifyText` method to include only the most relevant categories.

In summary, with sentiment analysis, entity analysis, entity sentiment analysis, content classification, and syntax analysis, Google's pre-trained models of the Natural Language API can help developers to apply natural language understanding to their applications and solve many business use cases.

The Google Cloud Conversation API

The **Google Cloud Conversation API** provides a way to have interactive natural language AI conversations. It has three aspects: Cloud Dialogflow, Cloud Text-to-Speech, and Cloud Speech-to-Text:

- **Dialogflow** provides a natural language understanding platform where you can design and integrate a conversational user interface.

- **Text-to-Speech** converts text input into audio data of natural human speech.

- **Speech-to-Text** converts audio or speech inputs to texts.

Google Cloud Dialogflow allows you to build virtual agents and chatbots. Dialogflow analyzes text or audio inputs and responds using text or speech.

Intents are at the core of Dialogflow. An intent categorizes an end user's intention. When a user adds an inputs, Dialogflow does intent classification by using training phrases – examples of what the end users may actually say – to train the model, and the training results are the mapping of the phrases to intents. Using user intents, a typical workflow for Dialogflow is as follows:

1. An end user will provide an input phrase, which will be sent to some type of agent. The agent performs intent classification and maps the input phrase into an intent.

2. From the intent, it will extract the relevant parameters and link actions to intents, such as retrieving a bank account balance.

3. The parameters and actions will be sent to create a response.

4. The response is speech or text that is returned to the end user.

Google Cloud Speech-to-Text enables the integration of Google speech recognition technologies into application development using Google's advanced AI technologies. There are three main methods in Speech-to-Text:

- **Synchronous recognition**: When the Speech-to-Text API receives speech audio data, it performs data recognition/processing and returns results after all audio data has been processed before it processes the next request.

- **Asynchronous recognition**: When the Speech-to-Text API receives audio data input, it initiates a long-running operation, which periodically polls for recognition results.

- **Streaming recognition**: Real-time audio recognition, such as capturing live audio from a microphone. Streaming recognition provides interim results while audio is being captured, allowing results to appear while a user is still speaking.

Speech-to-Text can use one of several machine learning models to transcribe your audio file. Google has trained these speech recognition models for specific audio types and sources. When you send an audio transcription request to Speech-to-Text, you can improve the results that you receive by specifying the source of the original audio. This allows the Speech-to-Text API to process your audio files using a machine learning model trained to recognize speech audio from that particular type of source.

The Google Cloud Text-to-Speech API allows you to convert text to human-like speech using WaveNet voices, which synthesize speech with more human-like emphasis and inflection on syllables, phonemes, and words. WaveNet produces speech audio that people prefer over other text-to-speech technologies.

Text-to-Speech uses a synthetic voice to create audio from the text that is presented to it. It creates natural-sounding human speech as playable audio. In addition to normal text, the Cloud Text-to-Speech API can convert **Speech Synthesis Markup Language** (**SSML**) to audio. SSML allows you to control the way in which text is converted to speech.

Summary

In this chapter, we have introduced the Google Cloud ML API services: the Cloud Sight API with Vision and Video APIs, the Cloud Language API with the Translation and NPL APIs, and the Cloud conversation API with Dialogflow, Speech-to-Text and Text-to-Speech. These Google pre-trained API services provide the best functions and interfaces for ML application development, and we have shown some sample business use cases leveraging Google ML APIs.

To master the Google ML API services, labs are an important part of the learning process, and we have provided some ML API hands-on demonstrations in *Appendix 5, Practicing with the Google Cloud ML API*. Please review and understand all the practice steps.

In the next chapter, we will discuss the best practices in implementing ML in Google Cloud.

Further reading

For further insights into the learnings of this chapter, you can refer to the following links:

- *Vision AI | Derive Image Insights via ML | Cloud Vision API*:

    `https://cloud.google.com/vision/`

- *Video AI - Video Content Analysis | Cloud Video Intelligence API*:

    `https://cloud.google.com/video-intelligence/`

- *Speech-to-Text: Automatic Speech Recognition*:

    `https://cloud.google.com/speech-to-text`

- *Text-to-Speech: Lifelike Speech Synthesis*:

    `https://cloud.google.com/text-to-speech`

- *Dialogflow*:

    `https://cloud.google.com/dialogflow/`

- *Appendix 5, Practicing with the Google Cloud ML API*

9
Using Google Cloud ML Best Practices

In this chapter, we will discuss the best practices for implementing **Machine Learning (ML)** in Google Cloud. We will go through an implementation of a customer-trained ML model development process in GCP and provide recommendations throughout.

In this chapter, we will cover the following topics:

- ML environment setup
- ML data storage and processing
- ML model training
- ML model deployment
- ML workflow orchestration
- ML model continuous monitoring

This chapter aims to integrate the knowledge we have learned so far in this book and apply it to a customer-trained ML project. We will start by setting up the ML environment.

ML environment setup

In *Chapter 4, Developing and Deploying ML Models*, in the *Preparing the platform* section, we learned about the ML platform in the Cloud. Then, in *Chapter 7, Exploring Google Cloud Vertex AI*, we introduced the Vertex AI services. For a customer-trained model development platform, we recommend **Vertex AI Workbench user-managed notebooks**. Let's look at the details from the prospects of performance, cost, and security.

With Vertex AI Workbench user-managed notebooks, you have the flexibility and options to implement **performance excellency**. You can create an instance with the existing deep learning VM images that have the latest ML and data science libraries preinstalled, along with the latest accelerator drivers. Depending on your data, model, and workloads, you can choose the right VM instance type to fit your environment and optimize performance, from general-purpose compute (E2, N1, N2, and N2D), to memory-optimized (M1 and M2), to compute-optimized (C2), and so on. You can also create a notebooks instance based on a custom container to tailor your ML environment.

With Vertex AI Workbench user-managed notebooks, you can go with GCP best practices and **reduce costs**. As with any Google Cloud services, treat your notebook's VM instances as flexible and disposable resources; when you train ML models on the VM instances, make sure that you store all your data in Cloud Storage or BigQuery, instead of storing it in the instances' local storage, such as persistent disks, so that you can stop or delete the instances when you are done with the ML experimenting or training. During the ML model development process, always monitor the VM instances' performances and costs, and scale out/in based on the workloads while utilizing Google's Managed instance groups (MIGs).

Security is always an important area we need to address in the Cloud. Some of the best security practices are as follows:

- With Vertex AI Workbench user-managed notebooks, we recommend that a user-managed notebooks instance is created for each member of the data science team. If a team member is involved in multiple projects, we recommend using multiple user-managed notebooks instances for the member and treating each instance as a virtual workspace.

- Operating Vertex AI requires collaboration among a variety of teams, and it is super important to determine which groups or systems will be responsible for which functions. From a networking point of view, you should configure user-managed notebooks to use shared VPCs if possible, to minimize access to the notebook instances. Restrictive firewall rules must also be enabled to limit access to notebook instances and other Vertex AI resources.

- For data and model storing, we also recommend storing the training data and training model in the same project for reproducibility. In a Google organization with multiple folders and multiple projects, the best practice is leveraging Google IAM roles and groups.

- For data protection, we recommend using Google Cloud organization policies and Data Loss Prevention (DLP) tools to protect Personal Identifiable Information (PII) data. Data encryption is also recommended for storing data at rest and in transit in the Vertex AI notebooks instances. Vertex AI supports **Customer-Managed Encryption Keys (CMEK)** across most of its components.

Now that we have understood the environment setup, let's move to data storage and processing.

ML data storage and processing

As we discussed in *Chapter 4, Developing and Deploying ML Models*, storing data involves collecting raw data from various data sources and storing it in a centralized repository. On the other hand, data processing includes both data engineering and feature engineering. Data engineering is the process of converting raw data (the data in its source form) into prepared data (the dataset in the form that is ready to be input into ML tasks). Feature engineering then tunes the prepared data to create the features expected by the ML model.

For structured data, we recommend using **Google Cloud BQ** to store and process it. For unstructured data, videos, audio, and image data, we recommend using **Google Cloud** object storage to store them and **Google Cloud Dataflow** or **Dataproc** to process them. As we have discussed, **Dataflow** is a managed service that uses the **Apache Beam** programming model to convert unstructured data into binary formats and can improve data ingestion performance. Dataproc is a managed **Apache Spark** and **Apache Hadoop** service that leverages open source data tools for batch processing, querying, streaming, and ML.

For supervised ML, which needs labeled datasets, we recommend using the **Google Vertex AI Data Labeling** service, especially for unstructured data. From a security point of view, we recommend using **Google Cloud IAM** to manage data access in Cloud Storage and BQ, using GCP DLP to manage PII and other sensitive data, and using GCP Key Management Services (KMS) for data encryption key management.

Once the data has been preprocessed, we recommend using a Vertex AI-managed dataset to create a link between your data and custom-trained models and provide descriptive statistics to split data into training, validation, and testing subsets.

Depending on the ML model features, many methods can be utilized in feature engineering. We recommend using **Vertex AI Feature Store**, which can be used to create new features from the data lakes, schedule data processing, and feature engineering jobs, ingest them into Vertex Feature Store for online or batch serving, and share the common features within the data science team.

ML model training

ML model training is a critical phase in ML development, which is why we recommend using GCP Vertex AI Training. Instead of manually adjusting hyperparameters with numerous training runs for optimal values, we recommend the automated Vertex AI training model enhancer to test different hyperparameter configurations, and **Google Vertex AI TensorBoard** to track, share, and compare model metrics such as loss functions to visualize model graphs. This allows you to compare various experiments for parameter tuning and model optimization.

Using Vertex AI Workbench user-managed notebooks, you can develop your code conveniently and interactively, and we recommend operationalizing your code for reproducibility and scalability and running your code in either Vertex training or **Vertex AI Pipelines**.

After model training, it is recommended that you use **Vertex Explainable AI** to study and gain insights regarding feature contributions and understand your model's behavior. Vertex Explainable AI helps you understand your model's outputs – it tells you how much each feature in the data contributed to the predicted result. Then, you can use this information to see whether your model is behaving as expected, to recognize bias (if there is any) in your models, and get some ideas to improve your model and your training data.

ML model deployment

ML model deployment refers to putting a model into production. Once an ML model has been deployed into production, it can be used to predict new data. We recommend using the Vertex AI console or API to deploy a trained ML model. With Vertex AI, we can serve the model in production with batch prediction; we recommend specifying the appropriate hardware for your model and determining how to pass inputs to the model. With Vertex AI, we can also serve the model with online endpoint prediction; we recommend using Vertex AI Feature Store's online serving API and turning on automatic scaling with a minimum of two nodes.

ML workflow orchestration

As we discussed in *Chapter 7, Exploring Google Cloud Vertex AI*, Vertex AI Pipelines is a fully managed service that allows you to retrain your models as often as necessary so that you can adapt to changes and maintain performance over time. We recommend Vertex AI Pipelines for Cloud ML workflow orchestration.

If you're using the **Google TensorFlow framework**, we recommend using **TensorFlow Extended** to define your pipeline and the operations for each step, then executing it on Vertex AI's serverless pipeline system. TensorFlow provides pre-built components for common steps in the Vertex AI workflow, such as data ingestion, data validation, and training.

If you are using other frameworks, we recommend using **Kubeflow Pipeline**, which is very flexible and allows you to use simple code to construct pipelines. Kubeflow Pipeline also provides Google Cloud pipeline components such as Vertex AI AutoML.

ML model continuous monitoring

Once you've deployed your model into production, you need to monitor model performance continuously to ensure that it is performing as expected. We recommend using Vertex AI, which provides two ways to monitor your ML models:

- **Skew detection**, which looks for the degree of distortion between your model training and production data.

- **Drift detection**, which looks for drift in your production data. Drift occurs when the statistical properties of the inputs and the target change over time and cause predictions to become less accurate as time passes.

For skew and drift detection, we recommend setting up a model monitoring job by providing a pointer to the training data that you used to train your model, and then tuning the thresholds that are used for alerting to measure skew or drift occurring in your data.

You can also use feature attributions in Vertex Explainable AI to detect data drift or skew as an early indicator that model performance may be degrading. For example, let's say that your model originally relied on five features to make predictions in training and test data, but when going into production, it began to rely on entirely different features.

Summary

In this chapter, we discussed the best practices for implementing ML in Google Cloud, with a focus on custom-trained models based on your data and code.

This chapter concludes *Part 3* of this book, in which we have discussed Google BQ and BQML for training ML models from structured data, Google ML training frameworks such as TensorFlow and Keras, the Google ML training suite Vertex AI, Google Cloud ML APIs, and the best ML practices in Google Cloud.

In the fourth part of this book, we will prepare for the Google Cloud Certified Professional ML Engineer certification by understanding the certification's requirements and deep diving into some of the certification's practice questions.

Further reading

To learn more about what was covered in this chapter, take a look at the following resources:

- `https://www.tensorflow.org/tfx`
- `https://www.kubeflow.org/`
- `https://cloud.google.com/architecture/ml-on-gcp-best-practices`
- `https://cloud.google.com/architecture/mlops-continuous-delivery-and-automation-pipelines-in-machine-learning`

Part 4:
Accomplishing GCP
ML Certification

In this part, we focus on the Google Cloud Professional Machine Learning Engineer certification. We introduce the GCP ML certification and Google's official guides. We study the certification exam questions by integrating the knowledge and skills learned from the book.

This part comprises the following chapter:

- Chapter 10, Achieving the GCP ML Certification

10

Achieving the GCP ML Certification

Congratulations! You have gone through all the chapters thus far and built a strong knowledge base and skillset for **Machine Learning** (**ML**) in Google Cloud. Now, it is time to integrate what you have learned so far and take the GCP ML certification exam – the last part of our learning roadmap.

The Google Professional Machine Learning Engineer certification exam is a very important part of your journey to becoming a Google Cloud Certified Machine Learning Engineer. To prepare for and pass the exam, you must review all the contents in this book and integrate them to deeply understand them and connect all the dots.

We recommend that you take the following steps to prepare for and achieve the Google Professional ML Engineer certification:

1. Read the official Google ML certification exam guide.

2. Read all the chapters in this book.

3. Complete all the hands-on labs in this book.

4. Practice and review all the practice questions in this chapter.

To get you prepared, we have provided some practice questions for the ML certification exam, along with the analysis of the questions in this chapter. Make sure you fully understand each question and all the answers to the questions, and why the right answer is right and the wrong answers are wrong. Keep in mind that the questions set here are just examples and we aim to provide a pilot sample for you to follow. You will need to do more research on the internet to reach a comprehensive level for the exam.

GCP ML exam practice questions

Please read each question carefully and thoroughly, and fully understand it. Please also review all the docs that are related to the question at the reference links provided:

- **Question 1**: Space Y is launching its hundredth satellite to build its StarSphere network. They have designed an accurate orbit (launching speed/time/and so on) for it based on the existing 99 satellite orbits to cover the Earth's scope. What's the best solution to forecast the position of the 100 satellites after the hundredth launch?

  A. Use ML algorithms and train ML models to forecast

  B. Use neural networks to train the model to forecast

  C. Use physical laws and actual environmental data to model and forecast

  D. Use a linear regression model to forecast

  Analysis: This is an ML problem framing question. To decide whether ML is the best method for a problem, we need to see whether traditional science modeling would be very difficult or impossible to solve the problem and whether plenty of data exists. When we start, science modeling will be our first choice since it builds the most accurate model based on science and natural laws. For example, given the initial position and speed of an object, as well as its mass and the forces acting on it, we can precisely predict its position at any time. For this case, the mathematical model works much better than any ML model!

  To forecast the hundredth satellite's orbit, answer C is the best choice here.

  Reference: Section *Is ML the best solution?* in *Chapter 3, Preparing for ML Development*

- **Question 2**: A financial company is building an ML model to detect credit card fraud based on their historical dataset, which contains 20 positives and 4,990 negatives.

  Due to the imbalanced classes, the model training is not working as desired. What's the best way to resolve this issue?

  A. Data augmentation

  B. Early stopping

  C. Downsampling and upweighting

  D. Regularization

  Analysis: This question is about class imbalance when preparing data for classification problems. When the data is imbalanced, it will be very difficult to train the ML model and get good forecasts. We need to use *downsampling and upweighting* to balance the classes, so the answer is C.

  Reference: Section *Data sampling and balancing* in *Chapter 3, Preparing for ML Development*

- **Question 3**: A chemical manufacturer is using a GCP ML pipeline to detect real-time sensor anomalies by queuing the inputs and analyzing and visualizing the data. Which one will you choose for the pipeline?

  A. Dataproc | AI Platform | BQ

  B. Dataflow | AutoML | Cloud SQL

  C. Dataflow | AI Platform | BQ

  D. Dataproc | AutoML | Bigtable

  Analysis: This is an ML pipeline question. We need to understand the difference between Dataflow and Dataproc, AI Platform and AutoML, as well as the various GCP databases: Cloud SQL, Bigtable, and BQ.

  Dataproc and Dataflow are GCP data processing services, and both can process batch or streaming data. However, Dataproc is designed to run on clusters for jobs that are compatible with MapReduce (Apache Hadoop, Hive, and Spark). Dataflow is based on parallel data processing and works better if your data has no implementation with Spark or Hadoop.

  AI Platform involves "human-performed" ML training – using your own data and model. AutoML is "automated" ML training with Google's model and your own data, with no coding.

  Out of the GCP database/warehouse products, Cloud SQL is for relational data online transaction processing, Bigtable is more for NoSQL transaction processing, and BQ is great for analyzing and visualizing data (integrating with Data Studio).

  Based on this, we will choose C as the answer.

- **Question 4**: A real estate company, Zeellow, does great business buying and selling properties in the United States. Over the past few years, they have accumulated a big amount of historical data for US houses.

  Zeellow is using ML training to predict housing prices, and they retrain the models every month by integrating new data. The company does not want to write any code in the ML process. What method best suits their needs?

  A. AutoML tables

  B. BigQuery ML

  C. AI Platform

  D. AutoML classification

  Analysis: This question is also about the difference between AutoML and AI Platform, as well as between regression and classification. Since AutoML serves the purpose of no coding during the ML process, and this is a structured data ML problem, the correct answer is A.

- **Question 5**: The data scientist team is building a deep learning model for a customer support center of a big **Enterprise Resource Planning** (**ERP**) company, which has many ERP products and modules. The DL model will input customers' chat texts and categorize them into products before routing them to the corresponding team. The company wants to minimize the model development time and data preprocessing time. What strategy/platform should they choose?

  A.   AI Platform

  B.   Auto ML

  C.   NLP API

  D.   Vertex AI Custom notebooks

  Analysis: The key point here is that *the company wants to minimize the model development time and data preprocessing time*. AutoML is the best choice, so the correct answer is B.

- **Question 6**: A real estate company, Zeellow, does great business buying and selling properties in the United States. Over the past few years, they have accumulated a big amount of historical data for US houses.

  Zeellow wants to use ML to forecast future sales by leveraging their historical sales data. The historical data is stored in cloud storage. You want to rapidly experiment with all the available data. How should you build and train your model?

  A.   Load data into BigQuery and use BigQuery ML

  B.   Convert the data into CSV and use AutoML Tables

  C.   Convert the data into TFRecords and use TensorFlow

  D.   Convert and refactor the data into CSV format and use the built-in XGBoost library

  Analysis: The key point here is that we need to experiment quickly with all the structured datasets stored in cloud storage. BQ and BQML are the best options here since all the others will take a long time to build and train the model. Thus, the correct answer is A.

- **Question 7**: A real estate company, Zeellow, uses ML to forecast future sales by leveraging their historical data. New data is coming in every week, and Zeellow needs to make sure the model is continually retrained to reflect the marketing trend. What should they do with the historical data and new data?

  A.   Only use the new data for retraining

  B.   Update the datasets weekly with new data

  C.   Update the datasets with new data when model evaluation metrics do not meet the required criteria

  D.   Update the datasets monthly with new data

Analysis: Model retraining is the key term here. Since data changes over time and causes trained models to become obsolete, model retraining is the norm in the ML process. In this case, when do we need to retrain the model? The answer is when the performance metrics do not meet the requirements. How do we retrain the model? The answer is to use the integrated datasets, including existing and new data. Therefore, the correct answer is C.

- **Question 8**: A real estate company, Zeellow, uses ML to forecast future sales by leveraging their historical data. Their data science team trained and deployed a DL model in production half a year ago. Recently, the model is suffering from performance issues due to data distribution changes.

  The team is working on a strategy for model retraining. What is your suggestion?

  A.   Monitor data skew and retrain the model

  B.   Retrain the model with fewer model features

  C.   Retrain the model to fix overfitting

  D.   Retrain the model with new data coming in every month

  Analysis: Model retraining is based on data value skews, which are significant changes in the statistical properties of data. When data skew is detected, this means that data patterns are changing, and we need to retrain the model to capture these changes. The question did not mention any overfitting issues, nor did it mention feature reduction. The retraining strategy will be monitoring data skew and retraining the model with the new inputs. Thus, the correct answer is A.

  Reference: https://developers.google.com/machine-learning/guides/rules-of-ml/#rule_37_measure_trainingserving_skew.

- **Question 9**: Recent research has indicated that when a certain kind of cancer, X, is developed in a human liver, there are usually other symptoms that can be identified as objects Y and Z from CT scan images. A hospital is using this research to train ML models with a label map of (X, Y, Z) on CT images. What cost functions should be used in this case?

  A.   Binary cross-entropy

  B.   Categorical cross-entropy

  C.   Sparse categorical cross-entropy

  D.   Dense categorical cross-entropy

Analysis: The correct answer is B.

In *Chapter 5, Understanding Neural Networks and Deep Learning, in The cost function* section, we discussed the use cases for different cost functions. Binary cross-entropy is used for binary classification problems. Categorical entropy is better to use when you want to prevent the model from giving more importance to a certain class – the same as the one-hot encoding idea. Sparse categorical entropy is more optimal when your classes are mutually exclusive (for example, when each sample belongs exactly to one class).

- **Question 10**: The data science team in your company has built a DNN model to forecast the sales value for an automobile company, based on historical data. As a Google ML Engineer, you need to verify that the features selected are good enough for the ML model.

  A. Train the model with L1 regularization and verify that the loss is constant

  B. Train the model with no regularization and verify that the loss is constant

  C. Train the model with L2 regularization and verify that the loss is decreasing

  D. Train the model with no regularization and verify that the loss is close to zero

  Analysis: The correct answer is D.

  The loss function is the measurement for model prediction accuracy and is used as an index for the ML training process. To verify that the model that's been built has enough features, we need to make sure that the loss function is close to zero when no regularizations are used.

  Reference: Section *Regularization* in *Chapter 4, Developing and Deploying ML Models*

- **Question 11**: The data science team in your company has built a DNN model to forecast the sales value for a real estate company, based on historical data. As a Google ML Engineer, you find that the model has over 300 features and that you wish to remove some features that are not contributing to the target. What will you do?

  A. Use Explainable AI to understand the feature contributions and reduce the non-contributing ones.

  B. Use L1 regularization to reduce features.

  C. Use L2 regularization to reduce features.

  D. Drop a feature at a time, train the model, and verify that it does not degrade the model. Remove these features.

  Analysis: The correct answer is A. This question is discussing feature selection, and Explainable AI is one of the ways to understand which features are contributing and which ones are not. It is important to understand that L1 and L2 are methods for resolving model overfitting issues and not feature selection in data engineering.

- **Question 12**: The data science team in your company has built a DNN model to forecast the sales value for a real estate company, based on historical data. They found that the model fits the training dataset well, but not the validation dataset. What would you do to improve the model?

  A.   Apply a dropout parameter of 0.3 and decrease the learning rate by a factor of 10

  B.   Apply an L2 regularization parameter of 0.3 and decrease the learning rate by a factor of 10

  C.   Apply an L1 regularization parameter of 0.3 and increase the learning rate by a factor of 10

  D.   Tune the hyperparameters to optimize the L2 regularization and dropout parameters

  Analysis: The correct answer is D.

  This question is discussing techniques to avoid model overfitting. While L1/L2 regularization, dropout parameters, and learning rate are all ways to help, we must tune the hyperparameters and find the optimized values. A hint here is that the correct answer would be fitting to the general case and thus will not have concrete numbers such as 0.3, 10, and so on.

- **Question 13**: You are building a DL model for a customer service center. The model will input customers' chat text and analyze their sentiments. What algorithm should be used for the model?

  A.   MLP

  B.   Regression

  C.   CNN

  D.   RNN

  Analysis: The correct answer is D.

  This question tests the different algorithms used for ML/DL. Since text processing for sentiment analysis needs to process sequential data (time series), the best option is **Recurrent Neural Networks (RNNs)**.

- **Question 14**: A health insurance company scans customers' hand-filled claim forms and stores them in Google Cloud Storage buckets in real time. They use ML models to recognize the handwritten texts. Since the claims may contain **Personally Identifiable Information (PII)**, company policies require only authorized persons to access the information. What's the best way to store and process this streaming data?

  A.   Create two buckets and label them as sensitive and non-sensitive. Store data in the non-sensitive bucket first. Periodically scan it using the DLP API and move the sensitive data to the sensitive bucket.

  B.   Create one bucket to store the data. Only allow the ML service account access to it.

C. Create three buckets – quarantine, sensitive, and non-sensitive. Store all the data in the quarantine bucket first. Then, periodically scan it using the DLP API and move the data to either the sensitive or non-sensitive bucket.

D. Create three buckets – quarantine, sensitive, and non-sensitive. Store all the data in the quarantine bucket first. Then, once the file has been uploaded, trigger the DLP API to scan it, and move the data to either the sensitive or non-sensitive bucket.

Analysis: The correct answer is D.

This is a business use case for PII/private data storage and processing, and a typical solution is to create three buckets and utilize DLP to scan and then move the raw data into different buckets and control their access.

- **Question 15**: A real estate company, Zeellow, uses ML to forecast future sales by leveraging their historical data. The recent model training was able to achieve the desired forecast accuracy objective, but it took the data science team a long time. They want to decrease the training time without affecting the achieved model accuracy. What hyperparameter should the team adjust?

A. Learning rate

B. Epochs

C. Scale tier

D. Batch size

Analysis: The correct answer is C since changing the other three parameters will change the model's prediction accuracy.

- **Question 16**: The data science team has built a DNN model to monitor and detect defective products using the images from the assembly line of an automobile manufacturing company. As a Google ML Engineer, you need to measure the performance of the ML model for the test dataset/images. Which of the following would you choose?

A. The AUC value

B. The recall value

C. The precision value

D. The TP value

Analysis: The correct answer is A because it measures how well the predictions are ranked rather than their absolute values. It is a classification threshold invariant and thus is the best way to measure the model's performance.

- **Question 17**: The data science team has built a DL model to monitor and detect defective products using the images from the assembly line of an automobile manufacturing company. Over time, the team has built multiple model versions in AI Platform. As a Google ML Engineer, how will you compare the model versions?

A.   Compare the mean average precision for the model versions

B.   Compare the model loss functions on the training dataset

C.   Compare the model loss functions on the validation dataset

D.   Compare the model loss functions on the testing dataset

Analysis: The correct answer is A because it measures how well the different model versions perform over time: deploy your model as a model version and then create an evaluation job for that version. By comparing the mean average precision across the model versions, you can find the best performer.

References: `https://cloud.google.com/ai-platform/prediction/docs/ continuous-evaluation/view-metrics#compare_mean_average_precision_ across_models`.

- **Question 18**: The data science team is building a recommendation engine for an e-commerce website using ML models to increase its business revenue, based on users' similarities. What model would you choose?

A.   Collaborative filtering

B.   Regression

C.   Classification

D.   Content-based filtering

Analysis: For this recommendation engine question, the correct answer is A.

Content-based filtering uses the similarity between items to recommend items that are similar to what the user likes. Collaborative filtering uses similarities between users to provide recommendations. The question specifies "based on users' similarities."

References: `https://developers.google.com/machine-learning/ recommendation/overview/candidate-generation`.

- **Question 19**: The data science team is building a fraud-detection model for a credit card company, whose objective is to detect as much fraud as possible and avoid as many false alarms as possible. What confusion matrix index would you maximize for this model performance evaluation?

A.   Precision

B.   Recall

C.   The area under the PR curve

D.   The area under the ROC curve

Analysis: In this fraud-detection problem, it asks you to focus on detecting fraudulent transactions - maximize True Positive rate and minimize False Negative - maximize recall (*Recall = TruePositives / (TruePositives + FalseNegatives)*). It also asks you to minimize false alarms (false positives) - maximize precision (*Precision = TruePositives / (TruePositives + FalsePositives)*).

So, since you want to maximize both precision and recall, the correct answer is C (maximize the area under the PR curve).

References: https://machinelearningmastery.com/roc-curves-and-precision-recall-curves-for-imbalanced-classification/.

- **Question 20**: The data science team is building a data pipeline for an auto manufacturing company, whose objective is to integrate all the data sources that exist in their on-premise facilities, via a codeless data ETL interface. What GCP service will you use?

  A. Dataproc

  B. Dataflow

  C. Dataprep

  D. Data Fusion

  Analysis: Since the question asks for data integration with a codeless interface, Data Fusion is the best choice here. Thus, the correct answer is D.

  References: https://cloud.google.com/data-fusion/docs/concepts/overview#using_the_code-free_web_ui.

- **Question 21**: The data science team has built a TensorFlow model in BigQuery for a real estate company, whose objective is to integrate all their data models into the new Google Vertex AI platform. What's the best strategy?

  A. Export the model from BigQuery ML

  B. Register the BQML model to Vertex AI

  C. Import the model into Vertex AI

  D. Use AI Platform as the middle stage

  Analysis: Since the question asks for model integration with Vertex AI, which allows you to register a BQML model in it, the correct answer is B.

  References: https://cloud.google.com/bigquery-ml/docs/managing-models-vertex.

- **Question 22**: A real estate company, Zeellow, uses ML to forecast future house sale prices by leveraging their historical data. The data science team needs to build a model to predict US house sale prices based on the house location (US city-specific) and house type. What strategy is the best for feature engineering in this case?

A. One feature cross: [latitude X longitude X housetype]

B. Two feature crosses: [binned latitude X binned housetype] and [binned longitude X binned housetype]

C. Three separate binned features: [binned latitude], [binned longitude], [binned housetype]

D. One feature cross: [binned latitude X binned longitude X binned housetype]

Analysis: Crossing binned latitude with binned longitude enables the model to learn city-specific effects on house types. It prevents a change in latitude from producing the same result as a change in longitude. Depending on the granularity of the bins, this feature cross could learn city-specific housing effects. So, the correct answer is D.

References: `https://developers.google.com/machine-learning/crash-course/feature-crosses/check-your-understanding`.

- **Question 23**: A health insurance company scans customer's hand-filled claim forms and stores them in Google Cloud Storage buckets in real time. The data scientist team has developed an AI documentation model to digitize the images. By the end of each day, the submitted forms need to be processed automatically. The model is ready for deployment. What strategy should the team use to process the forms?

A. Vertex AI batch prediction

B. Vertex AI online prediction

C. Vertex AI ML pipeline prediction

D. Cloud Run to trigger prediction

Analysis: As specified in the question, we need to run the process at the end of each day, which implies batch processing using AI Platform or Vertex AI. The correct answer is A.

- **Question 24**: A real estate company, Zeellow, uses GCP ML to forecast future house sale prices by leveraging their historical data. Their data science team has about 30 members and each member has developed multiple versions of models using Vertex AI customer notebooks. What's the best strategy to manage these different models and different versions developed by the team members?

A. Set up IAM permissions to allow each member access to their notebooks, models, and versions

B. Create a GCP project for each member for clean management

C. Create a map from each member to their GCP resources using BQ

D. Apply label/tags to the resources when they're created for scalable inventory/cost/access management

Analysis: Resource tagging/labeling is the best way to manage ML resources for medium/big data science teams. The best answer is D.

Resource: `https://cloud.google.com/resource-manager/docs/tags/tags-creating-and-managing`.

- **Question 25**: Starbucks is an international coffee shop selling multiple products A, B, C... at different stores (1, 2, 3... using one-hot encoding and location binning). They are building stores and want to leverage ML models to predict product sales based on historical data (A1 is the data for product A sales at store 1). Following the best practices of splitting data into a training subset, validation subset, and testing subset, how should the data be distributed into these subsets?

  A. Distribute data randomly across the subsets:

   - Training set: [A1, B2, F1, E2, ...]

   - Testing set: [A2, C3, D2, F4, ...]

   - Validation set: [B1, C1, D9, C2...]

  B. Distribute products randomly across the subsets:

   - Training set: [A1, A2, A3, E1, E2, ...]

   - Testing set: [B1, B2, C1, C2, C3, ...]

   - Validation set: [D1, D2, F1, F2, F3, ...]

  C. Distribute stores randomly across subsets:

   - Training set: [A1, B1, C1, ...]

   - Testing set: [A2, C2, F2, ...]

   - Validation set: [D3, A3, C3, ...]

  D. Aggregate the data groups by the cities where the stores are allocated and distribute cities randomly across subsets

  Analysis: This question is about dataset splitting to avoid data leakage. If we distribute the data randomly into the training, validation, and test sets, the model will be able to learn specific qualities about the products. If we divided things up at the product level so that the given products were only in the training subset, the validation subset, or the testing subset, the model would find it more difficult to get high accuracy on the validation since it would need to focus on the product characteristics/qualities. Therefore, the correct answer is B.

Reference: `https://developers.google.com/machine-learning/crash-course/18th-century-literature`.

- **Question 26**: You are building a DL model with Keras that looks as follows:

```
model = tf.keras.sequential
model.add(df.keras.layers.
Dense(128,activation='relu',input_shape=(200, )))
model.add(df.keras.layers.Dropout(rate=0.25))
model.add(df.keras.layers.Dense(4,activation='relu'))
model.add(df.keras.layers.Dropout(rate=0.25))
model.add(Dense(2))
```

How many trainable weights does this model have?

A.   200x128+128x4+4x2

B.   200x128+128x4+2

C.   200x128+129x4+5x2

D.   200x128x0.25+128x4x0.25+4x2

Analysis: This question is testing the concept of trainable weights in a Keras model. As you can see, the correct answer is D.

- **Question 27**: The data science team is building a DL model for a customer support center of a big ERP company, which has many ERP products and modules. The company receives over a million customer service calls every day and stores them in GCS. The call data must not leave the region in which the call originated and no PII can be stored/analyzed. The model will analyze calls for customer sentiments. How should you design a data pipeline for call processing, analyzing, and visualizing?

A.   GCS -> Speech2Text -> DLP -> BigQuery

B.   GCS -> Pub/Sub -> Speech2Text -> DLP -> Datastore

C.   GCS -> Speech2Text -> DLP -> BigTable

D.   GCS -> Speech2Text -> DLP -> Cloud SQL

Analysis: Since the question asks for a data pipeline to process, analyze, and visualize, the best answer is A. BigQuery is the best tool here to analyze and visualize.

- **Question 28**: The data science team is building an ML model to monitor and detect defective products using the images from the assembly line of an automobile manufacturing company, which does not have reliable Wi-Fi near the assembly line. As a Google ML Engineer, you need to reduce the amount of time spent by quality control inspectors utilizing the model's fast defect detection. Your company wants to implement the new ML model as soon as possible. Which model should you use?

    A. AutoML Vision

    B. AutoML Vision Edge mobile-versatile-1

    C. AutoML Vision Edge mobile-low-latency-1

    D. AutoML Vision Edge mobile-high-accuracy-1

    Analysis: Since the question asks for a quick inspection time and prioritizes latency reduction, the correct answer is C.

    Reference: `https://cloud.google.com/vision/automl/docs/train-edge`.

- **Question 29**: A national hospital is leveraging Google Cloud and a cell phone app to build an ML model to forecast heart attacks based on age, gender, exercise, heart rate, blood pressure, and more. Since the health data is highly sensitive personal information and cannot be stored in cloud databases, how should you train and deploy the ML model?

    A. IoT with data encryption

    B. Federated learning

    C. Encrypted BQML

    D. DLP API

    Analysis: Federated learning is the best choice here due to the restrictions. With federated learning, all the data is collected, and the model is trained with algorithms across multiple decentralized edge devices such as cell phones or websites, without exchanging them. Therefore, the best answer is B.

- **Question 30**: You are an ML engineer at a media company. You need to build an ML model to analyze video content frame by frame, identify objects, and alert users if there is inappropriate content. Which Google Cloud products should you use to build this project?

    A. Pub/Sub, Cloud Functions, and Cloud Vision API

    B. Pub/Sub, Cloud IoT, Dataflow, Cloud Vision API, and Cloud Logging

    C. Pub/Sub, Cloud Functions, Video Intelligence API, and Cloud Logging

    D. Pub/Sub, Cloud Functions, AutoML Video Intelligence, and Cloud Logging

Analysis: Since this question involves video analysis, this will eliminate A and B. AutoML video intelligence is for cases where you wish to customize models with Google's model and your data. Therefore, C is the correct answer since the Video Intelligence API can be used to meet the requirements.

Summary

In this chapter, we discussed the Google Cloud Professional Machine Learning Engineer certification exam and some practice questions. Since GCP ML is a changing domain, many new services have been developed and released by Google while this book was being written. By no means does this book cover all the exam topics in this domain. You will need to refer to the Google certification page for the certification exam guides and updates.

This chapter concludes part four of this book. In part five of this book, in the appendices, we will provide some labs and demos for practicing your hands-on skills. It is recommended that you go through each appendix and practice the labs step-by-step.

Part 5: Appendices

In this part, we provide hands-on practices for ML in Google Cloud, including the basic GCP services, the Python data science libraries, the scikit-learn library, the GCP Vertex AI suite, and the Google Cloud ML APIs.

This part comprises the following chapters:

- Appendix 1, Practicing with Basic GCP Services
- Appendix 2, Practicing with the Python Data Library
- Appendix 3, Practicing with Scikit-Learn
- Appendix 4, Practicing with Google Vertex AI
- Appendix 5, Practicing with Google Cloud ML API

Appendix 1
Practicing with Basic GCP Services

In this appendix, we will show some GCP resource provisioning examples, using the Google Cloud console and Cloud Shell. We will use the following architecture to practice using the Google Cloud console, as shown in *Figure 11.1*:

- A VPC network, VPC1, and two subnets in it: a public subnet1 and a private subnet2

- A **virtual machine (VM)** in the public subnet1 that has an external IP address and can be accessed from the internet

- A VM in the private subnet2 that does not have an external IP address and thus can only be accessed from the console browser, or from VMs within the same VPC

- Another VPC network, VPC2, and one subnet within VPC2: a private subnet8

- A VM in the private subnet8

- Peering between VPC1 and VPC2

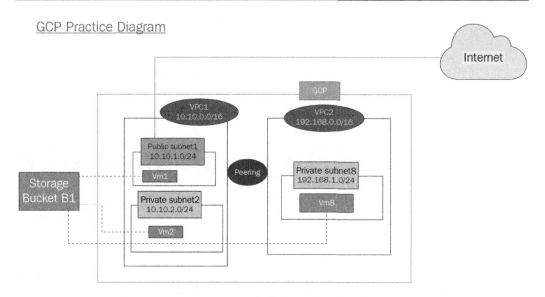

Figure 11.1 – A sample architecture for GCP console practice

In the GCP practice diagram in *Figure 11.1*, `public subnet1` is accessible from the internet. There is a Google Cloud Storage bucket called `B1`. If we want to have VM1, VM2, and VM8 access `B1`, what do we need to do? This is a great question to think about before reading further.

Practicing using GCP services with the Cloud console

In GCP, a project is the basic unit for resource provision. You can use the following steps to begin a project:

1. After you log into the GCP console (`https://console.cloud.google.com`) from your browser, you will see the following starting page:

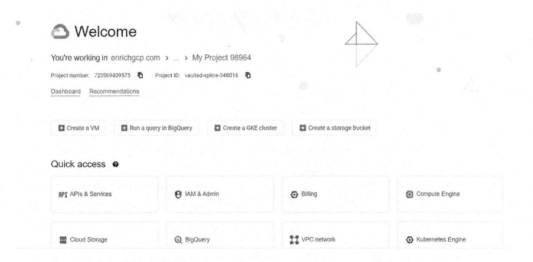

2. You can always create a new project by clicking the drop-down button next to **My First Project**.

Within the **My First Project** project, we will now create the network VPCs, subnets, and VMs.

Creating network VPCs using the GCP console

Use the following steps to create a VPC in the GCP console:

1. On the upper-left side of the window, there is the navigation drop-down menu that you will be able to use to choose the GCP services.

2.   From the navigation menu on the left side, go to **VPC network** and select **VPC networks** from the dropdown. It will prompt you to enable **Compute Engine API**. Go ahead and enable it.

You will be brought to the **VPC network** page, where you can create a VPC network.

3.   Click **CREATE VPC NETWORK**.

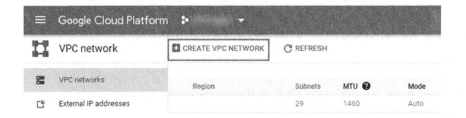

4. Then, fill in the network details and create VPC1:

    *   **Subnet name**: subnet1
    *   **IP v4 range**: 10.10.1.0/24
    *   **Region**: us-east1
    *   **Subnet name**: subnet2
    *   **IP v4 range**: 10.10.2.0/24
    *   **Region**: asia-east1

    Then, vpc1 is created with two subnets:

▾ vpc1		2	1460	Custom	None			
	asia-east1	subnet2			10.10.2.0/24	None	None	10.10.2.1
	us-east1	subnet1			10.10.1.0/24	None	None	10.10.1.1

5. Repeat *Steps 3* and *4* to create vpc2:

    *   **Subnet name**: subnet8
    *   **IP v4 range**: 192.168.1.0/24
    *   **Region**: europe-central2

▾ vpc1		2	1460	Custom	None			
	asia-east1	subnet2			10.10.2.0/24	None	None	10.10.2.1
	us-east1	subnet1			10.10.1.0/24	None	None	10.10.1.1
▾ vpc2		1	1460	Custom	None			
	europe-central2	subnet8			192.168.1.0/24	None	None	192.168.1.1

You now have two VPCs created: vpc1 with two subnets and vpc2 with one subnet.

Creating a public VM, vm1, within vpc1/subnet1 using the GCP console

Use the following steps to create a VM in the GCP console:

1. From the navigation menu on the left side, go to **Compute Engine** and then **VM instances**. Click the **CREATE INSTANCE** button.

VM Instances

Compute Engine lets you use virtual machines that run on Google's infrastructure. Create micro-VMs or larger instances running Debian, Windows, or other standard images. Create your first VM instance, import it using a migration service, or try the quickstart to build a sample app.

CREATE INSTANCE   TAKE THE QUICKSTART

Then, fill in the VM instance details:

*   **Name**: vm1
*   **Region**: us-east1
*   **Zone**: us-east1-b
*   **Machine configuration: GENERAL-PURPOSE, N1** series
*   **Machine type**: f1-micro
*   **Subnet name**: subnet1

This is shown in the following screenshot:

2. Select the defaults for the other options, and then click on **NETWORKING, DISKS, SECURITY, MANAGEMENT, SOLE-TENANCY**.

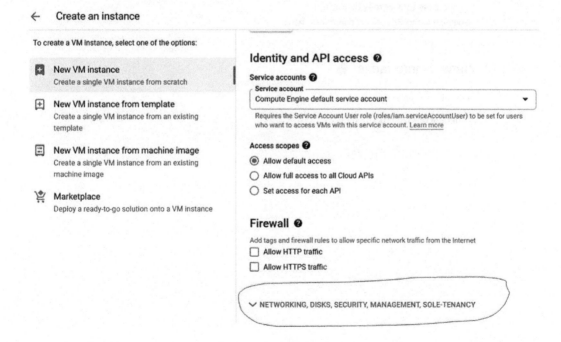

3.   Expand the **Networking** option, then go to **Network interfaces**.

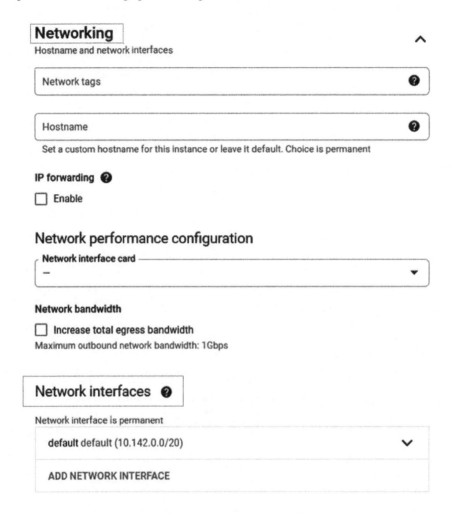

4. In the **Edit network interface** section, select `vpc1` for **Network** and `subnet1  Ipv4`
    (`10.10.1.0/24`) for **Subnetwork**, and leave everything else as the default.

5. Click **DONE** and then **CREATE**.

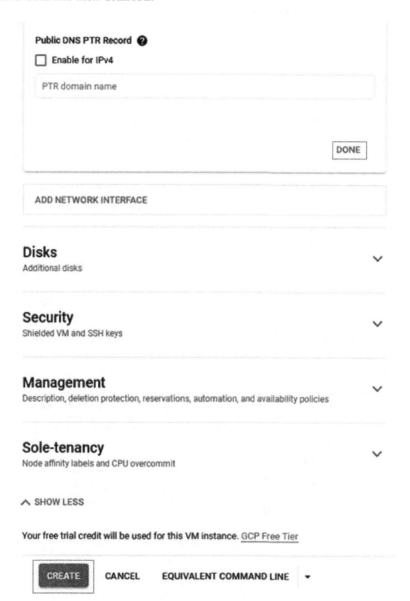

At this time, VM1 is created in `vpc1` and `subnet1` (`10.10.1.0/24`), with the internal IP address of `10.10.1.2` and the external IP address of `34.148.1.115`.

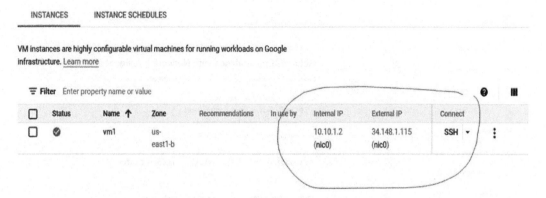

To allow **Secure Shell** (**SSH**) into this Linux VM, you need to create a firewall rule to allow inbound SSH traffic.

6. Select **View network details** from the three dots drop-down menu.

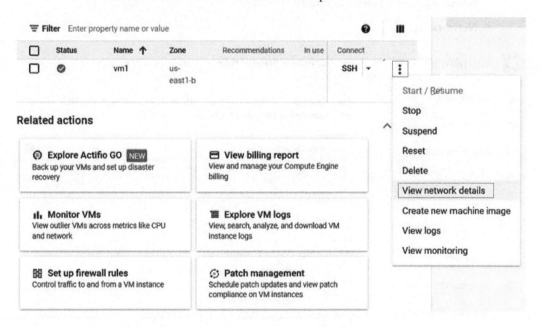

7. Select **Firewall** and then **CREATE FIREWALL RULE**.

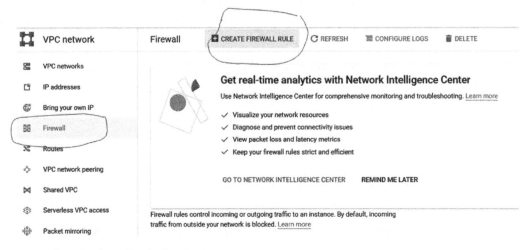

8. Fill in the firewall rule details:

    - **Name**: vpc1-firewall-rule2

    - **Network**: vpc1

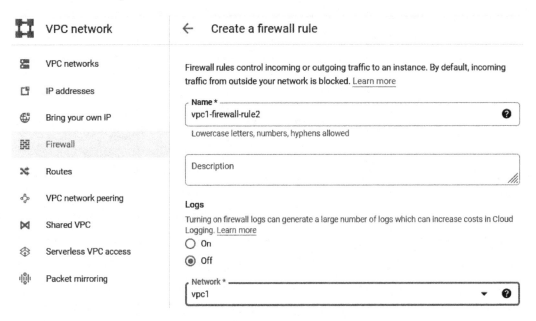

9. Select **All instances in the network** for **Targets**, enter 0.0.0.0/0 for **Source IPv4 ranges** (allow all the sources), and select **tcp :** and enter 22 as the port number (SSH uses port 22). Then, click **CREATE**.

10. After the firewall rule is created successfully, go back to the **VM instances** page. Select **Open in browser window** from the **SSH** drop-down menu (make sure you allow pop-up windows from the browser).

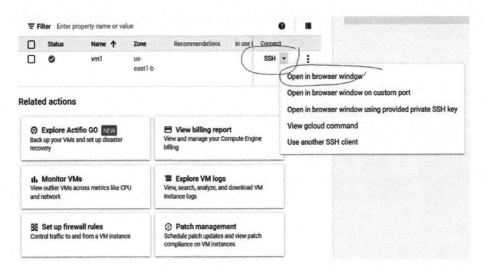

Now you are able to SSH into the VM instance.

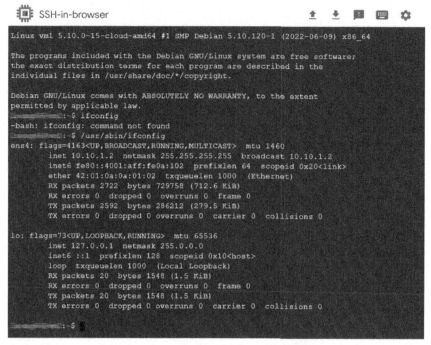

You now have a GCP VM, called `vm1`, created in `subnet1` of `vpc1`.

Creating a private VM, vm2, within vpc1/subnet2 using the GCP console

1. Repeat the steps in *the previous section* to create a VM in `vpc1/subnet2`. The only changes are as follows:

    *   Choose `asia-east1` as the region where `subnet2` sits.

    *   Choose `subnet2` as the subnetwork.

    *   Choose **None** for **External IPv4 address** since this is a private VM and no external IP address is assigned.

Network interface is permanent

Now, vm2 is provisioned in `vpc1/subnet2` with the IP address of `10.10.2.2`.

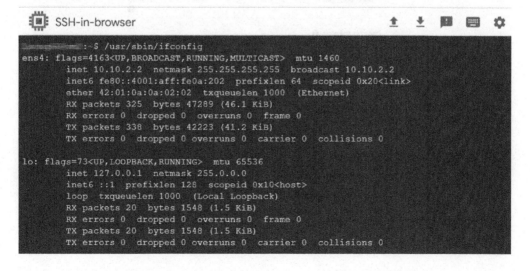

2. Repeat the steps in *Creating a public virtual machine vm1 within the vpc1/subnet1 using GCP console* to create a firewall rule to allow `ping` within `vpc1` (`10.10.0.0/16`) so `vm1` and `vm2` can ping each other since they are in the same VPC.

3. Ping vm2 (`10.10.1.2`) from vm1.

```
          @vm2:~$ ping 10.10.1.2
PING 10.10.1.2 (10.10.1.2) 56(84) bytes of data.
64 bytes from 10.10.1.2: icmp_seq=1 ttl=64 time=188 ms
64 bytes from 10.10.1.2: icmp_seq=2 ttl=64 time=184 ms
64 bytes from 10.10.1.2: icmp_seq=3 ttl=64 time=183 ms
64 bytes from 10.10.1.2: icmp_seq=4 ttl=64 time=183 ms
^C
--- 10.10.1.2 ping statistics ---
4 packets transmitted, 4 received, 0% packet loss, time 3004ms
rtt min/avg/max/mdev = 183.399/184.599/188.020/1.975 ms
```

At this time, you have a GCP VM, vm2, created in `subnet2` of vpc1, and vm1 can ping vm2.

Creating a private VM, vm8, within vpc2/subnet8 using the GCP console

Repeat the steps in *Creating a private virtual machine vm2 within the vpc1/subnet2 using GCP console* to create a VM in `vpc2/subnet8` (`192.168.1.0/24`), with no public IP addresses. The only changes are as follows:

- Choose `europe-central2` as the region where `subnet3` sits.

- Choose `subnet8` as the subnetwork.

Notice that vm1/vm2 cannot ping vm8 even if you create firewall rules allowing pinging from vpc1 to vpc2, since there are no routes between vpc1 and vpc2. That's why we need to create peering between vpc1 and vpc2.

Creating peering between vpc1 and vpc2 using the GCP console

Use the following steps to create VPC network peering between vpc1 and vpc2:

1.   From the navigation menu, go to **VPC network** and then **VPC network peering**.

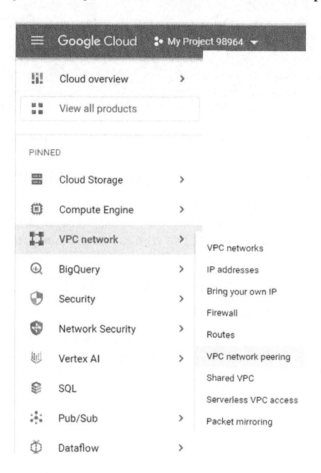

2. Create `vpc12-peering` from `vpc1` to `vpc2`.

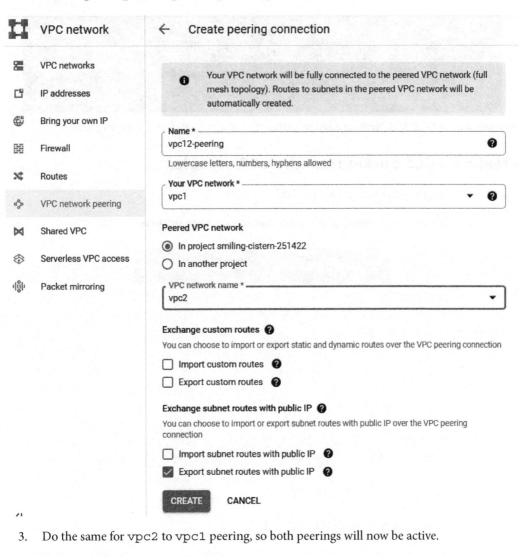

3. Do the same for `vpc2` to `vpc1` peering, so both peerings will now be active.

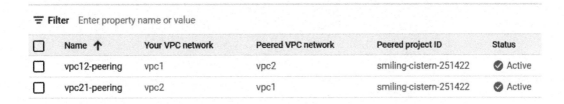

4.   Ping vm8 (`192.168.1.2`) from vm1.

```
        @vm1:~$ ping 192.168.1.2
PING 192.168.1.2 (192.168.1.2) 56(84) bytes of data.
64 bytes from 192.168.1.2: icmp_seq=1 ttl=64 time=111 ms
64 bytes from 192.168.1.2: icmp_seq=2 ttl=64 time=110 ms
64 bytes from 192.168.1.2: icmp_seq=3 ttl=64 time=110 ms
```

You now have a GCP VM, vm8, created in `subnet8` of `vpc2`, and vm1 can ping vm8.

Creating a GCS bucket from the GCP console

Use the following steps to create a GCS bucket:

1.   From the navigation menu, go to **Cloud Storage** and then **Buckets**.

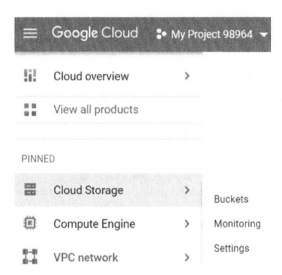

2.   From the new window, click **CREATE BUCKET**.

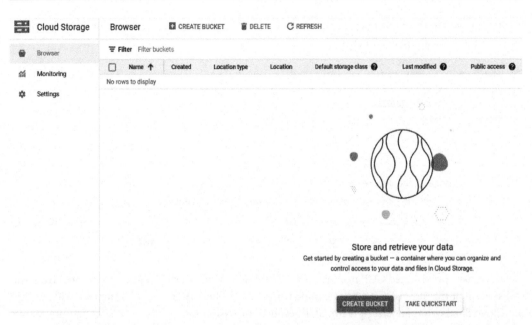

3. Choose a globally unique name for the GCP bucket. Here, we use `bucket-08282022`. Select **Region** under **Choose where to store your data**, and select **us-east1** as the storage bucket region. Click the **CREATE** button.

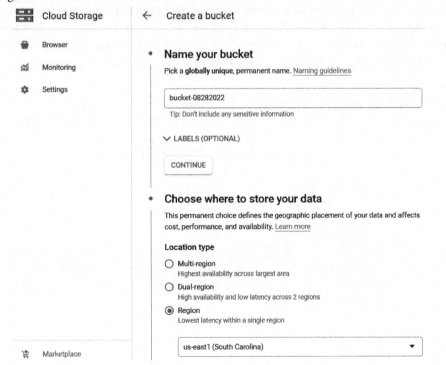

It will bring you to the bucket page, where you can create a subfolder, upload files, or upload a folder under the previously created bucket.

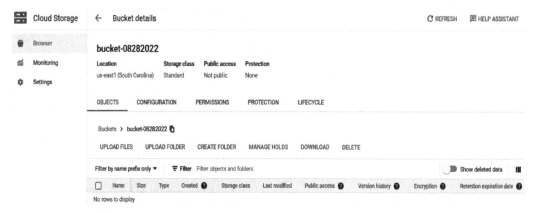

So far, we have provisioned GCP resources (VPCs/subnets, VPC peering, VMs, and storage) from the console. All of this provisioning can be done using Cloud Shell. In the next section, we will provide the Cloud Shell commands/scripts for GCP resource provisioning.

Provisioning GCP resources using Google Cloud Shell

Instead of using the GCP console, we can use Google Cloud Shell to provision all the resources. In the following example, the GCP architecture is shown in *Figure 11.2*, and we use the Cloud Shell commands to provision GCP resources, including network VPCs/subnets, VMs, and VPC peering. Please practice using them in Cloud Shell, and make sure you understand each step.

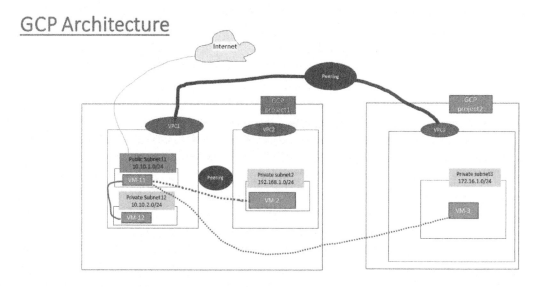

Figure 11.2 – A sample architecture for GCP Cloud Shell practice

1. Create a project,VPC, and subnet:

```
gcloud projects create test10122021 --folder 464105225938
gcloud compute networks create vpc1 --project corvel-
032021  --subnet-mode=custom
gcloud compute networks subnets create subnet11
--network=vpc1 --range=10.10.1.0/24 --project corvel-
032021 --region us-west1
gcloud compute networks subnets create subnet12
--network=vpc1 --range=10.10.2.0/24 --project corvel-
032021 --region us-east1
gcloud compute networks create vpc2 --project corvel-
032021  --subnet-mode=custom
gcloud compute networks subnets create subnet2
--network=vpc2 --range=192.168.1.0/24 --project corvel-
032021 --region us-central1
gcloud compute networks create vpc3 --project
test10122021  --subnet-mode=custom
gcloud compute networks subnets create subnet3
--network=vpc3 --range=172.16.1.0/24 --project
test10122021 --region us-central1
```

2. Create VMs:

```
gcloud compute instances create myvm11 --project corvel-
032021 --machine-type=f1-micro --zone=us-west1-a
--subnet=subnet11
gcloud compute instances create myvm12 --project
corvel-032021 --machine-type=f1-micro --network-
interface=subnet=subnet12,no-address  --zone=us-east1-b
gcloud compute instances create myvm2 --project
corvel-032021 --machine-type=f1-micro --network-
interface=subnet=subnet2,no-address  --zone=us-central1-b
gcloud compute instances create myvm3 --project
test10122021 --machine-type=f1-micro --network-
interface=subnet=subnet3,no-address --zone=us-central1-b
```

3. List all the VMs and write down their IP addresses:

```
gcloud compute instances list --project corvel-032021
gcloud compute instances list --project test10122021
```

4. Open the firewall for VPC1:

    ```
    gcloud compute firewall-rules create fw1 --network vpc1
    --allow tcp:22,icmp --source-ranges 0.0.0.0/0 --project
    corvel-032021
    ```

5. SSH from the console to myvm11, and you should be able to ping vm12 from vm11.

6. But how can we ping from myvm11 to myvm2? You need to create VPC peering between VPC1 and VPC2 (they are in the same project):

    ```
    gcloud compute networks peerings create peer12
    --project=corvel-032021   --network=vpc1 --peer-
    project=corvel-032021 --peer-network=vpc2
    gcloud compute networks peerings create peer21
    --peer-project=corvel-032021   --network=vpc2
    --project=corvel-032021 --peer-network=vpc1
    gcloud compute networks peerings list
    --project=corvel-032021
    ```

7. Open a firewall for vpc2:

    ```
    gcloud compute firewall-rules create fw2 --network vpc2
    --allow tcp:22,icmp --source-ranges 0.0.0.0/0 --project
    corvel-032021
    ```

8. Now you shall be able to ping vm2 from vm11. But how can we ping from myvm11 to myvm3? You need to create VPC peering between vpc1 and vpc3 (they are in different projects):

    ```
    gcloud compute networks peerings create peer13
    --project=corvel-032021   --network=vpc1 --peer-
    project=test10122021 --peer-network=vpc3
    gcloud compute networks peerings create peer31
    --project=test10122021 --network=vpc3 --peer-
    project=corvel-032021 --peer-network=vpc1
    gcloud compute networks peerings list
    --project=corvel-032021
    ```

9. Open a firewall for vpc3:

    ```
    gcloud compute firewall-rules create fw3 --network
    vpc3 --allow tcp:22,icmp --source-ranges 10.10.1.0/24
    --project test10122021
    ```

Now you shall be able to ping vm3 from vm11.

Summary

In this appendix, we have provided practice examples to provision GCP services/resources from the GCP console. We have also shown how to create these basic resources using Google Cloud Shell.

Appendix 2
Practicing Using the Python Data Libraries

In *Chapter 2*, *Mastering Python Programming*, we covered the Python data libraries, including NumPy, Pandas, Matpotlib, and Seaborn. In this appendix, we will continue learning these libraries by practicing using them on the Google Colab platform (colab.research.google.com).

With a step-by-step approach, we will show how to use these libraries to manage and visualize data. For the NumPy library, we will discuss how to generate and operate NumPy arrays. For the Pandas library, we cover features including Series, DataFrames, missing data handling, GroupBy, and operations. For the Matpotlib and Seaborn libraries, we will show their features by exploring multiple data visualization examples.

Follow these examples and make sure you understand each of them. Practicing each example on Google Colab will yield the best results.

NumPy

NumPy is a library for Python that adds support for large, multi-dimensional arrays and matrices, along with a large collection of high-level mathematical functions to operate on these arrays.

In this section, we will go over the following topics:

- Generating NumPy arrays
- Operating NumPy arrays

We will start with how to generate NumPy arrays.

Generating NumPy arrays

In this section, we will demonstrate various ways to create NumPy arrays. Arrays might be one-dimensional or two-dimensional.

Let's convert a list into a one-dimensional array by using the following code (the first line imports the NumPy library and and gives it the alias of np):

```
import numpy as np
my_list = [1,2,3]
my_list
[1, 2, 3]


import numpy as np
my_list = [1,2,3]
arr = np.array(my_list)
arr
array([1, 2, 3])
```

Now, let's make our list a little complicated with the following code:

```
import numpy as np
my_mat =[[10,20,30],[40,50,60],[70,80,90]]
np.array(my_mat)
array([[10, 20, 30],
       [40, 50, 60],
       [70, 80, 90]])
```

Note that there are two sets of brackets that represent the two-dimensional array.

One of the basic functions in NumPy is arange(), where you can provide start and stop values. For example, with 0 as the start value and 10 as the stop value, np.arange() will generate a one-dimensional array with values from 0 to 10 (the last value provided in the function is not included):

```
import numpy as np
np.arange(0,10)
array([0, 1, 2, 3, 4, 5, 6, 7, 8, 9])
```

Let's use the same function with some other values/arguments. In the following example, we add an additional argument called **step size** to create a one-dimensional array, with even numbers:

```
import numpy as np
np.arange(0,11,2)
array([ 0, 2, 4, 6, 8, 10])
```

The first argument in the arange function is the start value, the second is the stop value, and the last one is the step size.

The other built-in function in NumPy is to generate an array with all zeros. We need to provide the argument with how many zeros we want to generate in the array, as shown in the following snippet:

```
import numpy as np
np.zeros(5)
array([0., 0., 0., 0., 0.])
```

You can also provide a tuple as an argument:

```
import numpy as np
np.zeros((4,4))
array([[0., 0., 0., 0.],
       [0., 0., 0., 0.],
       [0., 0., 0., 0.],
       [0., 0., 0., 0.]])
```

Similarly, if we need to generate an array with pure ones, we can use the ones function and provide a number as an argument, as shown here:

```
import numpy as np
np.ones((3,4))
array([[1., 1., 1., 1.],
       [1., 1., 1., 1.],
       [1., 1., 1., 1.]])
```

Another useful built-in function is linspace, where we enter arguments as the first number and the last number, evenly spaced between specified intervals. Remember that the arange function returns all integers between the start and stop points, but linspace takes a third argument, the number of points we want:

```
import numpy as np
np.linspace(0,5,10)
array([0.        , 0.55555556, 1.11111111, 1.66666667,
2.22222222,
       2.77777778, 3.33333333, 3.88888889, 4.44444444, 5.
])
```

In the previous example, there is a one-dimensional array (specified with a single bracket), with 10 evenly spaced points between 0 and 5:

```
import numpy as np
np.linspace(0,5,25)
array([0.        , 0.20833333, 0.41666667, 0.625      ,
0.83333333,
       1.04166667, 1.25      , 1.45833333, 1.66666667, 1.875
    ,
       2.08333333, 2.29166667, 2.5       , 2.70833333,
2.91666667,
       3.125     , 3.33333333, 3.54166667, 3.75       ,
3.95833333,
       4.16666667, 4.375     , 4.58333333, 4.79166667, 5.
```

Note that, using the same example with different space points (25), the array looks like a two-dimensional array, but it is one-dimensional, proven by there only being one bracket in front of the array.

If you are dealing with linear algebra problems, it is basically a two-dimensional square matrix (the same number of rows and columns), where we have a diagonal of ones and everything else is zero. That's why it takes a single digit as an argument:

```
import numpy as np
np.eye(5)
array([[1., 0., 0., 0., 0.],
       [0., 1., 0., 0., 0.],
       [0., 0., 1., 0., 0.],
       [0., 0., 0., 1., 0.],
       [0., 0., 0., 0., 1.]])
```

One of the most used functions that will be used here generates an array with random numbers, such as the following:

```
import numpy as np
np.random.rand(4,5)
array([[0.44698983, 0.46938684, 0.66609426, 0.95168835,
0.48775195],
       [0.17627195, 0.98549358, 0.69526343, 0.44981183,
0.11574242],
       [0.09377203, 0.35856856, 0.38228733, 0.6129268 ,
0.16385609],
```

```
        [0.79041234, 0.9281485 , 0.72570369, 0.46438003,
0.3159711 ]])
```

If we need to return from the standard normal distribution, instead of rand, we can use the randn function:

```
import numpy as np
np.random.randn(4)
array([ 1.57461921, -1.47658163, 0.38070033, -1.43224982])
```

The other function is randint, which returns a random single integer between the lowest and highest integer values, provided as an argument (the lowest inclusive and the highest exclusive):

```
import numpy as np
np.random.randint(1,100)
29
```

If we need a particular number of random integers between the provided interval, we need to provide a third argument:

```
import numpy as np
np.random.randint(1,100,10)
array([29, 7, 33, 85, 83, 34, 5, 50, 53, 39])
```

Now, let's do some conversion. In the following example, we have generated a one-dimensional array with 25 values, saved it in an array variable, and then reshaped it into a two-dimensional array:

```
import numpy as np
array = np.arange(25)
array
array([ 0, 1, 2, 3, 4, 5, 6, 7, 8, 9, 10, 11, 12, 13, 14, 15,
16, 17, 18, 19, 20, 21, 22, 23, 24])
array.reshape(5,5)
array([[ 0, 1, 2, 3, 4],
       [ 5, 6, 7, 8, 9],
       [10, 11, 12, 13, 14],
       [15, 16, 17, 18, 19],
       [20, 21, 22, 23, 24]])
```

If we want to get the maximum or minimum value in the randomly generated array, we can use the array.max() or array.min() function respectively:

```
import numpy as np
array = np.random.randint(0,50,10)
array
array([ 2, 8, 31, 2, 25, 34, 49, 8, 49, 42])
array.max()
49
array.min()
2
```

If we want to pick a single value (or a set of values) from the array provided in the preceding example, we can specify this with brackets, as shown here:

```
import numpy as np
array = np.random.randint(0,50,10)
array
array([42, 38, 43, 22, 39, 4, 20, 30, 49, 13])
array[3]
22
array[0:4]
array([42, 38, 43, 22])
```

If we want to replace a single value or a set of values in an array, we need to set those values as shown here:

```
import numpy as np
array = np.random.randint(0,50,100)
array
array([42, 10, 14, 34, 45, 18, 21, 11, 33, 32, 22, 13, 11, 42,
16, 20, 10,
        1, 36, 41, 45, 21, 45, 45, 41,  0, 38, 39, 16, 10, 18,
45, 43, 42,
       23, 31, 20, 14,  9, 46, 44, 33, 24, 35,  6,  6, 26, 13,
20, 20, 28,
       23, 46, 40, 15, 43, 17, 31, 15, 48,  9, 17, 46, 28, 48,
41, 30, 28,
       32, 40, 35,  8, 10,  5, 33, 30,  4, 38, 47, 22, 13, 14,
29,  1, 15,
```

```
        48, 18, 48, 18, 21, 45,  9,  6,  1, 31, 28,  5, 42,  8,
28])
array[0:3] = 100
array
array([100, 100, 100,  34,  45,  18,  21,  11,  33,  32,  22,
13,  11,
        42,  16,  20,  10,   1,  36,  41,  45,  21,  45,  45,
41,   0,
        38,  39,  16,  10,  18,  45,  43,  42,  23,  31,  20,
14,   9,
        46,  44,  33,  24,  35,   6,   6,  26,  13,  20,  20,
28,  23,
        46,  40,  15,  43,  17,  31,  15,  48,   9,  17,  46,
28,  48,
        41,  30,  28,  32,  40,  35,   8,  10,   5,  33,  30,
4,  38,
        47,  22,  13,  14,  29,   1,  15,  48,  18,  48,  18,
21,  45,
         9,   6,   1,  31,  28,   5,  42,   8,  28])
```

As you can see, values that are in the 0, 1, and 2 indexes are replaced with values of 100.

Operating NumPy arrays

Now, we are going a little deeper and working with a two-dimensional array. In the following example, we generated an array with 25 random numbers and reshaped it into a two-dimensional array. It then shows a value, which is located on row 1 and column 1:

```
import numpy as np
array = np.random.randint(0,50,25).reshape(5,5)
array
array([[15, 21, 34, 39, 18],
       [42, 41, 28, 24,  2],
       [43, 25, 38, 42, 35],
       [ 3,  4, 27,  2, 49],
       [17,  5, 33, 11, 30]])
array[0:3]
array([[15, 21, 34, 39, 18],
       [42, 41, 28, 24,  2],
       [43, 25, 38, 42, 35]])
```

The following is a function to return a Boolean (`True` or `False`) of the array, based on a specific condition:

```
import numpy as np
array = np.random.randint(0,50,25).reshape(5,5)
array
array([[47, 25,  1, 33,  7],
       [31, 18,  9, 13, 41],
       [28, 33, 34, 19,  2],
       [ 1, 32, 45, 34, 48],
       [27, 34, 38, 18,  9]])
array > 25
array([[ True, False, False,  True, False],
       [ True, False, False, False,  True],
       [ True,  True,  True, False, False],
       [False,  True,  True,  True,  True],
       [ True,  True,  True, False, False]])
```

We can also apply some math, such as addition, subtraction, multiplication, and division operations, to an array, as well as applying some functions, such as `sin`, `cos`, and `log`:

```
import numpy as np
array = np.arange(10)
array
array([0, 1, 2, 3, 4, 5, 6, 7, 8, 9])
array + array
array([ 0,  2,  4,  6,  8, 10, 12, 14, 16, 18])
array * 2
array([ 0,  2,  4,  6,  8, 10, 12, 14, 16, 18])
np.sin(array)
array([ 0.        ,  0.84147098,  0.90929743,  0.14112001,
-0.7568025 ,
        -0.95892427, -0.2794155 ,  0.6569866 ,  0.98935825,
0.41211849])
```

We have shown some examples using the NumPy library; for more information about the library, please refer to https://numpy.org/.

Pandas

Pandas is an open source library that is built on top of NumPy. Pandas allows for quick data analysis and data preparation. It excels in performance and productivity.

In this section, we will discuss the following topics:

- Series
- DataFrames
- Missing data handling
- GroupBy
- Operations

Depending on the environment, you may need to install Pandas first by going to your command line or terminal and running the following commands:

```
conda install pandas
pip install pandas
```

We will start by looking at the Series data type.

Series

Series is the first main data type that we will be using with Pandas. Series is almost the same as the NumPy array. The difference is that with Series, a series of axis labels can be indexed by a label.

We are going to make four different Python objects and form a list:

```
import numpy as np
import pandas as pd
labels = ['A', 'B','C']
my_data = [100,200,300]
array = np.array(my_data)
d = {'A':100, 'B':200, 'C':300}
pd.Series(data = my_data)
A    100
B    200
C    300
dtype: int64
```

By default, if we do not specify the index values, it will assign 0, 1, 2, ... Therefore, we can change those labels into labels we created earlier (labels):

```
pd.Series(my_data, labels)
A     100
B     200
C     300
dtype: int64
```

If you want to provide a dictionary in a Series, you do not need to provide an index, since the dictionary already has its keys and values:

```
pd.Series(d)
A     100
B     200
C     300
dtype: int64
```

A Series can hold any data types, and we can provide labels too:

```
pd.Series(labels, my_data)
100     A
200     B
300     C
dtype: object


Next we will examine Dataframes.
```

DataFrames

A DataFrame is a two-dimensional labeled data structure with columns of different types. In this section, we will start building our first DataFrame using Pandas. In the following example, we have created a random number generated by NumPy and built a nice view with labels (rows and columns) with Pandas:

```
import numpy as np
import pandas as pd
from numpy.random import randn
np.random.seed(101)
```

```
df = pd.DataFrame(randn(5,4),['a','b','c','d','e'],['x','y','z
','t'])
df
```

	x	y	z	t
a	2.706850	0.628133	0.907969	0.503826
b	0.651118	-0.319318	-0.848077	0.605965
c	-2.018168	0.740122	0.528813	-0.589001
d	0.188695	-0.758872	-0.933237	0.955057
e	0.190794	1.978757	2.605967	0.683509

If you want to display a specific row of a DataFrame, specify the name of the row in the brackets:

```
df['x']
a     2.706850
b     0.651118
c    -2.018168
d     0.188695
e     0.190794
Name: x, dtype: float64
```

Note that the output is a Series, which we have covered before. If you want to check the type of the output, use the type syntax, as shown here:

```
type(df['x'])
pandas.core.series.Series
```

If you want to display multiple columns from the DataFrame, you can specify them in brackets as a list:

```
df[['x','y']]
```

	x	y
a	2.706850	0.628133
b	0.651118	-0.319318
c	-2.018168	0.740122
d	0.188695	-0.758872
e	0.190794	1.978757

Another feature of the DataFrame is being able to add new columns to it. When adding a new column, we need to specify the values of the new column. In the following example, we are creating a new column, new, and we will sum all the values from x and y and add them to it:

```
df['new'] = df['x'] + df['y']
df
```

	x	y	z	t	new
a	2.706850	0.628133	0.907969	0.503826	3.334983
b	0.651118	-0.319318	-0.848077	0.605965	0.331800
c	-2.018168	0.740122	0.528813	-0.589001	-1.278046
d	0.188695	-0.758872	-0.933237	0.955057	-0.570177
e	0.190794	1.978757	2.605967	0.683509	2.169552

If you want to delete a particular column or row, you can use the built-in drop function:

```
df.drop('new', axis=1)
```

	x	y	z	t
a	2.706850	0.628133	0.907969	0.503826
b	0.651118	-0.319318	-0.848077	0.605965
c	-2.018168	0.740122	0.528813	-0.589001
d	0.188695	-0.758872	-0.933237	0.955057
e	0.190794	1.978757	2.605967	0.683509

If you need to get output from a specific row, you can use the loc syntax, which stands for location, and you need to specify a row name as an argument:

```
df
```

	x	y	z	t	new
a	2.706850	0.628133	0.907969	0.503826	3.334983
b	0.651118	-0.319318	-0.848077	0.605965	0.331800
c	-2.018168	0.740122	0.528813	-0.589001	-1.278046
d	0.188695	-0.758872	-0.933237	0.955057	-0.570177
e	0.190794	1.978757	2.605967	0.683509	2.169552

```
df.loc['a']
```

x	2.706850
y	0.628133
z	0.907969
t	0.503826

```
new     3.334983
Name: a, dtype: float64
```

Conditional selection is also a feature of Pandas, where you can call data as a Boolean (`True or False`) in a DataFrame:

```
df
          x           y           z           t           new
a    2.706850    0.628133    0.907969    0.503826    3.334983
b    0.651118   -0.319318   -0.848077    0.605965    0.331800
c   -2.018168    0.740122    0.528813    0.589001   -1.278046
d    0.188695   -0.758872   -0.933237    0.955057   -0.570177
e    0.190794    1.978757    2.605967    0.683509    2.169552
df > 0
          x        y        z        t        new
a     True     True     True     True     True
b     True    False    False     True     True
c    False     True     True    False    False
d     True    False    False     True    False
e     True     True     True     True     True
```

Missing data handling

In the DataFrame we created earlier, if we apply some conditions (such as greater than zero), data that is less than zero will be displayed as `NaN` (null data). If you need to display only rows and columns that do not have `null` data, use the `dropna` syntax, as shown here:

```
df
          x           y           z           t           new
a    2.706850    0.628133    0.907969    0.503826    3.334983
b    0.651118   -0.319318   -0.848077    0.605965    0.331800
c   -2.018168    0.740122    0.528813   -0.589001   -1.278046
d    0.188695   -0.758872   -0.933237    0.955057   -0.570177
e    0.190794    1.978757    2.605967    0.683509    2.169552
df[df > 0].dropna()
          x           y           z           t           new
a    2.706850    0.628133    0.907969    0.503826    3.334983
e    0.190794    1.978757    2.605967    0.683509    2.169552
```

Now, we are going to apply a condition and save a new DataFrame (new_df) with values that are greater than zero, as shown here:

```
new_df = df[df > 0]
new_df
```

	x	y	z	t	new
a	2.706850	0.628133	0.907969	0.503826	3.334983
b	0.651118	NaN	NaN	0.605965	0.331800
c	NaN	0.740122	0.528813	NaN	NaN
d	0.188695	NaN	NaN	0.955057	NaN
e	0.190794	1.978757	2.605967	0.683509	2.169552

For the cells that do not have any value (NaN), we are going to replace them with the mean (average) of all values in that column:

```
new_df['x'].fillna(value=new_df['x'].mean())
a    2.706850
b    0.651118
c    0.934364
d    0.188695
e    0.190794
Name: x, dtype: float64
```

Note that the value in the x column and c row is not null and is replaced with a value.

GroupBy

GroupBy allows you to group together rows based on columns and perform an aggregate function on them.

In the next example, we will create a new DataFrame using the dictionary, as shown here:

```
import numpy as np
import pandas as pd
data = {'Country': ['USA', 'USA', 'France',
'France','Germany','Germany'],
        'Person':
['Sam','Amy','Carhile','Richard','John','Frank'],
        'Sales': [250, 300, 125, 500, 350, 200]}
df = pd.DataFrame(data)
```

```
df
      Country      Person      Sales
0     USA          Sam         250
1     USA          Amy         300
2     France       Carhile     125
3     France       Richard     500
4     Germany      John        350
5     Germany      Frank       200
```

If you are working with a large DataFrame and want to print the sum of the sales of each country, use the `groupby` built-in function, as shown here:

```
df.groupby('Country').sum()
Country      Sales
France       625
Germany      550
USA          550
```

Operations

In this section, we will show some real-life data operations. In the next examples, we are going to use a CSV file, `Salaries.csv` (taken from `https://www.kaggle.com/kaggle/sf-salaries?select=Salaries.csv`).

After downloading the file to a local computer and uploading it to Google Colab, you can visualize the DataFrame and explore the data using the Pandas library.

Use the `read_csv` function to read the CSV file, as shown here:

```
import pandas as pd
df = pd.read_csv('Salaries.csv')
df
```

	Id	EmployeeName	JobTitle	BasePay	OvertimePay	OtherPay	Benefits	TotalPay	TotalPayBenefits	Year	Notes	Agency	Status
0	1	NATHANIEL FORD	GENERAL MANAGER-METROPOLITAN TRANSIT AUTHORITY	167411.18	0.0	400184.25	NaN	567595.43	567595.43	2011	NaN	San Francisco	NaN
1	2	GARY JIMENEZ	CAPTAIN III (POLICE DEPARTMENT)	155966.02	245131.88	137811.38	NaN	538909.28	538909.28	2011	NaN	San Francisco	NaN
2	3	ALBERT PARDINI	CAPTAIN III (POLICE DEPARTMENT)	212739.13	106088.18	16452.6	NaN	335279.91	335279.91	2011	NaN	San Francisco	NaN
3	4	CHRISTOPHER CHONG	WIRE ROPE CABLE MAINTENANCE MECHANIC	77916.0	56120.71	198306.9	NaN	332343.61	332343.61	2011	NaN	San Francisco	NaN
4	5	PATRICK GARDNER	DEPUTY CHIEF OF DEPARTMENT,(FIRE DEPARTMENT)	134401.6	9737.0	182234.59	NaN	326373.19	326373.19	2011	NaN	San Francisco	NaN
...	...	...	...	...	...	...	...	...	...	...	...	...	...
148649	148650	Roy I Tillery	Custodian	0.00	0.00	0.00	0.00	0.00	0.00	2014	NaN	San Francisco	PT
148650	148651	Not provided	Not provided	Not Provided	Not Provided	Not Provided	Not Provided	0.00	0.00	2014	NaN	San Francisco	NaN
148651	148652	Not provided	Not provided	Not Provided	Not Provided	Not Provided	Not Provided	0.00	0.00	2014	NaN	San Francisco	NaN
148652	148653	Not provided	Not provided	Not Provided	Not Provided	Not Provided	Not Provided	0.00	0.00	2014	NaN	San Francisco	NaN
148653	148654	Joe Lopez	Counselor, Log Cabin Ranch	0.00	0.00	-618.13	0.00	-618.13	-618.13	2014	NaN	San Francisco	PT

```
df.info()
<class 'pandas.core.frame.DataFrame'>
RangeIndex: 148654 entries, 0 to 148653
Data columns (total 13 columns):
 #   Column            Non-Null Count    Dtype
---  ------            --------------    -----
 0   Id                148654 non-null   int64
 1   EmployeeName      148654 non-null   object
 2   JobTitle          148654 non-null   object
 3   BasePay           148049 non-null   object
 4   OvertimePay       148654 non-null   object
 5   OtherPay          148654 non-null   object
 6   Benefits          112495 non-null   object
 7   TotalPay          148654 non-null   float64
 8   TotalPayBenefits  148654 non-null   float64
 9   Year              148654 non-null   int64
 10  Notes             0 non-null        float64
 11  Agency            148654 non-null   object
 12  Status            38119 non-null    object
dtypes: float64(3), int64(2), object(8)
memory usage: 14.7+ MB
df["TotalPay"].mean()
74768.32197169267
df[df["EmployeeName"] == "Joseph Driscoll"]["JobTitle"]
36198    Captain, Fire Suppression
Name: JobTitle, dtype: object
```

In the preceding sections, we have shown the basic features of the Pandas library. For more information on Pandas features, please refer to `https://pandas.pydata.org`.

Matplotlib

Matplotlib is one of the essential libraries of data visualization in Python. It is an excellent two-dimensional and three-dimensional graphics library for generating scientific figures.

Some of the major pros of Matplotlib are as follows:

- Generally easy to get started with simple plots
- Support for custom labels and text
- Great control of every element in a figure
- High-quality output in many formats
- Very customizable in general

We will start with simple data generated by the NumPy library:

```
import matplotlib.pyplot as plt
import numpy as np
a = np.linspace(1,10,15)
a
array([ 1.        ,  1.64285714,  2.28571429,  2.92857143,
3.57142857,
        4.21428571,  4.85714286,  5.5       ,  6.14285714,
6.78571429,
        7.42857143,  8.07142857,  8.71428571,  9.35714286, 10. ])
```

We have generated data using the `linspace` function in the NumPy library. We can also play with all our data (in our case, it is an array), such as taking each number in an array and squaring it:

```
b = a ** 2
b
array([  1.        ,   2.69897959,   5.2244898 ,   8.57653061,
         12.75510204,  17.76020408,  23.59183673,  30.25       ,
         37.73469388,  46.04591837,  55.18367347,  65.14795918,
         75.93877551,  87.55612245, 100.        ])
```

We can plot the data in a graph with a simple function in Matplotlib:

```
plt.plot(a,b)
```

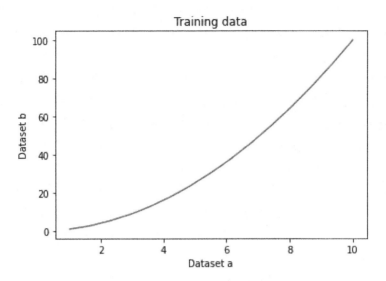

You can rearrange the x and y axes with a and b values, as shown here:

```
plt.subplot(1,2,1)
plt.plot(a,b)
plt.title("Dito training 1")
plt.subplot(1,2,2)
plt.plot(b,a,"r")
plt.title("Dito training 2")
```

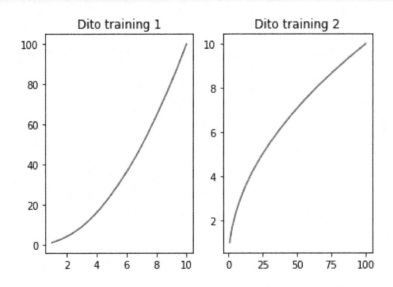

So far, we have demonstrated how to plot using the `plot` and `subplot` methods. Now, we are going to dive into object-oriented methods, where we will break down all for a more formal introduction of the `matplotlib` object-oriented API method. In the following example, we run a built-in `figure` function, which builds an imaginary blank canvas, and later on, we will add a set to this canvas so that it will work more flexibly:

```
import matplotlib.pyplot as plt
fig = plt.figure()
<Figure size 432x288 with 0 Axes>

import matplotlib.pyplot as plt
fig = plt.figure()
axes = fig.add_axes([0.1,0.1,0.8,0.8])
```

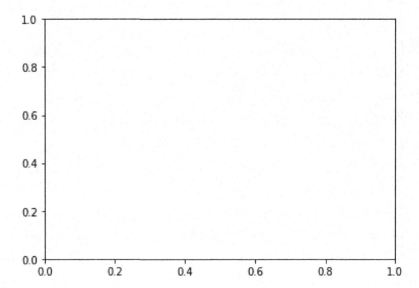

The very first step is to add axes to the canvas using the `add_axes` function. The numbers in the brackets represent the left, the button, the width, and the height of the axes.

Each number should be between zero and one, representing a percentage, numbers representation:

- The first number (0.1) represents 10 percent from the left of the canvas.
- The second number (0.1) represents 10 percent from the bottom.
- The third number (0.8) represents the percentage of axes from the canvas (width).
- The fourth number (0.8) represents the percentage of axes from the canvas (height).

In the preceding example, we generated a and b values using NumPy and plotted them in our custom canvas/axes using object-oriented methods, which gives us more control. Using some other functions, we can set names for each axis and title, as shown here:

```
import matplotlib.pyplot as plt
import numpy as np
a = np.linspace(1,10,15)
b = a ** 2
fig = plt.figure()
axes = fig.add_axes([0.1,0.1,0.8,0.8])
axes.plot(a,b)
```

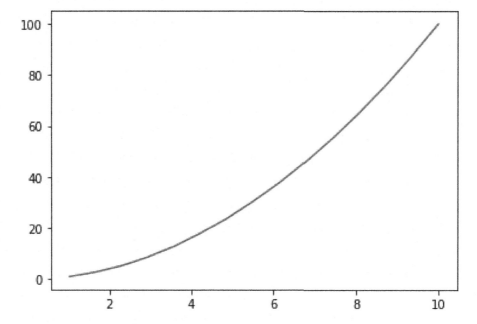

Now, let's put two sets of figures on the same canvas:

```
import matplotlib.pyplot as plt
import numpy as np
a = np.linspace(1,10,15)
b = a ** 2
fig = plt.figure()
axes1 = fig.add_axes([0.1,0.1,0.8,0.8])
axes2 = fig.add_axes([0.2,0.5,0.4,0.3])
```

```
axes1.plot(a,b)
axes2.plot(b,a)
axes1.set_xlabel("X1 Label")
axes1.set_ylabel("Y1 Label")
axes1.set_title("Title 1")
axes2.set_xlabel("X2 Label")
axes2.set_ylabel("Y2 Label")
axes2.set_title("Title 2")
```

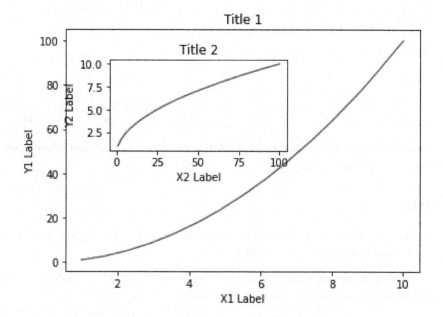

In the next example, we have plotted two sets in the same figure and also added some labels, using the label and legend methods:

```
import matplotlib.pyplot as plt
import numpy as np
a = np.linspace(1,10,15)
b = a ** 2
fig = plt.figure()
ax = fig.add_axes([0,0,1,1])
ax.plot(a, a**2, label = 'a squared')
ax.plot(a, a**3, label = 'a cubed')
ax.legend()
```

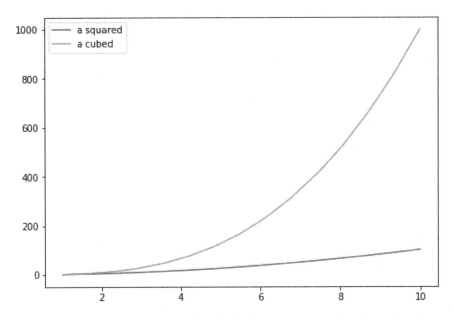

We have shown some examples using the Matplotlib library; for more detailed information, please refer to `https://matplotlib.org`.

Seaborn

Seaborn is a statistical library built on top of the Matplotlib library, and all the Matplotlib knowledge that we have learned can be applied to Seaborn.

We will start with a simple importing library. One of the useful features of Seaborn is its built-in datasets. In our case, we are going to use the `tips` dataset:

```
import seaborn as sns
tips = sns.load_dataset('tips')
tips.head()
```

You can also check out some other details (such as the number of columns and rows, and data types) by using the `.info()` function, as shown here:

	total_bill	tip	sex	smoker	day	time	size
0	16.99	1.01	Female	No	Sun	Dinner	2
1	10.34	1.66	Male	No	Sun	Dinner	3
2	21.01	3.50	Male	No	Sun	Dinner	3
3	23.68	3.31	Male	No	Sun	Dinner	2
4	24.59	3.61	Female	No	Sun	Dinner	4

```
tips.info()
<class 'pandas.core.frame.DataFrame'>
RangeIndex: 244 entries, 0 to 243
Data columns (total 7 columns):
 #   Column      Non-Null Count   Dtype
---  ------      --------------   -----
 0   total_bill  244 non-null     float64
 1   tip         244 non-null     float64
 2   sex         244 non-null     category
 3   smoker      244 non-null     category
 4   day         244 non-null     category
 5   time        244 non-null     category
 6   size        244 non-null     int64
dtypes: category(4), float64(2), int64(1)
memory usage: 7.4 KB
```

The example here shows a very basic histogram, where we set the dataset name as `tips` and the `total_bill` data (one of the columns of our dataset):

```
sns.displot(tips['total_bill'])
```

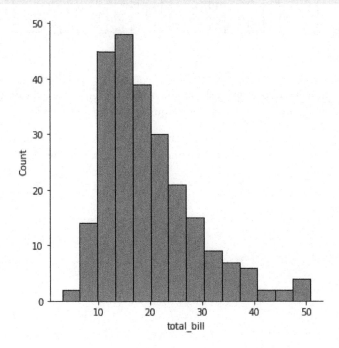

```
sns.displot(tips['total_bill'], kde=True, bins = 40)
```

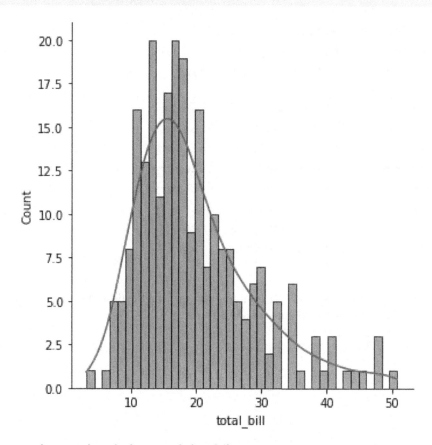

The displot function described previously has different arguments that you can set to modify your graph/histogram. Note that we have entered two arguments, kde and bins.

Next, we are going to explore different types of graphs using the jointplot function. You need to provide the x value, the y value, and the data name as arguments, as shown here:

```
sns.jointplot('total_bill', 'tip', data=tips)
```

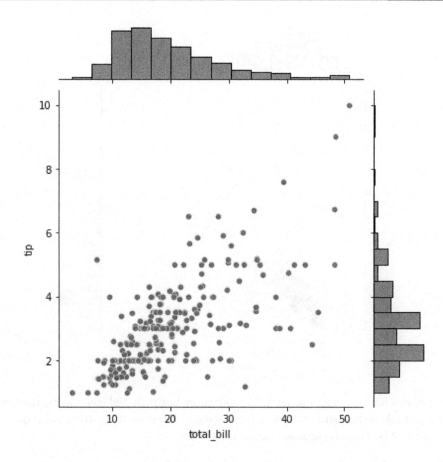

Note that the arguments we provided (`total_bill` and `tips`) are from data we imported, and they are the column names. It is a two-distribution plot, and in between, we have a scatter plot. As the bill value increases on the plot, the tip value also increases. `jointplot` also has other arguments that can help you to modify the graph (by default, it is a scatter plot, but you can also pass the hex argument), as shown here:

```
sns.jointplot('total_bill', 'tip', data=tips, kind = 'hex')
```

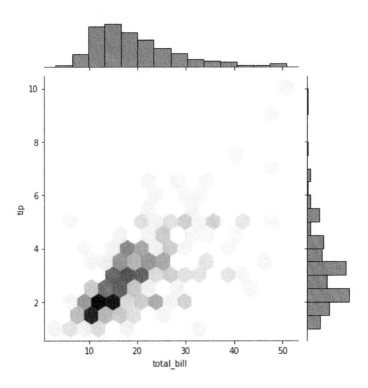

The next Seaborn features/functions we will introduce are box plots and violin plots. These types of plots are used to show the distribution of categorical data. They show the distribution of quantitative data in a way that facilitates comparison between variables:

```
sns.boxplot(x='day', y='total_bill', data=tips)
```

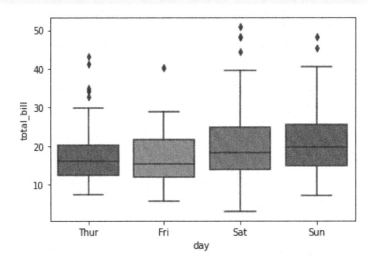

The violin plot, unlike the box plot, allows you to actually plot all the components that correspond to actual data points, and it essentially shows the kernel density estimation of the underlying distribution:

```
sns.violinplot(x='day', y='total_bill', data=tips)
```

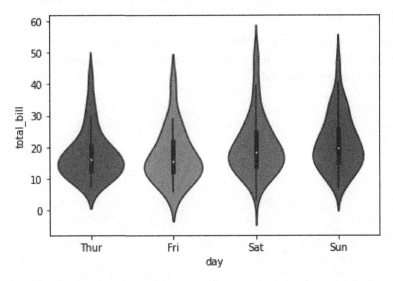

By adding more arguments to the `violinplot` function, you can add different features and details to the graph, as shown here.

```
sns.violinplot(x='day', y='total_bill', data=tips,
               hue = 'sex', split=True)
```

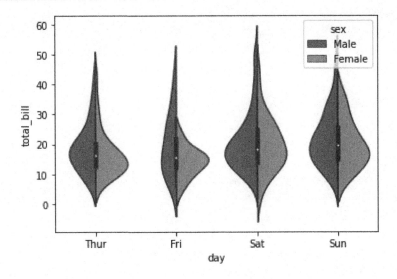

So far, we have shown the Seaborn library features via several examples. There are many different visual representations that use the Seaborn library in Python. Check out the Seaborn website (`https://seaborn.pydata.org/index.html`) for more details

Summary

In this appendix, we practices using the Python data libraries, including NumPy, Pandas, Matpotlib, and Seaborn. Thoroughly understanding these examples will help you to understand the data libraries and master Python programming skills.

Appendix 3
Practicing with Scikit-Learn

In *Chapter 3*, *Preparing for ML Development*, and *Chapter 4*, *Developing and Deploying ML Models*, we discussed the data preparation and ML model development process. In this appendix, we will continue learning about ML modeling skills by practicing using the scikit-learn package on the Google Colaboratory platform (`colab.research.google.com`).

With a step-by-step approach, we will show you how to develop ML models leveraging the scikit-learn library. We will cover the following practices:

- Data preparation
- Regression
- Classification

It is a best practice to follow these examples and make sure you understand each of them. Practicing each example on Google Colab will yield the best results.

Data preparation

In the previous chapters, we discussed Python libraries such as NumPy, Pandas, Matplotlib, and Seaborn for processing and visualizing data. Let's start with simply importing the libraries:

```
import numpy as np
import pandas as pd
import matplotlib.pyplot as plt
```

We will use a simple dataset that has only 4 columns and 10 rows.

Country	Age	Salary	Purchased
France	44	72000	No
Spain	27	48000	Yes
Germany	30	54000	No
Spain	38	61000	No
Germany	40		Yes
France	35	58000	Yes
Spain		52000	No
France	48	79000	Yes
Germany	50	83000	No
France	37	67000	Yes

Notice that some of the columns are categorical and others are numerical, and some of them have missing values that we need to fix. The dataset `.csv` file is uploaded to Google Colab.

Using the `pandas` library and the `read_csv` function, we read the data and save it to a variable dataset, assign the first three columns (**Country, Age, and Salary**) as features, assign the feature dataset to X, and assign the last column dataset to y, as the prediction:

```
dataset = pd.read_csv('Data.csv')
X = dataset.iloc[:,:-1].values
y = dataset.iloc[:, -1].values
print(X)
[['France' 44.0 72000.0]
['Spain' 27.0 48000.0]
['Germany' 30.0 54000.0]
['Spain' 38.0 61000.0]
['Germany' 40.0 nan]
['France' 35.0 58000.0]
```

```
['Spain' nan 52000.0]
['France' 48.0 79000.0]
['Germany' 50.0 83000.0]
['France' 37.0 67000.0]]
```

Note that it has some missing values. In the ML training process, we need to minimize the number of missing values, so you can either delete the rows containing missing data cells or replace the missing values with an input value, for example, the average of all values in that column. The following example is the filling of missing values with the mean/average of that particular column:

```
from sklearn.impute import SimpleImputer
imputer = SimpleImputer(missing_values=np.nan, strategy='mean')
imputer.fit(X[:, 1:3])
X[:, 1:3] = imputer.transform(X[:,1:3])
print(X)
[['France' 44.0 72000.0]
['Spain' 27.0 48000.0]
['Germany' 30.0 54000.0]
['Spain' 38.0 61000.0]
['Germany' 40.0 63777.77777777778]
['France' 35.0 58000.0]
['Spain' 38.77777777777778 52000.0]
['France' 48.0 79000.0]
['Germany' 50.0 83000.0]
['France' 37.0 67000.0]]
```

The next step is to convert categorical values to numerical values. In our loaded dataset (`data.cvs`), the name of the column is `Country` and it has three different values (`France`, `Spain`, and `Germany`). We are going to convert it to three columns with binary values using one-hot encoding:

```
from sklearn.compose import ColumnTransformer
from sklearn.preprocessing import OneHotEncoder
ct = ColumnTransformer(transformers=[('encoder',
OneHotEncoder(), [0])],
remainder = 'passthrough')
X = np.array(ct.fit_transform(X))
print(X)
[[1.0 0.0 0.0 44.0 72000.0]
[0.0 0.0 1.0 27.0 48000.0]
```

```
    [0.0 1.0 0.0 30.0 54000.0]
    [0.0 0.0 1.0 38.0 61000.0]
    [0.0 1.0 0.0 40.0 63777.77777777778]
    [1.0 0.0 0.0 35.0 58000.0]
    [0.0 0.0 1.0 38.77777777777778 52000.0]
    [1.0 0.0 0.0 48.0 79000.0]
    [0.0 1.0 0.0 50.0 83000.0]
    [1.0 0.0 0.0 37.0 67000.0]]
```

We also need to encode the very last column of our dataset (where values are Yes or No only) to zeros and ones:

```
from sklearn.preprocessing import LabelEncoder
le = LabelEncoder()
y = le.fit_transform(y)
print(y)
[0 1 0 0 1 1 0 1 0 1]
```

The next step is to split them into training and testing datasets:

```
from sklearn.model_selection import train_test_split
X_train, X_test, y_train, y_test = train_test_split(X, y ,
test_size = 0.2, random_state = 1)
print(X_train)
[[0.0 0.0 1.0 38.77777777777778 52000.0]
 [0.0 1.0 0.0 40.0 63777.77777777778]
 [1.0 0.0 0.0 44.0 72000.0]
 [0.0 0.0 1.0 38.0 61000.0]
 [0.0 0.0 1.0 27.0 48000.0]
 [1.0 0.0 0.0 48.0 79000.0]
 [0.0 1.0 0.0 50.0 83000.0]
 [1.0 0.0 0.0 35.0 58000.0]]
print(X_test)
[[0.0 1.0 0.0 30.0 54000.0]
 [1.0 0.0 0.0 37.0 67000.0]]
print(y_train)
```

```
[0 1 0 0 1 1 0 1]
print(y_test)
[0 1]
```

Now we have practiced the basic data processing skills, let's get into feature scaling before starting training ML models. There are two types of feature scaling: standardization and normalization. The goal is to have all values of the features in the same range. Let's examine the train data:

```
1 print(X_train)

[[0.0 0.0 1.0 38.77777777777778 52000.0]
 [0.0 1.0 0.0 40.0 63777.77777777778]
 [1.0 0.0 0.0 44.0 72000.0]
 [0.0 0.0 1.0 38.0 61000.0]
 [0.0 0.0 1.0 27.0 48000.0]
 [1.0 0.0 0.0 48.0 79000.0]
 [0.0 1.0 0.0 50.0 83000.0]
 [1.0 0.0 0.0 35.0 58000.0]]
```

We find that the very first three rows were encoded previously, so we will apply feature scaling for rows 4 and 5 only:

```
from sklearn.preprocessing import StandardScaler
sc  = StandardScaler()
X_train[:, 3:] = sc.fit_transform(X_train[:, 3:])
X_test[:, 3:] = sc.transform(X_test[:, 3:])
print(X_train)
[[0.0 0.0 1.0 -0.1915918438457856 -1.0781259408412427]
 [0.0 1.0 0.0 -0.014117293757057902 -0.07013167641635401]
 [1.0 0.0 0.0 0.5667085065333239 0.6335624327104546]
 [0.0 0.0 1.0 -0.3045301939022488 -0.30786617274297895]
 [0.0 0.0 1.0 -1.901801144700799 -1.4204636155515822]
 [1.0 0.0 0.0 1.1475343068237056 1.2326533634535488]
 [0.0 1.0 0.0 1.4379472069688966 1.5749910381638883]
 [1.0 0.0 0.0 -0.7401495441200352 -0.5646194287757336]]
```

Note that the outcome of X_train is between -2 and +2 (avery short range).

Regression

Now we have split the datasets and transformed the data, we will show you how to use the scikit-learn library to build up ML models. We will start with regression and show you the following examples:

- Simple linear regression
- Multiple linear regression
- Polynomial/non-linear regression

Simple linear regression

First things first, we need to prepare the dataset:

```python
import numpy as pd
import pandas as pd
import matplotlib.pyplot as plt


dataset = pd.read_csv('Salary_Data.csv')
X = dataset.iloc[:,:-1].values
y = dataset.iloc[:, -1].values


from sklearn.model_selection import train_test_split
X_train, X_test, y_train, y_test = train_test_split(X, y ,
test_size = 0.2, random_state = 1)
```

Now we can start training our regression model. We need to import a class and feed our training data:

```python
from sklearn.linear_model import LinearRegression
regressor = LinearRegression()
regressor.fit(X_train, y_train)
```

Next, we are going to predict the results of the observation in the test set:

```python
y_pred = regressor.predict(X_test)
```

Let's plot our prediction and real data to see how close they are:

```
plt.scatter(X_train, y_train, color = 'red')
plt.plot(X_train, regressor.predict(X_train), color='blue')
plt.title("Salary vs Experiment (Training Set")
plt.xlabel("Years of Experience")
plt.ylabel("Salary")
plt.show()
```

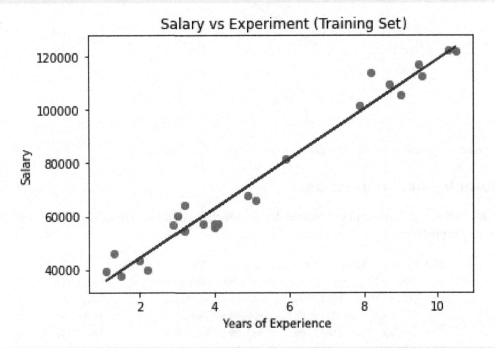

```
plt.scatter(X_test, y_test, color = 'red')
plt.plot(X_train, regressor.predict(X_train), color='blue')
plt.title("Salary vs Experiment (Training Set")
plt.xlabel("Years of Experience")
plt.ylabel("Salary")
plt.show()
```

As you can see, the simple linear regression model fits well with our datasets.

Multiple linear regression

In this section, we are going to use another dataset, which has multiple columns as data features and one for the predictor:

R&D Spend	Administration	Marketing Spend	State	Profit
165349.2	136897.8	471784.1	New York	192261.83
162597.7	151377.59	443898.53	California	191792.06
153441.51	101145.55	407934.54	Florida	191050.39
144372.41	118671.85	383199.62	New York	182901.99
142107.34	91391.77	366168.42	Florida	166187.94
131876.9	99814.71	362861.36	New York	156991.12
134615.46	147198.87	127716.82	California	156122.51
130298.13	145530.06	323876.68	Florida	155752.6
120542.52	148718.95	311613.29	New York	152211.77

First, we perform the data preparation:

1. Import the necessary libraries and/or classes.

2. Split the dataset into X (features) and y (predictors).

3. Encode column index 3 (state names have been converted to binary values and saved as three additional columns).

4.   Split the data into training and testing:

```
import numpy as np
import pandas as pd
import matplotlib.pyplot as plt


dataset = pd.read_csv('50_Startups.csv')
X = dataset.iloc[:,:-1].values
y = dataset.iloc[:, -1].values


from sklearn.compose import ColumnTransformer
from sklearn.preprocessing import OneHotEncoder
ct = ColumnTransformer(transformers=[('encoder',
OneHotEncoder(), [3])], remainder='passthrough')
X = np.array(ct.fit_transform(X))


from sklearn.model_selection import train_test_split
X_train, X_test, y_train, y_test = train_test_split(X, y ,
test_size = 0.2, random_state=1)
```

We can start training our model now:

```
from sklearn.linear_model import LinearRegression
regressor = LinearRegression()
regressor.fit(X_train, y_train)
```

And now is the time to validate/test our model. We cannot visualize as we did in the simple linear regression, since we have four different features and cannot plot them in a 5-dimensional graph. However, we can display two vectors: vectors of the *real profit* in the test set, and the *predicted profit*:

```
y_pred = regressor.predict(X_test)
np.set_printoptions(precision=2)
print(np.concatenate((y_pred.reshape(len(y_pred),1), y_test.
reshape(len(y_test),1)),1))
[[114664.42 105008.31]
 [ 90593.16  96479.51]
 [ 75692.84  78239.91]
 [ 70221.89  81229.06]
 [179790.26 191050.39]
```

```
[171576.92 182901.99]
[ 49753.59  35673.41]
[102276.66 101004.64]
[ 58649.38  49490.75]
[ 98272.03  97483.56]]
```

The left side of the output indicates the predicted profits, and the right side indicates the real profits.

Polynomial/non-linear regression

In this section, we will show examples of non-linear regression, where the relationship between the target and the feature(s) is not linear, that is, it is polynomial. We will use a linear model and a non-linear model, and compare how they fit to the real datasets.

We will start with the data preparation:

```
import numpy as np
import pandas as pd
import matplotlib.pyplot as plt


dataset = pd.read_csv('Position_Salaries.csv')
X = dataset.iloc[:, 1:-1].values
y = dataset.iloc[:, -1].values
```

Now, we are going to train two models: linear regression and polynomial regression. The following example shows both regression models:

```
from sklearn.linear_model import LinearRegression
lin_reg = LinearRegression()
lin_reg.fit(X,y)


from sklearn.preprocessing import PolynomialFeatures
poly_reg = PolynomialFeatures(degree = 2)
X_poly = poly_reg.fit_transform(X)
lin_reg_2 = LinearRegression()
lin_reg_2.fit(X_poly, y)
```

Next, we will visualize both regressions.

This is the linear regression:

```
plt.scatter(X, y, color = 'red')
plt.plot(X, lin_reg.predict(X), color = 'blue')
plt.title("Linear Regression")
plt.xlabel("Position Level")
plt.ylabel("Salary")
plt.show()
```

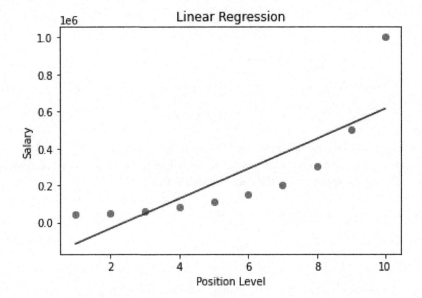

Then, this is the polynomial regression:

```
plt.scatter(X, y, color = 'red')
plt.plot(X, lin_reg_2.predict(X_poly), color = 'blue')
plt.title("Linear Regression")
plt.xlabel("Position Level")
plt.ylabel("Salary")
plt.show()
```

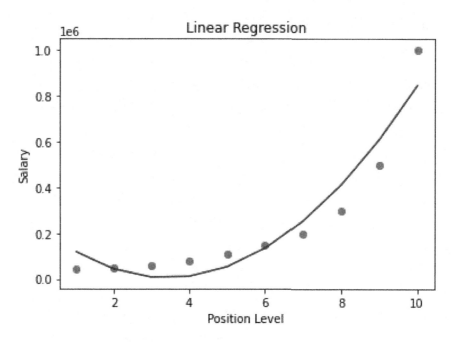

As we can see, polynomial regression (we used the power of 2) yields accurate predictions. If we go with higher powers, we will harvest better results. In the following examples, we will change the power to 4 (see line 2), and the result will fit the dataset much better:

```
from sklearn.linear_model import LinearRegression
lin_reg = LinearRegression()
lin_reg.fit(X,y)

from sklearn.preprocessing import PolynomialFeatures
poly_reg = PolynomialFeatures(degree = 4)
X_poly = poly_reg.fit_transform(X)
lin_reg_2 = LinearRegression()
lin_reg_2.fit(X_poly, y)
```

```
plt.scatter(X, y, color = 'red')
plt.plot(X, lin_reg_2.predict(X_poly), color = 'blue')
plt.title("Linear Regression")
plt.xlabel("Position Level")
plt.ylabel("Salary")
plt.show()
```

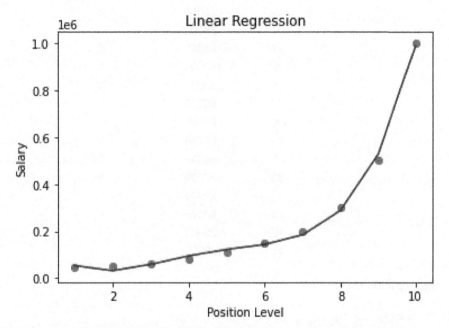

So far, we have covered the regression modeling process by practicing simple linear regression, multiple linear regression, and non-linear regression. In the next section, we will discuss classification models.

Classification

Unlike regression, where you predict a continuous number, you use classification to predict a category. We will cover logistic regression here.

We will use a dataset of historical data of iPhone purchases, based on the age and the salary of the buyers, to predict whether a new potential buyer will purchase an iPhone.

Age	EstimatedSalary	Purchased
19	19000	0
35	20000	0
26	43000	0
27	57000	0
19	76000	0
27	58000	0
27	84000	0
32	150000	1
25	33000	0
35	65000	0
26	80000	0
26	52000	0
20	86000	0
32	18000	0
18	82000	0
29	80000	0
47	25000	1
45	26000	1

Let's do the preparation first:

```
import numpy as np
import pandas as pd
import matplotlib.pyplot as plt


dataset = pd.read_csv('Social_Network_Ads.csv')
X = dataset.iloc[:,:-1].values
y = dataset.iloc[:, -1].values


from sklearn.model_selection import train_test_split
X_train, X_test, y_train, y_test = train_test_split(X, y ,
test_size = 0.2, random_state=1)


from sklearn.preprocessing import StandardScaler
sc = StandardScaler()
```

```
X_train = sc.fit_transform(X_train)
X_test = sc.transform(X_test)
print(X_train)
[[-0.8  -1.19]
 [ 0.76 -1.37]
 [ 0.85  1.44]
 [-0.51 -1.49]
 [-1.49  0.38]
 [-1.19  0.55]
 [ 1.05 -1.04]
 [-0.22 -0.3 ]
 [ 0.95 -1.34]
 [-1.1  -1.07]
 [-0.51  1.97]
 [ 2.22 -1.01]
 [ 1.44 -1.4 ]
 [ 0.07 -0.39]
 [-1.19  0.64]
 [ 2.02 -0.9 ]
 [ 1.15  0.58]
 [-0.02  0.29]
 [-0.22  0.26]
 [-0.32 -0.75]
 [-1.68 -0.57]
 [ 0.85  0.58]
 [-0.61 -1.01]
 [ 0.95 -1.13]
 [-0.22 -0.54]
 [ 0.17  0.82]
 [-0.41  1.32]
 [ 1.15  0.52]
 [ 0.76  0.32]
 [ 0.66 -0.87]
 [ 0.37 -0.27]
 [ 0.46 -0.45]
 [-0.22  0.14]
```

```
[ 0.37   0.11]
[-1.     0.82]
[-0.71  1.41]
[ 0.37  -0.48]
[ 0.37  -0.48]
[-1.68  0.41]
[ 0.85  -0.81]
[-1.    -1.1 ]
[...]
```

Note that all values are between -3 and +3.

Next, we train the logistic regression model:

```
from sklearn.linear_model import LogisticRegression
classifier = LogisticRegression()
classifier.fit(X_train, y_train)
```

Let's predict a new result. Before running prediction scripts, let's take a look into our original dataset and pick up a random feature set (in our case, the age of 30 and salary of 87000), and the result is 0.

After running the prediction function, the result is also the same:

```
print(classifier.predict(sc.transform([[30, 87000]])))
[0]
```

The following example demonstrates the comparison of the actual and predicted results for the testing dataset so we can compare the accuracy/efficiency of the trained model:

```
y_pred = classifier.predict(X_test)
print(np.concatenate((y_pred.reshape(len(y_pred),1), y_test.
reshape(len(y_test),1)),1))
[[0 0]
[0 0]
[1 1]
[1 1]
[0 0]
[0 0]
[0 0]
[1 1]
[0 0]
```

```
[1 0]
[0 0]
[0 0]
[0 0]
[1 1]
[1 1]
[1 1]
[1 1]
[0 0]
[0 0]
[1 1]
[0 0]
[1 1]
[1 1]
[1 0]
[0 1]
[0 0]
[...]]
```

The output we have in the preceding code shows the comparison: the first column is the predicted value and the second column is the real value. To calculate the accuracy/efficiency of the model, we can divide the total of the correct number in the prediction by the total number of actual numbers in the testing dataset, and construct its confusion matrix:

```
from sklearn.metrics import confusion_matrix, accuracy_score
cm = confusion_matrix(y_test, y_pred)
print(cm)
accuracy_score(y_test, y_pred)
 [[41  7]
 [ 6 26]]
 0.8375
```

The output shows the following:

```
TP=41
FP=6
FN=7
TN=26
```

The accuracy/efficiency of the model is 83%.

Summary

In this appendix, we have shown examples of data preparation and model development (regression and classification) using the scikit-learn library. Going over these examples and understanding the process will help in your understanding of ML concepts and processes.

Appendix 4
Practicing with Google Vertex AI

In *Chapter 7, Exploring Google Cloud Vertex AI*, we discussed Google Cloud Vertex AI. This appendix contains some hands-on tutorials for Google Vertex AI in the Google Cloud console, step by step. We will cover the following labs:

- Vertex AI – enabling its API
- Vertex AI – datasets
- Vertex AI – labeling tasks
- Vertex AI – training
- Vertex AI – predictions (Vertex AI Endpoint)
- Vertex AI – predictions (Vertex AI Batch Prediction)
- Vertex AI – Workbench
- Vertex AI – Feature Store
- Vertex AI – pipelines and metadata
- Vertex AI – model monitoring

You are expected to follow these labs to practice Vertex AI and gain implementation skills.

Vertex AI – enabling its API

To start using Vertex AI in the Google Cloud console, you will need to set up a billing account and create a project. Once you have created a project (*Vertex AI – demo documentation*), you will be on the following project home dashboard:

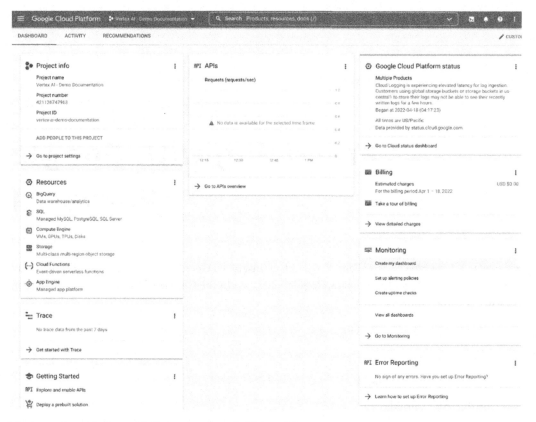

Navigate through the top-left menu to launch Vertex AI:

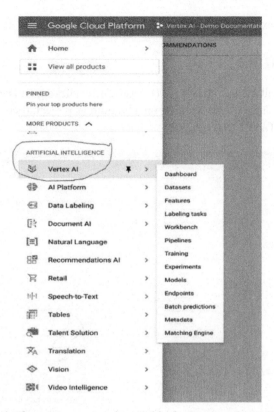

To launch Vertex AI for the first time, you need to enable the Vertex AI API. To do so, select a **Region** and click on the blue **ENABLE VERTEX AI API** button:

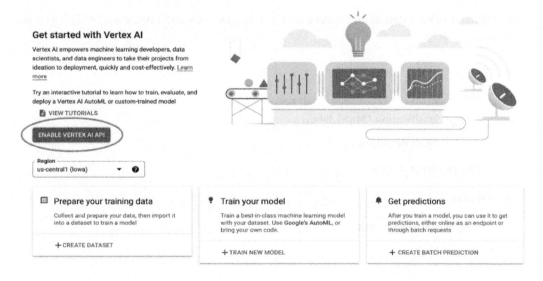

After enabling the Vertex AI API, by default, you will land on the Vertex AI API dashboard.

Vertex AI – datasets

The very first tool we will use in Vertex AI is **Datasets**. After clicking on **Datasets**, you will be taken to the respective page. Since we are working on a brand new project, there is no dataset to display. Click on **CREATE DATASET** to get started:

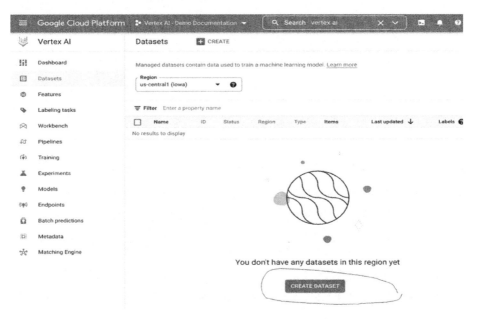

Enter the name of your dataset and select a dataset type to work with from the following four main categories:

- **Image**:
  - **Image classification (Single-label)**
  - **Image classification (Multi-label)**
  - **Image object detection**
  - **Image segmentation**
- **Tabular**:
  - **Regression/classification**
  - **Forecasting**

- **Text**:

  - **Text classification (Single-label)**

  - **Text classification (Multi-label)**

  - **Text entity extraction**

  - **Text sentiment analysis**

- **Video**:

  - **Video action recognition**

  - **Video classification**

  - **Video object tracking**

After selecting a dataset type, a bucket will be created in Google Cloud Storage as the default dataset repository. Here, you can specify the region where your bucket will be created:

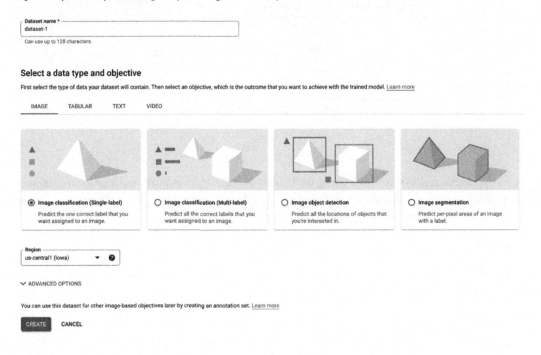

Click on the **CREATE** button. You will be brought to the next page, where you need to specify the import method. There are three options for importing data:

- **Upload images from your computer**
- **Upload import files from your computer**
- **Select import files from Cloud Storage**

To select a file(s) from your local computer, click on the **SELECT FILES** button:

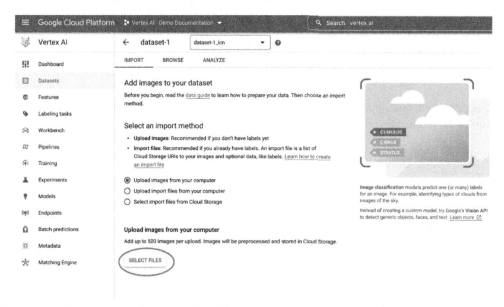

On the page that appears, navigate to the folder that contains your pictures on your local computer and then select one or more pictures that you want to upload to your dataset. Note that you can upload up to 500 images per upload. The pictures that you upload should be in one of the following formats:

- JPEG
- GIF
- PNG
- BMP
- ICO

If you need to upload more pictures, you need to click on the **SELECT FILES** button and specify which Google Cloud bucket you want to use for your dataset.

Once the pictures have been uploaded, you can browse all the images in the dataset and check their status (they will be either **Labeled** or **Unlabeled**). As shown in the following screenshot, we have a total of 20 images and all of them are unlabeled (labeling tasks will be covered in the next section):

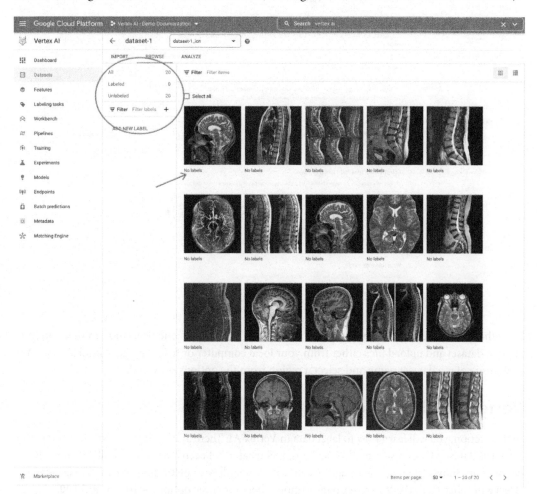

If you wish to use the other two options for adding images to a dataset – **Upload import files from your computer** and **Select import files from Cloud Storage** – you can simply provide a link to Cloud Storage, as shown in the following screenshot:

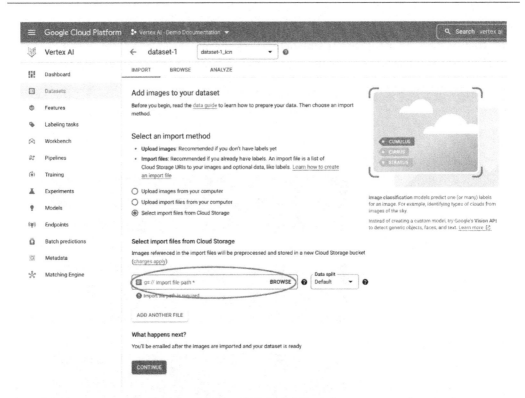

The other three categories (**Tabular**, **Text**, and **Video**) follow the same procedure in that you must create a dataset and upload files either from your local computer or from Google Cloud Storage. You must also enter a dataset name and select a region from the options provided.

Vertex AI – labeling tasks

In this section, you will learn how to label data in Vertex AI. There are several ways to label data within a created dataset. If you use a small-size dataset, you can label each dataset manually. By default, the dataset only shows 10 images per page. If you want to see all your pictures on the same page, you can select a number from the **Items per page** option. There are three options – **10**, **50**, and **100**:

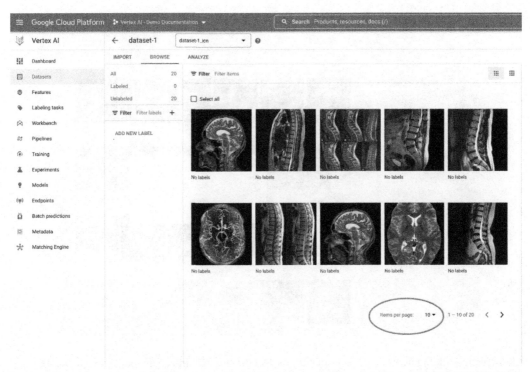

Since we haven't created a label yet, we need to define/create a label name. Click on **ADD NEW LABEL** and enter the name for a new label in the pop-up that appears. Then, click **Done**. In this example, we will create two new labels – `Brain` and `Spine`:

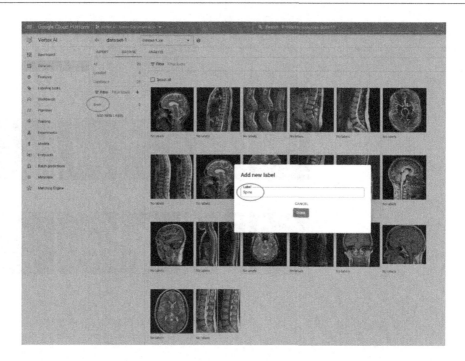

After creating/adding new labels, you can either select every single image and label it or make multiple selections and label them as a group (following each step from *Steps 1* to *4*):

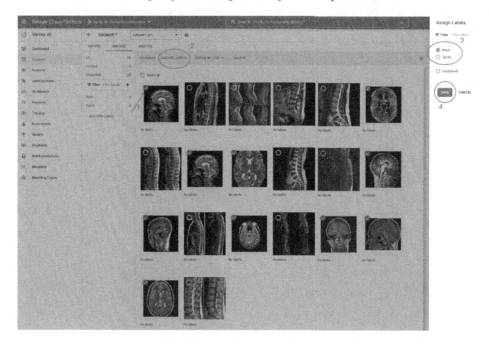

After labeling all the images, you can check if any of the images have been left unlabeled by going to the summary page:

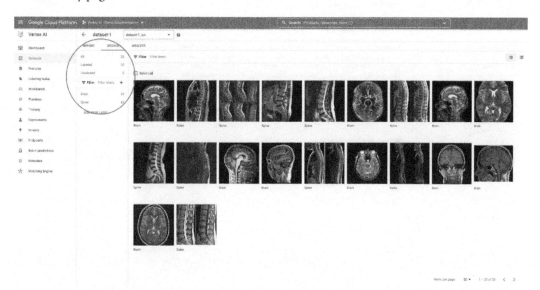

If you have a very large dataset, you can create a labeling task and assign it to a team to label the dataset.

Vertex AI – training

Now that you have a labeled dataset, it is ready for model training. Vertex AI provides different methods for training your model:

- AutoML

- Custom training (advanced)

To start AutoML training, in the Vertex AI console, click on **Training** and then the **CREATE** button, which is located at the top of the page (in our case, we are going to perform AutoML training using the dataset of MRI images that we created in the previous section):

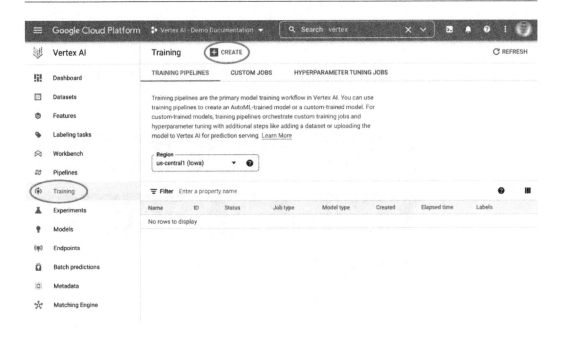

On the page that appears, you need to define some specifications for the model you are trying to train:

- **Select Dataset**: Here, you will be able to see all the datasets you created previously.

- **Annotation Set**: Labels are saved in collections called annotations. You can change annotation sets to apply a different group of labels to the same dataset.

On the **Training method** page, select **AutoML** (this will be selected by default). Then, click **CONTINUE**:

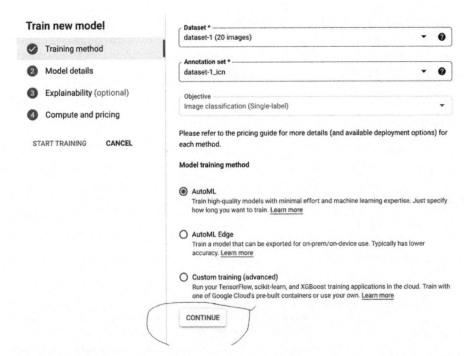

Since we are working on training a new ML model, we need to select **Train new model**. But in case you already have a trained model and want to retrain *or* train a model as a version of an existing model, select **Train new version**.

Next, enter the name of the model and provide a description (the description is optional).

In the **Advanced options** section, you will be given two options for data splitting: **Randomly assigned** and **Manual (Advanced)**. In terms of **Randomly assigned**, your dataset will be automatically randomized and split into training, validation, and testing sets using the following ratios:

- **Training**: 80%
- **Validation**: 10%
- **Testing**: 10%

You can change values as needed for your training mode. For more details, check out the Google documentation at `https://cloud.google.com/vertex-ai/docs/general/ml-use?_ga=2.140326960.-2030104523.1635276817&_gac=1.58794719.1650385127.CjwKCAjwu_mSBhAYEiwA5BBmf84zVxwFEpx-VaeJRusJFGq8rVNEovNnLhJ3vLYGMK3Eao6yJhRY5BoCdKgQAvD_BwE`:

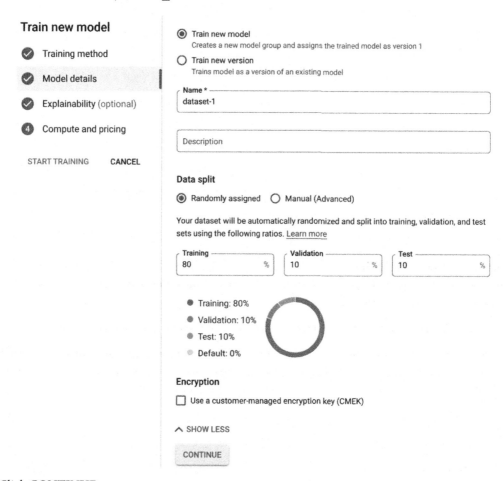

Click **CONTINUE**.

On the next and last page, you will be prompted to enter an amount in the **Budget** section. Here, you need to specify the maximum amount of time that will be used to train a particular model. Click on the **START TRAINING** option:

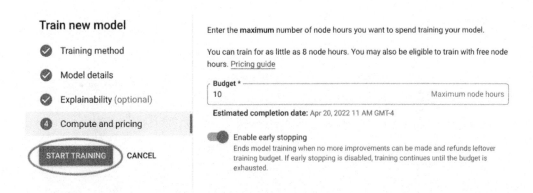

When the training is done, you will receive an email confirming this and you will be able to see its status. Now, you can analyze the trained model from the training page (the same page where we trained our model) or click on **Models** from the left menu and click on the model you want to analyze:

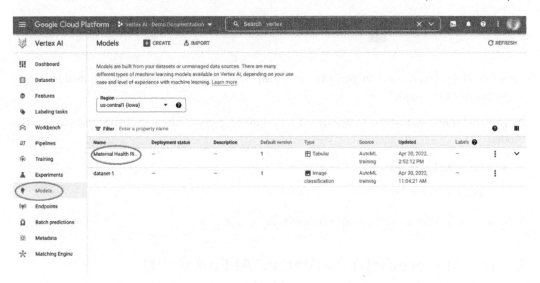

When you click on the model you want to analyze, you will be prompted to select the version of the model. Since we have trained a brand new model, we only have one version. The following screenshot shows a summary of the training model for our tabular dataset:

From this chart, you can see the performance of the trained model, as well as the confusion matrix of our classification model.

After model training, it is time to deploy the model for prediction. There are two ways to deploy the model:

- Vertex AI Endpoint
- Vertex AI Batch Prediction

We will discuss these in more detail in the next few sections.

Vertex AI – predictions (Vertex AI Endpoint)

In this section, we are going to deploy our model via Vertex AI Endpoint. There are two ways to deploy a model:

- From **Models**
- From **Endpoints**

Let's look at these options in detail.

Deploying the model via Models

Go to the **Models** section from the left menu, select the model you want to deploy, and select the version you want to deploy (remember, we have only one version since we have built/trained a brand-new model). Then, at the top of the page, click on **DEPLOY & TEST**:

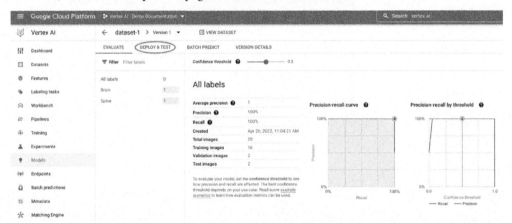

After clicking on **DEPLOY & TEST**, you will be taken to the next page. Here, click on the blue **DEPLOY TO ENDPOINT** button:

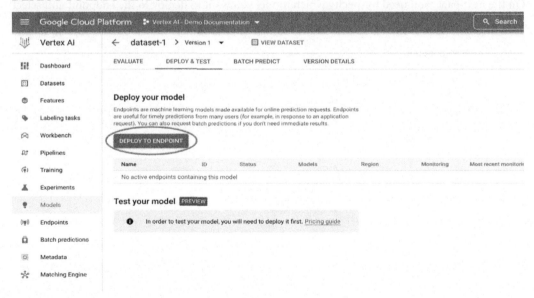

Deploying the model via Endpoints

Go to the **Endpoints** section from the left menu. By doing so, you will be navigated to a pop-up page where you need to define your endpoint:

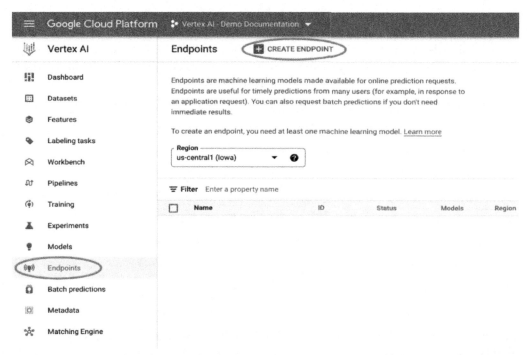

On the next page, you need to specify which model you want to deploy to the endpoint and select the version of the model:

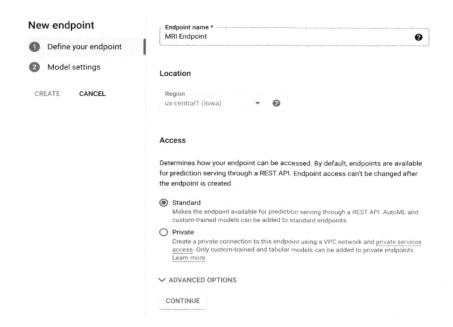

Specify the number of compute nodes and leave the other settings as-is. Then, click **DONE** and then **CREATE**:

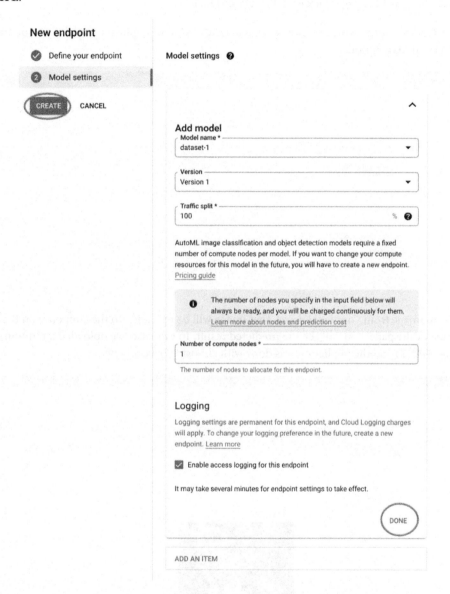

Upon completing the deployment, you will receive an email specifying the status of the endpoint deployment. Now, we can start making predictions:

1. Go to **Models**.

2. Select the model you wish to use.

3.   Select the model's version.

4.   At the top of the page, click on **DEPLOY & TEST**.

You will land on a page where you can start trying/testing your deployed model. Click on the blue **UPLOAD IMAGE** button:

Choose an image from your local drive. That image will be uploaded to the endpoint; on the right-hand side of the page, you will see the predicted result. In our case, we uploaded a random image (`spine MARI`) and the prediction was done with almost 99% accuracy:

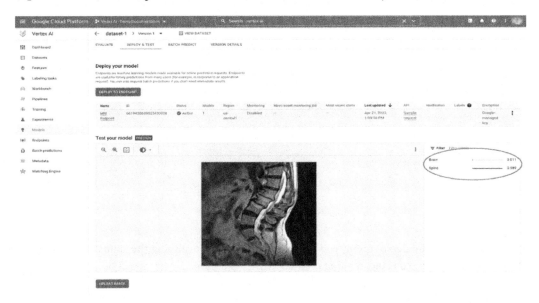

If you need to use your endpoint in mobile/web applications, you can request a sample API. From the same page, click on **Sample request**:

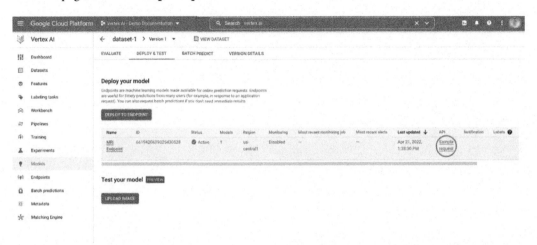

From the menu that appears, you can copy the script from the **REST** or **PYTHON** section based on your needs:

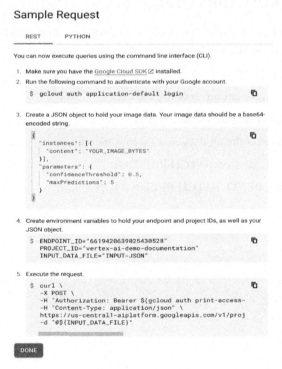

After several attempts, the system will start generating graphs based on the logs that have been collected from the endpoint:

So far, we have deployed our model to Vertex AI Endpoint. Now, let's learn how to use batch prediction.

Vertex AI – predictions (Batch Prediction)

Batch prediction is used when you don't require an immediate response and want to get predictions from the accumulated data via a single request. Follow these steps to perform batch prediction for the models we trained earlier:

1. Go to **Models** from the left menu of the console.

2. Click on the model you want to work with.

3. Click on the version of the model you want to work with.

4. From the top menu, click on **BATCH PREDICT**.

5. Click on the blue **CREATE BATCH PREDICTION** button:

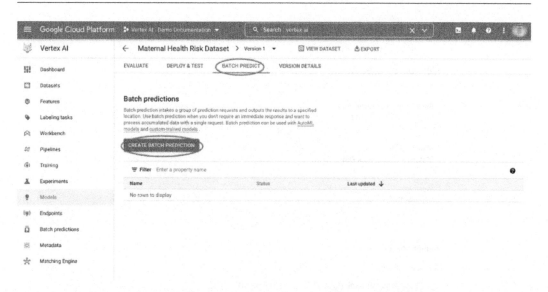

After clicking on **CREATE BATCH PREDICTION**, you need to define some parameters, such as the batch prediction's name, source, output, and so on. Let's analyze each of them:

- **Batch prediction name**: Enter a name for the batch prediction.

- **Select source**: Here, you need to specify the source of the value that will be used in batch prediction. You can source either the BigQuery table *or* the file in Cloud Storage. Remember that since we are using the tabular dataset, the format must be CSV, JSONL, or TFRecord.

- **Batch prediction output**: Select the format of output (BigQuery table, CSV, TFRecord, or JSONL) and provide the path (BigQuery *or* Cloud Storage).

- **Explainability options**: Optionally, you may check **Enable feature attributions** for this model to get feature attributions as part of the output.

Using a BigQuery dataset and the table we have created, we can create a new batch prediction to predict the **Risk Level** column:

New batch prediction

Batch prediction name *

batch-prediction-health

Model name *

Maternal Health Risk Dataset   ▼

Version

Version 1   ▼

Select source

◉ BigQuery table

○ File on Cloud Storage (CSV, JSONL, and TFRecord)

BigQuery path *

☑ vertex-ai-demo-documentation.batchprediction.a   BROWSE

Use the following format: projectId.datasetId.tableId. If an optional field is left blank, a new
one will be created.

Batch prediction output

Select a format and output location for the prediction results

Output format

BigQuery table   ▼

BigQuery path *

☑ vertex-ai-demo-documentation.batchprediction   BROWSE

Use the following format: projectId.datasetId(optional).tableId(optional). If an optional field is
left blank, a new one will be created.

Explainability options

☐ Enable feature attributions for this model

EDIT

∨ ADVANCED OPTIONS

[CREATE]   CANCEL

After defining all the parameters, click on **CREATE**; the batch prediction will start processing. It will take some time to complete this process and you will receive an email upon completion.

Vertex AI – Workbench

Vertex AI Workbench is a single development environment for the entire data science workflow. You can use Vertex AI Workbench's notebook-based environment to query and explore data, develop and train a model, and run your code as part of a pipeline. Vertex AI workbench offers the following features:

- **Managed notebooks** are Google-managed environments with integrations and features that help you set up and work in an end-to-end notebook-based production environment.

- **User-managed notebooks** are deep learning VM image instances that are heavily customizable and are therefore ideal for users who need a lot of control over their environment.

To launch Vertex AI Workbench, navigate to the Vertex AI console and click on **Workbench**:

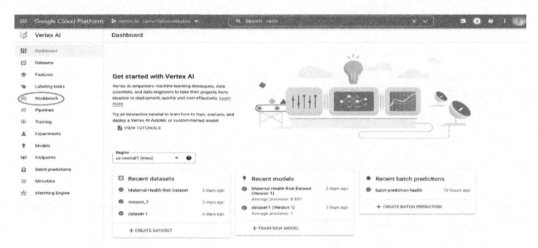

If you are using Vertex AI Workbench for the first time, you will need to enable Notebook API, which you will be prompted for after you click on **Workbench**. Click on **ENABLE**:

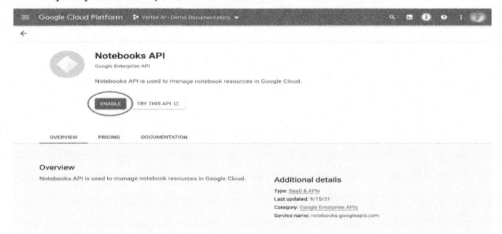

In this lab, we are going to create a user-managed notebook. Vertex AI provides different types of Jupyter notebooks with various pre-installed libraries and dependencies. In this example, we will create a simple Python 3 notebook. Follow these steps:

1. From the left menu of the console, click on **Workbench**.

2. Click on **NEW NOTEBOOK** at the top of the page.

3. From the drop - down menu, click on **Python 3**:

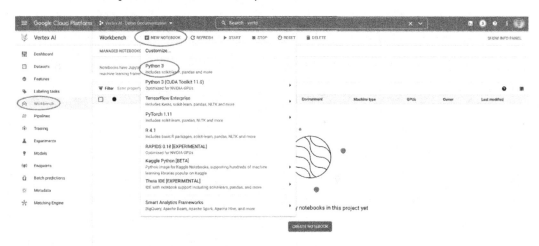

From the popup menu, you need to identify the notebook by providing its **Notebook name**, **Region**, **Zone**, and so on. Then, click on **CREATE**:

New notebook

Notebook name *

netobook-demo

63-char limit with lowercase letters, digits, or '-' only. Must start with a letter. Cannot end with a '-'.

Region *	Zone *
us-west1 (Oregon)	us-west1-b

Notebook properties ✏️

Environment ❓	Python 3 (with Intel® MKL)
Machine type	4 vCPUs, 15 GB RAM
Boot disk	100 GB Standard persistent disk
Data disk	100 GB Standard persistent disk
Subnetwork	default(10.138.0.0/20)
External IP	Ephemeral(Automatic)
Permission	Compute Engine default service account
Estimated cost ❓	$102.70 monthly, $0.141 hourly

ADVANCED OPTIONS   **CANCEL**   (**CREATE**)

Now, let's check and analyze the notebook we created earlier and what features are available in Vertex AI Notebook(s). Vertex AI provides a Jupyter notebook environment. Click on **OPEN JUPYTERLAB**, as shown in the following screenshot:

You will be navigated to a new tab containing the JupyterLab environment. On the left-hand side of the page, you will see all your folders. By default, there are two folders, but you can create, upload, or clone a folder from different sources such as GitHub. On the right-hand side of the page, you have **Notebook**, **Console**, and **Other**, which includes options for **Terminal**, **Text File**, and so on. Click on **Python 3** under Notebook. You will be taken to a blank notebook where you can start programming using Python:

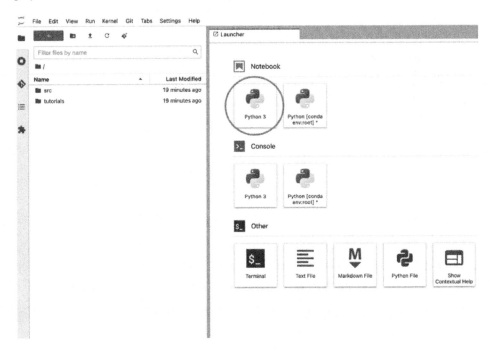

After clicking on **Python 3**, the Jupyter notebook will create a new `.ipynb` file (on the left) so that you can start inputting your scripts on the right:

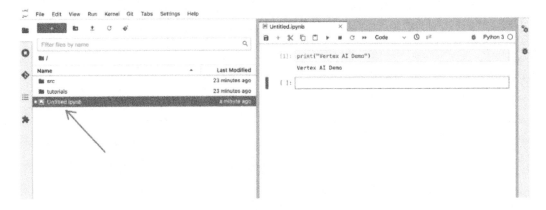

With that, you have created the training platform and are ready to start running Jupyter notebooks.

Vertex AI – Feature Store

Feature Store in Vertex AI is where you can create entities and features and add values that can be used later as needed. In this demo, we are going to explore creating a Feature Store with entities and features in the Jupyter notebook by running some Python scripts. Before diving into the notebook, let's create a Feature Store and entities via the Google Cloud console. From the left menu of the console, click on **Features**:

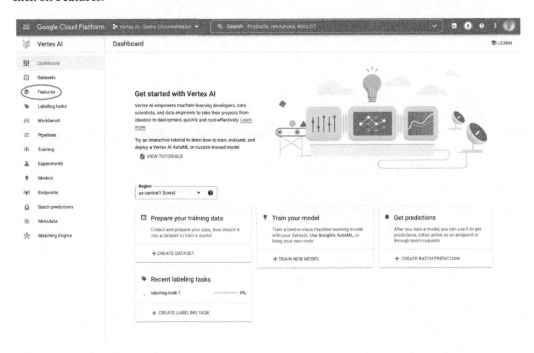

Since we haven't created any Feature Store(s) yet, this section will be empty. To create a new entity, click on **CREATE ENTITY TYPE**, which is located at the top of the page:

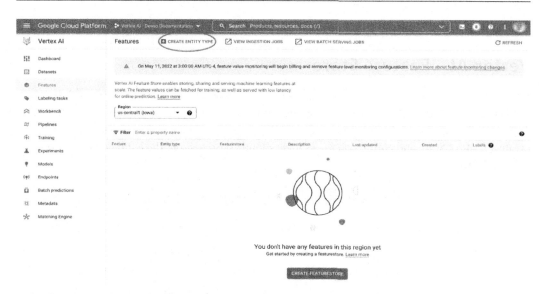

From the popup menu, enter all the necessary information and click the **CREATE** button, as shown here:

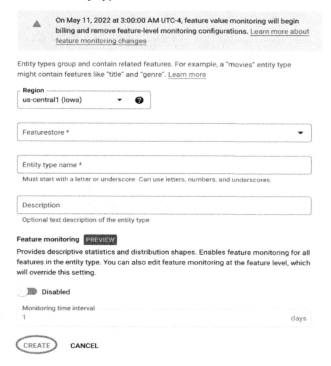

Next, we are going to create a new notebook and clone a repository from GitHub (`https://github.com/GoogleCloudPlatform/vertex-ai-samples`). After creating a notebook and cloning the aforementioned repository, from the `cloned` folder, go to `Vertex-ai-samples | notebooks | official | feature_store` and click on `gapic-feature-store.ipynb`:

Overview

This Colab introduces Vertex AI Feature Store, a managed cloud service for machine learning engineers and data scientists to store, serve, manage and share machine learning features at a large scale.

This Colab assumes that you understand basic Google Cloud concepts such as Project, Storage and Vertex AI. Some machine learning knowledge is also helpful but not required.

Dataset

This Colab uses a movie recommendation dataset as an example throughout all the sessions. The task is to train a model to predict if a user is going to watch a movie and serve this model online.

Objective

In this notebook, you will learn how to:

```
* How to import your features into Vertex AI Feature Store.
* How to serve online prediction requests using the imported features.
* How to access imported features in offline jobs, such as training jobs.
```

Costs

This tutorial uses billable components of Google Cloud:

- Vertex AI
- Cloud Storage
- Cloud Bigtable

Install all additional packages and enter your project ID, as shown in the following screenshot:

Set your project ID

If you don't know your project ID, you may be able to get your project ID using `gcloud`.

```
[1]: import os

     PROJECT_ID = ""

     # Get your Google Cloud project ID from gcloud
     if not os.getenv("IS_TESTING"):
         shell_output = !gcloud config list --format 'value(core.project)' 2>/dev/null
         PROJECT_ID = shell_output[0]
         print("Project ID: ", PROJECT_ID)
```

```
     Project ID:  vertex-ai-demo-documentation
```

Otherwise, set your project ID here.

```
[2]: if PROJECT_ID == "" or PROJECT_ID is None:
         PROJECT_ID = "python-docs-samples-tests"   # @param {type:"string"}
```

Run all the scripts as you go through (in this demo document, we will not go over every single line, but we will highlight important points related to the Vertex AI Feature Store).

These scripts will do the following:

1. Prepare a dataset for output. It will create a dataset in BigQuery to host the output.

2. Import libraries and define constants.

3. Create the feature store, as well as its entities and features.

4. Import values.

After running all the scripts, you can check the created Feature Store (along with its entities and features) in the Google console. From the console, go to **Vertex AI** and click on **Features** from the left menu:

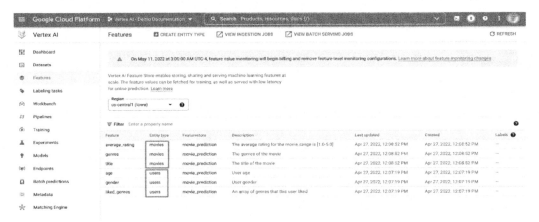

You will notice that we have created a Feature Store with two entities (`movies` and `users`). Each entity has three features. If you click on any entity provided, you will see some details about that particular entity (in our case, the entity is `movies`):

As a fully managed solution, Vertex AI Feature Store provides a centralized repository for you to organize, store, and serve ML features, and for your team to share, discover, and reuse ML features at scale. It greatly helps in developing and deploying new ML applications. For more detailed information about Feature Store, check out `https://cloud.google.com/vertex-ai/docs/featurestore`.

Vertex AI – pipelines and metadata

Pipelines help you automate and reproduce your ML workflow. Vertex AI integrates its ML offerings across Google Cloud into a seamless development experience. Previously, models trained with AutoML and custom models were accessible via separate services. Vertex AI combines both into a single API, along with other new products. In this demo, we will create and run ML pipelines with Vertex Pipelines.

We are going to use the Vertex AI SDK and create a Jupyter notebook. After creating a notebook, click on **OPEN JUPYTERLAB**, as shown in the following screenshot:

The new notebook will open in a new tab. Clone the repository (`https://github.com/GoogleCloudPlatform/vertex-ai-samples`).

From the cloned folder, go to `Vertex-ai-samples | notebooks | official | pipelines`. After clicking on the `automl_tabular_classification_beans.ipynb` file, the notebook will open on the left-hand side, as shown here:

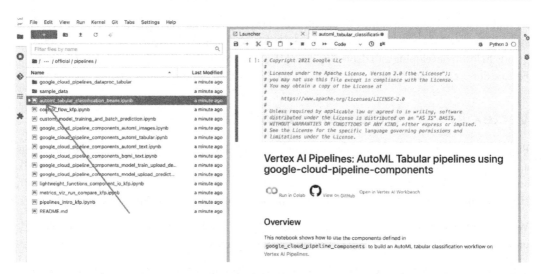

From the given notebook, read the overview and look at the dataset, objectives, and the cost of the particular demo. Run all commands as you go (we will not describe every single script but will focus on the main parts that are related to Vertex AI Pipeline).

The scripts you are going to run will do the following:

1. Set the project ID and bucket (where all the data will be stored).

2. Import the necessary libraries.

3. Define the constants and create the necessary components.

4. Create an end-to-end ML pipeline. This process will take over 2 hours since it is going to perform the following tasks:

    A. Create a dataset in Vertex AI.

    B. Train a tabular classification model with AutoML.

    C. Get evaluation metrics on this model.

    D. Based on the evaluation metrics, it will decide whether to deploy the model using conditional logic in Vertex Pipelines.

    E. Deploy the model to an endpoint using Vertex prediction.

After creating a pipeline, to view and analyze it, from the left menu of Vertex AI, click on **Pipelines**, as shown here:

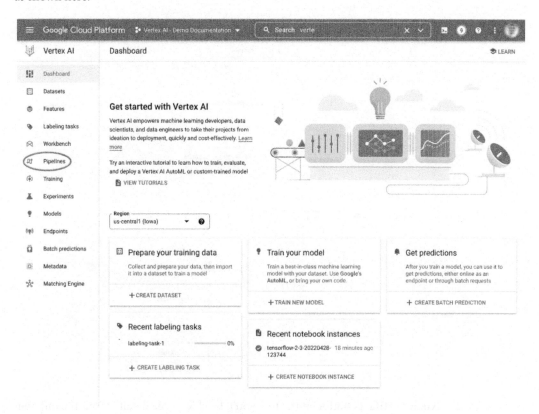

After clicking on **Pipelines**, you will be taken to a page where you can select a pipeline you want to view. You will see the following diagram of the pipeline:

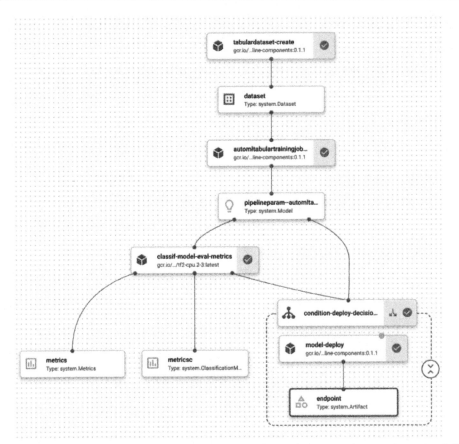

If you click the **Expand artifacts** button at the top, you'll be able to see details about the different artifacts that have been created from your pipeline. For example, if you click on the dataset artifact, you'll see details about the Vertex AI dataset that was created. You can click the link specified next to **URI** to go to the page for that dataset:

Artifact info

VIEW LINEAGE

Name	dataset
Type	system.Dataset
URI	aiplatform://v1/projects/462141068491/locations/us-central1/datasets/460712964224188416

To check the resulting metric visualizations from your custom evaluation component, click on the `metrics` artifact. On the right-hand side of your dashboard, you'll be able to see the confusion matrix for this model:

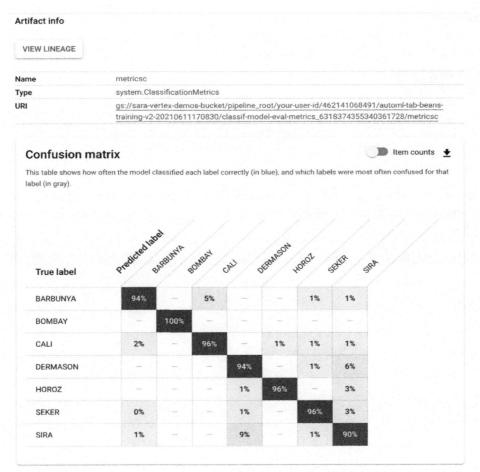

Artifact info

VIEW LINEAGE

Name	metricsc
Type	system.ClassificationMetrics
URI	gs://sara-vertex-demos-bucket/pipeline_root/your-user-id/462141068491/automl-tab-beans-training-v2-20210611170830/classif-model-eval-metrics_6318374355340361728/metricsc

Confusion matrix   Item counts

This table shows how often the model classified each label correctly (in blue), and which labels were most often confused for that label (in gray).

True label / Predicted label	BARBUNYA	BOMBAY	CALI	DERMASON	HOROZ	SEKER	SIRA
BARBUNYA	94%	–	5%	–	–	1%	1%
BOMBAY	–	100%	–	–	–	–	–
CALI	2%	–	96%	–	1%	1%	1%
DERMASON	–	–	–	94%	–	1%	6%
HOROZ	–	–	–	1%	96%	–	3%
SEKER	0%	–	–	1%	–	96%	3%
SIRA	1%	–	–	9%	–	1%	90%

To check the model and endpoint that was created from this pipeline run, go to the **Models** section and click on the `automl-beans` model. There, you should see this model deployed to an endpoint:

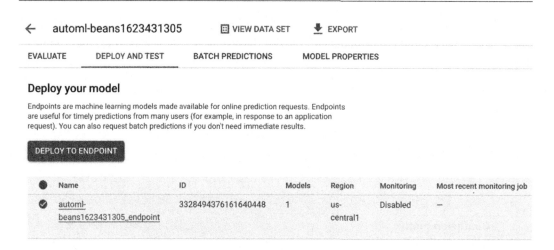

Remember that each section in the pipeline will produce output that will be used as input for the next section. Later, if those outputs/inputs need to be modified, click on the **Metadata** button from the left menu:

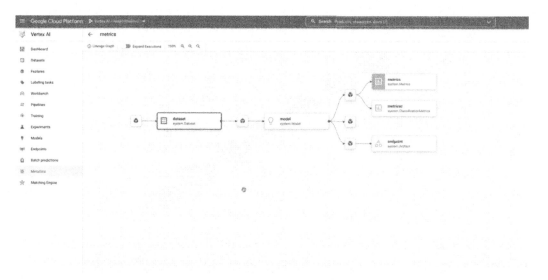

With that, we have covered Vertex AI Pipelines and metadata. In the next section, we will discuss model monitoring for Vertex AI.

Vertex AI – model monitoring

After model deployment, we need to monitor it since the data and environment may change and cause the model to deteriorate over time. Two concepts of monitoring should be considered: **feature skew** and **drift detection**.

In our demo documentation, we are going to build a brand-new tabular dataset and train the model. In this example, we will be using the *Women's International Football Results* (`https://www.kaggle.com/datasets/martj42/womens-international-football-results`) dataset.

We have created a tabular dataset where we have uploaded a CSV file that's been downloaded from Kaggle. The following screenshot shows a summary of the dataset:

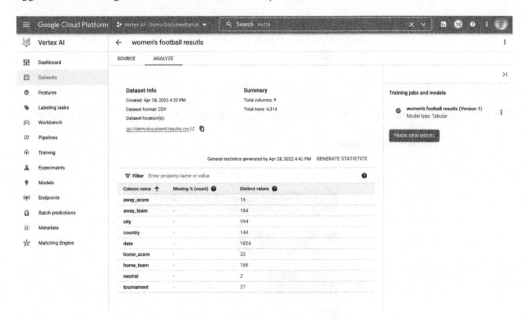

We have also trained a model using the AutoML method, and as the target, we have used the `neutral` column, which has two values (either `False` or `True`). The following screenshot shows the summary of the trained model:

With Explainable AI, we can see that the `tournament` column has the most impact on our model:

Feature Importance

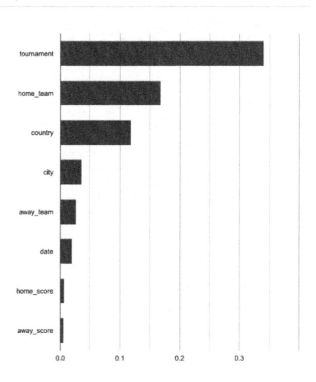

Next, we need to deploy our model to Endpoint. Click on the **DEPLOY TO ENDPOINT** button, as shown here:

In the popup menu that appears (on the right-hand side), fill out all the fields:

- **Monitoring job display name**: The name of the monitoring job.

- **Monitoring windows length**: How many hours the model will be monitored for.

- **Alert emails**: Enter at least 1 email that is going to receive an alert (you can enter multiple email addresses).

- **Sampling rate**: The percentage of the sampling.

Leave the rest of the fields as-is and click **CONTINUE**:

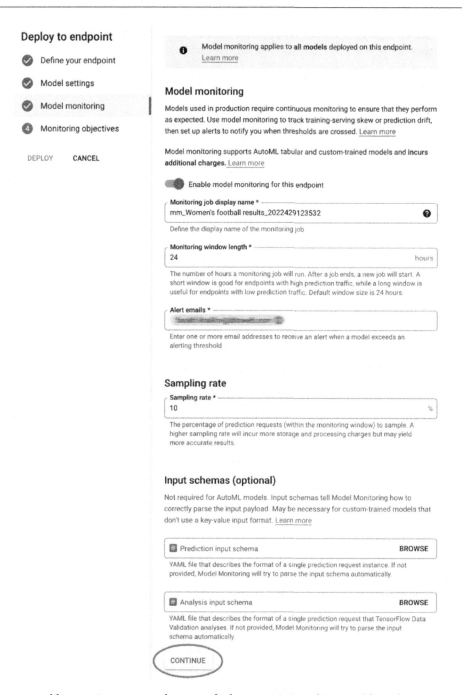

In the next and last section, you need to specify the monitoring objective (skew detection or drift detection). If you select the **Training-serving skew detection** option, you need to specify the training data source and target column. However, if you select the **Prediction drift detection** option, you need to specify alert thresholds. In our case, we will select **Prediction drift detection**. Next, click on the **DEPLOY** button:

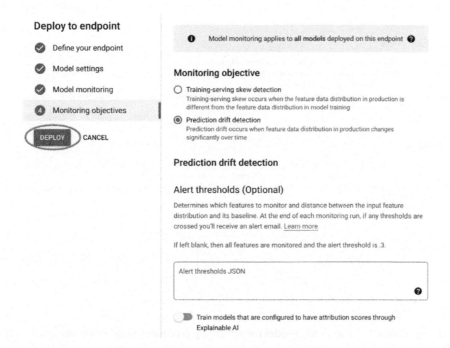

It will take a while to process the deployment to the endpoint. Once the deployment has finished, you will receive emails about the *notification and status of the deployment,* and the *monitoring job being created* (in two separate emails):

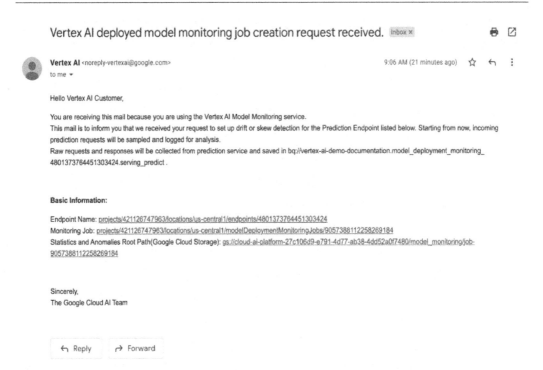

The preceding screenshot shows the model monitoring job request email notification. Note that the request has been submitted and is based on the incoming prediction request. It will be sampled and logged for analysis.

Summary

In this appendix, we looked at examples based on the Google Cloud Vertex AI suite, which provides end-to-end services for data scientists. We covered Vertex AI datasets, labeling tasks, training, prediction, Workbench, Feature Store, pipelines, metadata, and model monitoring.

In the next appendix, we will discuss how to use various Google Cloud ML APIs, including the Vision API, NLP API, Speech-to-Text API, Text-to-Speech API, Translation API, and Dialogflow API.

Appendix 5
Practicing with Google Cloud ML API

In *Chapter 8*, *Discovering Google Cloud ML API*, we explored the Google Cloud ML API, which is the API interface provided by Google, based on pre-trained models. The Google Cloud ML API includes the following APIs, all of which will be covered as topics in this appendix:

- Google Cloud Vision API

- Google Cloud NLP API

- Google Cloud Speech-to-Text API

- Google Cloud Text-to-Speech API

- Google Cloud Translation API

- Google Cloud Dialogflow API

In this appendix, we will provide implementation examples for each of these APIs. Let's get started.

Google Cloud Vision API

In this appendix, we will show you how to use the Vision API via Google Cloud Shell and the Python SDK.

Before we can start using the Vision API, we need to enable the Vision API from the Google console. From the left menu of the console, navigate to **APIs and Services | Library** and search for Vision API. After clicking on **Vision API**, you will be prompted to enable the API. In our case, the API is already enabled, as shown here:

Cloud Vision API

Google Enterprise API

Image Content Analysis

MANAGE   TRY THIS API ⬀   ✓ API Enabled

We will start by using the Vision API via Google Cloud Shell. From the Google console, from the top-right corner, click on the Cloud Shell icon, as shown here:

After clicking the Cloud Shell icon, the Shell Terminal will appear at the bottom of the console, as shown here:

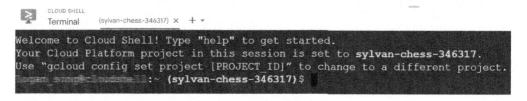

Now, let's look at some examples to show how the Vision API works in Google Cloud Shell:

- **Example 1** is an image of a tree:

To upload a file to Google Cloud Shell, click on the three dots icon highlighted in the following screenshot and click **Upload**:

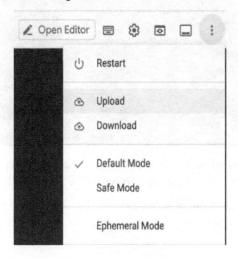

On the page that appears, you will be prompted to either upload a file or a folder. Navigate to your browser and select the image that you want to upload – in our case, tree.jpeg. Run the following command in Google Cloud Shell:

```
gcloud ml vision detect-objects tree.jpeg
```

```
                                    :~ (abcproject-341419)$ gcloud ml vision detect-objects tree.jpeg
{
  "responses": [
    {
      "localizedObjectAnnotations": [
        {
          "boundingPoly": {
            "normalizedVertices": [
              {
                "x": 0.35709468,
                "y": 0.16453059
              },
              {
                "x": 0.9865663,
                "y": 0.16453059
              },
              {
                "x": 0.9865663,
                "y": 0.7795686
              },
              {
                "x": 0.35709468,
                "y": 0.7795686
              }
            ]
          },
          "mid": "/m/0c9ph5",
          "name": "Flower",
          "score": 0.77939504
        }
      ]
    }
  ]
}
                             :~ (abcproject-341419)$ []
```

In the preceding screenshot, we can see *X* and *Y* values. These represent the corners of the object, and the object was detected as a flower with a 78% confidence level.

- **Example 2** is an image of the Google logo:

Now, we will try another option that's available from the Vision API and detect a logo. Upload the image of the Google logo, and type the following command in Google Cloud Shell:

```
gcloud ml vision detect-logos glogo.jpeg
```

```
_____:~ (abcproject-341419)$ gcloud ml vision detect-logos glogo.jpeg
{
  "responses": [
    {
      "logoAnnotations": [
        {
          "boundingPoly": {
            "vertices": [
              {
                "x": 68,
                "y": 57
              },
              {
                "x": 1212,
                "y": 57
              },
              {
                "x": 1212,
                "y": 1183
              },
              {
                "x": 68,
                "y": 1183
              }
            ]
          },
          "description": "Google",
          "mid": "/m/045c7b",
          "score": 0.97997874
        }
      ]
    }
  ]
}
_____:~ (abcproject-341419)$ []
```

You can also try using other options, such as detecting text on the *same* image. It will display the result, such as each character and the location of each character on the image:

```
gcloud ml vision detect-text glogo.jpeg
```

```
_____:~ (abcproject-341419)$ gcloud ml vision detect-text glogo.jpeg
{
  "responses": [
    {
      "fullTextAnnotation": {
        "pages": [
          {
            "blocks": [
              {
                "blockType": "TEXT",
                "boundingBox": {
                  "vertices": [
                    {
                      "x": 309,
                      "y": 149
                    },
                    {
                      "x": 1126,
                      "y": 212
                    },
                    {
                      "x": 1063,
```

Note that the preceding screenshot only displays part of the result since the output is long.

Now, let's interact with the Python SDK and the Vision API:

1. First, you must install Python's Google Cloud Vision API. Use the following command in Google Cloud Shell:

    ```
    pip3 install - -upgrade google-cloud-vision
    ```

2. Next, we will need some Python code. The following is a simple Python script where it detects the Google logo in the image:

    ```python
    import io
    import os
    # import the Google client library
    from google.cloud import vision
    # instantiates a client
    client = vision.ImageAnnotatorClient()
    # provide the name of the image file to annotate
    file_name = os.path.abspath('glogo.jpeg')
    # load the image into memoryview
    with io.open(file_name, 'rb') as image_file:
        content = image_file.read()
    image = vision.Image(content = content)
    # Performs label detection on the image file
    response = client.logo_detection(image=image)
    logos = response.logo_annotations
    for logo in logos:
        print(logo.description + " : " + str(logo.score))
    ```

Here, we have imported all the necessary libraries, then defined an image name (the same logo image we used earlier), detected the logo using the Vision API, and printed the result and the score.

Now, we need to upload the Python script to Cloud Shell. After uploading the Python script, we can execute it, as follows:

```
python3 main.py
Google: 0.979978402153015
```

The result indicates that the logo is **Google** and the score is 0.98, which means it has a confidence level of about 98%.

Google Cloud NLP API

The Google Cloud NLP API uses models to analyze text. There are several ways to use the NLP API. Here, we will show you how to use the NLP API via Google Cloud Shell and the Python SDK.

Before you can use the NLP API, you will need to enable it. Simply navigate to the Natural Language API from the left menu of the console *or* type `Natural Language API` in the search bar at the top of the page. After landing on the NLP API web page, you will be asked to **Enable API** (if you have already done this, you can skip this).

Now, let's start using the NLP API with Google Cloud Shell. Click on the Cloud Shell icon to activate it and type the following command:

```
gcloud ml language classify-text --content =
'If Roe is overturne, legislatures in 26 states have pending
laws indicating that they intent to ban abortions, according
to the Guttmacher Institure, a research organization that
supports abortion rights. That could leave many women in need
of abortion services hunders or thousands of miles away from
access to procedure - unaffordable for many.
Corporate America is increasingly being drawn from the
political sidelines on the abortion issue in response to
pressure from inverstors, customer and employees. Companies are
also struggling to attract and retain talent and worry about
the impact these states anti-abortion laws could have on their
workers.'
```

As output, you will see the result of the classification based on the text provided:

```
"categories": [
  {
    "confidence": 0.98,
    "name": "/People & Society/Social Issues & Advocacy"
  },
  {
    "confidence": 0.89,
    "name": "/Sensitive Subjects"
  }
]
}
```

The preceding output shows that it successfully identified the text in `People & Society / Social Issues & Advocacy` with 98% confidence and `Sensitive Subjects` with 89% confidence.

Let's try another option – that is, `analyze-sentiment`. Here, we can provide some text to analyze the sentiment. For this example, we will use a restaurant review from Google Maps:

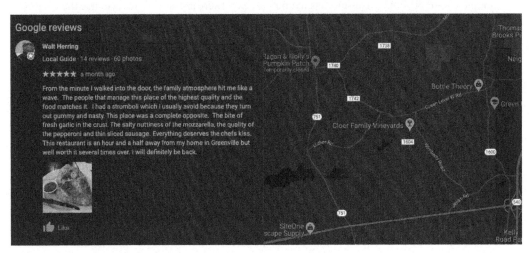

Enter the following command in Google Cloud Shell:

```
gcloud ml language analyze-sentiment - - content =
"From the minute I walked into the door, the family atmosphere
hit me like a wave. The people that manage this place of the
highest quality and the food matches it. I had a stromboli
which I usually avoid because they turn out gummy and nasty.
This place was a complete opposite. The bite of fresh garlic in
the crust. The salty nuttiness of the mozzarella, the quality
of the pepperoni and thin sliced sausage. Everything deserves
the chefs kiss. This restaurant is an hour and half away from
my home Greensville but well worth it several time over. I will
definitely be back."
```

The analysis will be displayed. The following screenshot shows part of the result:

```json
"documentSentiment": {
  "magnitude": 6.9,
  "score": 0.4
},
"language": "en",
"sentences": {
  {
    "sentiment": {
      "magnitude": 0.8,
      "score": 0.8
    },
    "text": {
      "beginOffset": 0,
      "content": "From the minute I walked into the door, the family atmosphere hit me like a wave."
    }
  },
  {
    "sentiment": {
      "magnitude": 0.9,
      "score": 0.9
    },
    "text": {
      "beginOffset": 83,
      "content": "The people that manage this place of the highest quality and the food matches it."
```

You can scroll through the result to view its details. There are two main concepts we need to understand: magnitude (the overall strength of the emotion – that is, either positive or negative) and score (the overall emotional leaning of the text).

Now, let's investigate the NLP API with the Python SDK. There are a few other SDKs available as well, such as Java, PHP, Go, and others:

First, we need to install the SDK. Type the following command:

```
pip install google-cloud-language
```

You need to have a credential to interact with Google Cloud. Therefore, create a service account, generate and upload the key, and activate it. We will skip this step here.

Next, we will need some Python code. The following is a simple Python script that analyzes sentiment from the given text:

```python
# Import ghe Google Cloud client library
from google.com import language_v1
#set a client variable
client = language_v1.LanguageServiceClient()
```

```
# The text to analyze
text = "We heard great review and thought we finally found a
Authentic Classy Italiant Restaurant... WRONG!"
document = language_v1.Document(content=text, type_ = language_
v1.Document.Type.PLAIN_TEXT)
#Detects the sentiment of the text
sentiment = client.analyze_
sentiment(request={'document':document}).document_sentiment
print("Text: {}".format(text))
print("Sentiment:{}".format(sentiment.score, sentiment.
magnitude))
```

Save the script on your local computer and upload it to Google Cloud Shell with a filename of `analyze_sentiment.py`. When all the files have been uploaded, you can run the `.py` file to execute the script and start the analysis process:

```
python3 analyze_sentiment.py
```

Using the `analyze-sentiment` method, we can retrieve the value of the sentiment and magnitude. We will let you execute it and get the results.

The NLP API can also be used to integrate with other APIs, such as the **Speech-To-Text (STT)** API. By using the STT API, we can convert a sound/voice file into text and apply the NLP API, as well as various methods, to analyze the sentiment/entity/syntax of the text.

Google Cloud Speech-to-Text API

The Google Cloud Speech-to-Text API is used to convert audio into text. The service is based on deep learning technology and supports 120 languages and variants. The service can be used to transcribe audio files as well as support voice-activated interfaces. Cloud Speech-to-Text automatically detects the language being spoken.

First, we need to enable the Speech-to-Text API. From the left menu, scroll down and click on **Speech-to-Text** or type `speech to text` in the search bar at the top of the page.

You will be taken to a page where you will be asked to enable the API. If you enabled it previously, you will see the following page:

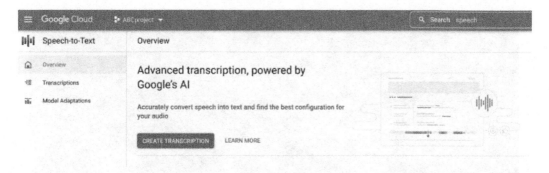

Since we are going to use `curl` to send a request to the Speech-To-Text API, we will need to generate an API key to pass in our request URL.

Create a request file named `request.json`:

```
{
    "config": {
        "encoding":"FLAC",
        "languageCode": "en-US"
    },
    "audio": {
        "uri":"gs://cloud-samples-data/speech/brooklyn_bridge.flac"
    }
}
```

Then, run the following command (note that we skipped the key creation step):

```
curl -s -X POST -H "Content-Type: application/json" -- data-
binay @request.json \ "http://speech.googleapis.com/v1/
speech:recognize?key=${API_KEY} > result.json
```

The preceding command calls the Speech-to-Text API, gets all the variables from the `request.json` file, uses the key we have generated, and sends/saves all the results to the `result.json` file. To view the `result.json` file, type the following command:

```
cat result.json
```

```
{
    "results": [
        {
            "alternatives": [
                {
                    "transcript": "how old is the Brooklyn Bridge",
                    "confidence": 0.98216057
                }
            ],
            "resultEndTime": "1.770s",
            "languageCode": "en-us"
        }
    ],
    "totalBilledTime": "15s"
}
```

The preceding screenshot shows the converted text from the given audio file, the confidence level (which is 98%), the time processed, and the language of the text.

Speech-to-Text supports different languages as well. Check out `https://cloud.google.com/speech-to-text/docs/languages` for more details about supported languages.

Google Cloud Text-To-Speech API

The Google Cloud Text-to-Speech API maps natural language texts to human-like speech. The initial step is to enable the Text-to-Speech API:

Cloud Text-to-Speech API

Google Enterprise API

Synthesizes natural-sounding speech by applying powerful neural network models.

Go to Cloud Shell by clicking on the Shell icon. Before diving into the API, check the list of the supported voices and languages. You can check the available languages and voices via Google Cloud Shell using the following command:

```
curl -H "Authorization: Bearer "$(gcloud auth application-
default print-access-token) \
    -H "Content-Type: application/json; charset=utf-8" \
    "https://texttospeech.googleapis.com/v1/voices"
```

The preceding command will list *all* possible languages and voices, along with their corresponding code. The following screenshot shows just a small part of the list:

```
{
  "languageCodes": [
    "en-US"
  ],
  "name": "en-US-Standard-B",
  "ssmlGender": "MALE",
  "naturalSampleRateHertz": 24000
},
{
  "languageCodes": [
    "en-US"
  ],
  "name": "en-US-Standard-C",
  "ssmlGender": "FEMALE",
  "naturalSampleRateHertz": 24000
},
```

Next, we need to create a JSON file named `synthesize-text.json`, where we will specify the language and voice codes and provide some full text that we want to convert into audio:

```
{
    'input':{
    'text':'This is a demo documentation for the Cloud Text-
to-Speech API. In this demo documentation we are using the
United States English language. The code of the language is:
"en-US-Standard-A". Thank you.'
    },
    'voice':{
    'languageCode':'en-us',
    'name':'en-US-Standard-A',
    'ssmlGender':'MALE'
    },
    'audioConfig':{
    'audioEncoding':'MP3'
    }
}
```

Use the following code to call the Text-to-Speech API using the `curl` command:

```
curl -H "Authorization: Bearer "$(gcloud auth application-
default print-access-token) \
  -H "Content-Type: application/json; charset=utf-8" \
```

```
   -d @synthesize-text.json "https://texttospeech.googleapis.
com/v1/text:synthesize" \
   > synthesize-text.txt
```

After running the preceding command, the result will be saved to a file called `synthesize-text.txt`.

Open the `synthesize-text.txt` file. You'll notice that the Text-to-Speech API provides the audio output in base64-encoded text and has been assigned to the `audioContent` field, as shown here:

```
{
  "audioContent": "//NExAASGoHwABhGudEACdzqFXfRE4EY3AACkD/
zX4ADf/6J/[...]"
}
```

Now, create a Python file named `tts_decode.py`:

```
import argparse
from base64 import decodebytes
import json
"""
Usage:
     python tts_decode.py --input "synthesize-text.txt" \
     --output "synthesize-text-audio.mp3"
"""
def decode_tts_output(input_file, output_file):
     """ Decode output from Cloud Text-to-Speech.
     input_file: the response from Cloud Text-to-Speech
     output_file: the name of the audio file to create
     """
     with open(input_file) as input:
     response = json.load(input)
     audio_data = response['audioContent']
     with open(output_file, "wb") as new_file:
     new_file.write(decodebytes(audio_data.encode('utf-8')))
if __name__ == '__main__':
     parser = argparse.ArgumentParser(
     description="Decode output from Cloud Text-to-Speech",
```

```
        formatter_class=argparse.RawDescriptionHelpFormatter)
    parser.add_argument('--input',
                    help='The response from the Text-to-Speech
API.',
                    required=True)
   parser.add_argument('--output',
                    help='The name of the audio file to
create',
                    required=True)
    args = parser.parse_args()
    decode_tts_output(args.input, args.output)
```

Finally, run the following command from Cloud Shell:

```
python tts_decode.py --input "synthesize-text.txt" --output
"synthesize-text-audio.mp3"
```

Now, our MP3 file is ready.

Google Cloud Translation API

Google's Cloud Translation API allows you to translate text that's in more than 100 languages. There are two ways to use the Translation API. From the main menu of the Google Cloud console, click on **Translation** (as shown in the following screenshot) or type `Translation API` into the search bar (at the top of the page):

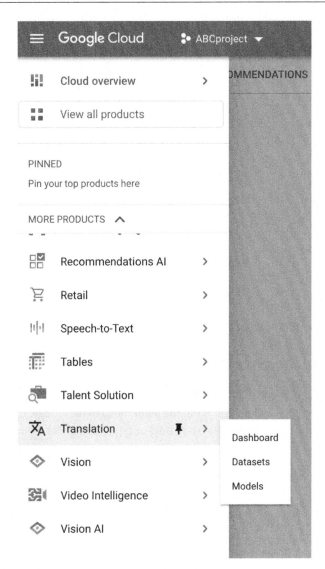

After clicking on the dashboard, you will be prompted to select one of three options:

- **AutoML Translation**
- **Cloud Translation API**
- **Translation Hub**

Since we are going to use `curl` to send a request to the Translation API, we will need to generate an API key to pass in our request URL.

First, let's define our text. Type TEXT= and type any sentence. Remember that the space between words should *not* be left blank; instead, in each space, type %20. In our example, we will type This is a demo documentation, as shown here:

```
TEXT = "This%20is%20a%20demo%20documentation"
```

Now that we've defined our TEXT variable, type the following command, which is underlined in red:

```
curl "https://translation.googleapis.com/language/translate/
v2?target=ru&key=${API_KEY}&q=${TEXT}"
```

That is a curl call for the API where we specified a target language (in our case, it is ru, which stands for Russian). Check out https://cloud.google.com/translate/docs/languages to view all the supported languages and ISO-639-1 codes.

After running the command provided, you will see the following output:

```
{
  "data": {
    "translations": [
      {
        "translatedText": "Это демонстрационная документация",
        "detectedSourceLanguage": "en"
      }
    ]
  }
}
```

The Google Cloud Translation API also has a feature that detects a language and translates it into *any* supported language.

In this example, we will provide two different texts in different languages, as shown here:

```
TEXT_ONE = "Merhaba%20Dostlar"
TEXT_TWO = "привет%20друзья"
```

Instead of using a space between words, we need to type %20.

After defining TEXT_ONE and TEXT_TWO, run the following command to call the Translation API to detect the language(s):

```
Curl "https://translation.googleapis.com/language/translate/v2/
detect?key=${API_KEY}&q=$"TEXT_TWO}"
```

This will return the language that was detected with a confidence level between zero and one (where zero stands for 0% and one stands for 100%):

```json
{
  "data": {
    "detections": [
      [
        {
          "language": "tr",
          "confidence": 1,
          "isReliable": false
        }
      ],
      [
        {
          "language": "ru",
          "confidence": 1,
          "isReliable": false
        }
      ]
    ]
  }
}
```

As we can see, the language of TEXT_ONE is Turkish (tr) with a 100% confidence level and the language of TEXT_TWO is Russian (ru) with a 100% confidence level as well.

Google Cloud Dialogflow API

The Dialogflow API is used for chatbots, **interactive voice response** (**IVR**), and other dialog-based interactions with human speech. First, we need to enable the Dialogflow API:

To start using the platform, open a new tab and type `https://dialogflow.cloud.google.com/#/login` `dialogflow.cloud.google.com` into your browser. You might be asked to sign in with your Google account.

You will be taken to the Dialogflow platform. This is the Dialogflow ES (essential) version. Here, we will mainly be using its **user interface** (**UI**). There is a section where you can type scripts (such as Google Functions), which will be covered in this demo documentation.

Now, let's become familiar with the Dialogflow UI. The following screenshot shows the page you'll see when you first start the Dialogflow platform:

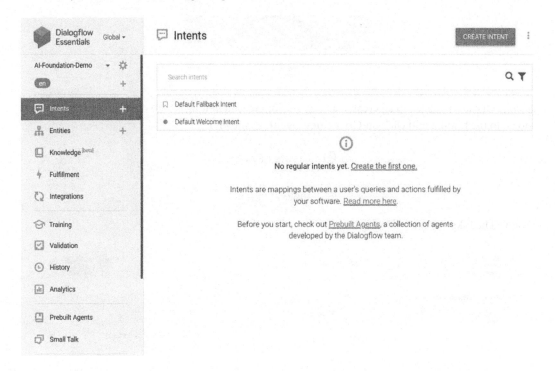

In Dialogflow, you can have multiple agents. If you have already created agents before, you can check them by clicking on the down arrow shown in the following screenshot:

Here, you can view a list of all created agents and/or create a new agent. To create a new agent, scroll down to the bottom and click on **Create new agent**, as shown here:

⊕   Create new agent

☰   View all agents

You will be taken to the following page:

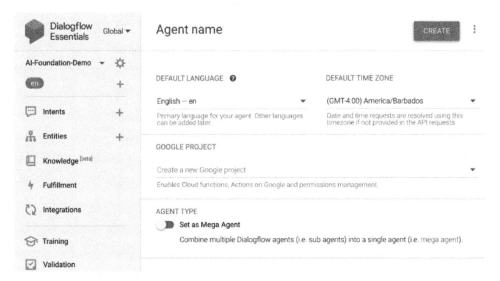

In our case, we will name our new agent `Test-Chatbot` and leave all the other settings as-is. Now, click **CREATE**:

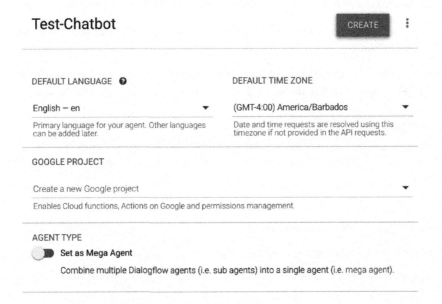

Once your agent has been created, you will see **Intents** on the left:

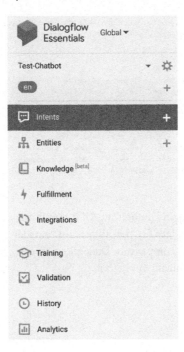

This option helps you understand the intent of the user. Then, we have **Entities**, which allows you to grab useful information from users. For example, when someone says "I want a veggie pizza," the chatbot can understand that they want a vegetarian pizza instead of a normal pizza.

At the time of writing, **Knowledge** is a beta feature. You can use this feature to create a knowledge base inside Dialogflow.

Fulfillment is where you can integrate Dialogflow with other systems such as your customer management system. The following screenshot shows an example script powered by Google Functions:

⚡ Fulfillment

Webhook

Your web service will receive a POST request from Dialogflow in the form of the response to a user query matched by intents with webhook enable

Inline Editor   (Powered by Google Cloud Functions)

Build and manage fulfillment directly in Dialogflow via Cloud Functions. Docs

ⓘ   Newly created cloud functions now use Node.js 10 as runtime engine. Check migration guide for more details.

index.js   package.json

```
1  // See https://github.com/dialogflow/dialogflow-fulfillment-nodejs
2  // for Dialogflow fulfillment library docs, samples, and to report issues
3  'use strict';
4
5  const functions = require('firebase-functions');
6  const {WebhookClient} = require('dialogflow-fulfillment');
7  const {Card, Suggestion} = require('dialogflow-fulfillment');
8
9  process.env.DEBUG = 'dialogflow:debug'; // enables lib debugging statements
10
11 exports.dialogflowFirebaseFulfillment = functions.https.onRequest((request, response) => {
12   const agent = new WebhookClient({ request, response });
13   console.log('Dialogflow Request headers: ' + JSON.stringify(request.headers));
14   console.log('Dialogflow Request body: ' + JSON.stringify(request.body));
15
```

Now, let's learn how to use intents in Dialogflow. An intent is an action a user wants to perform or a question a user has. For example, let's say that they want to order a pizza, book an appointment, or want more information about your company. In Dialogflow, we can create an agent that can understand the intent of the user and automatically reply to it.

When you create a new agent (as we did here), Dialogflow creates two intents by default:

- **Default Welcome Intent**

- **Default Fallback Intent**

  These can be seen in the following screenshot:

Let's see what's inside **Default Welcome Intent**. To do so, click on **Default Welcome Intent**. This intent is for understanding greetings such as Hello, Hi, and others:

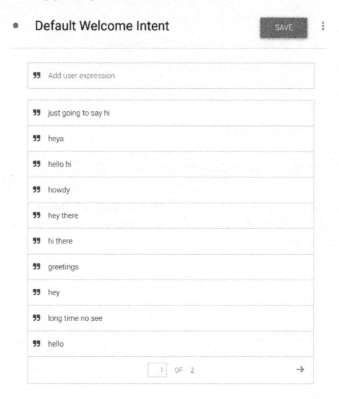

Each intent consists of two main parts:

- Training phases
- Response phases

Training phases help Dialogflow understand the intent of the user, whereas the response phase involves Dialogflow understanding the greeting. If it does, it will respond with some text, which will be provided in the **Responses** section:

The other default intent provided by Dialogflow is **Default Fallback Intent**. Here, when Dialogflow does not understand the user, it will respond with one of the pieces of text provided as a text response in **Default Fallback Intent**:

Responses ❓

DEFAULT ✚

Text Response	
1	I didn't get that. Can you say it again?
2	I missed what you said. What was that?
3	Sorry, could you say that again?
4	Sorry, can you say that again?
5	Can you say that again?
6	Sorry, I didn't get that. Can you rephrase?
7	Sorry, what was that?
8	One more time?
9	What was that?
10	Say that one more time?
11	I didn't get that. Can you repeat?
12	I missed that, say that again?
13	Enter a text response variant

ADD RESPONSES

🔘 Set this intent as end of conversation ❓

Now, let's dive into creating an intent (as mentioned previously, we will build a chatbot where the user will order a pizza).

To create a new intent, click **CREATE INTENT**, as shown here:

💬 **Intents**   CREATE INTENT   ⋮

🔍 Search intents   🔍 ▼

🔖 Default Fallback Intent

⬤ Default Welcome Intent

We will name our first intent `opening_times`, as shown here:

Click on **ADD TRAINING PHRASES**. This is where we will provide examples of how users can express their intent:

Train the intent with what your users will say

Provide examples of how users will express their intent in natural language. Adding numerous phrases with different variations and parameters will improve the accuracy of intent matching. Learn more

ADD TRAINING PHRASES

Let's add a couple of training phrases, as shown in the following screenshot:

> Add user expression

> Are you open every day?

> When are you open?

> Opening times

> What are your opening times?

Next, we need to add some responses. Click on **ADD RESPONSE**, as shown here:

Responses ❓   ⌃

Execute and respond to the user

Respond to your users with a simple message, or build
custom rich messages for the integrations you support.
Learn more

ADD RESPONSE

We will add just one response here, but remember you can add multiple responses for a particular intent:

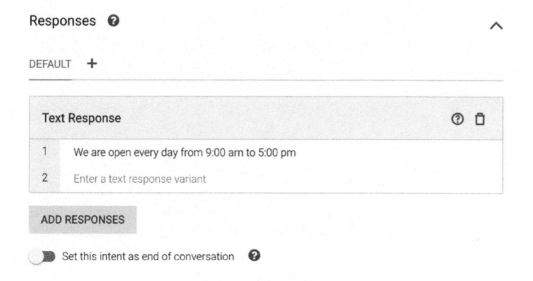

Responses ❓   ⌃

DEFAULT   **+**

Text Response	⑦ 🗑
1 We are open every day from 9:00 am to 5:00 pm	
2 Enter a text response variant	

ADD RESPONSES

🔘 Set this intent as end of conversation ❓

When you've finished with the training phrases and responses, save them; they will automatically start training the agent. Dialogflow needs to train the agent to respond to the question. This will take a couple of seconds (or minutes if you have a long input); you will be notified when training has been completed.

Now, let's try our trained agent. On the right-hand side of the page, you will see a small section where you can try your trained agent.

Let's type a question for our agent. Let's ask if they are open today and see what response we get:

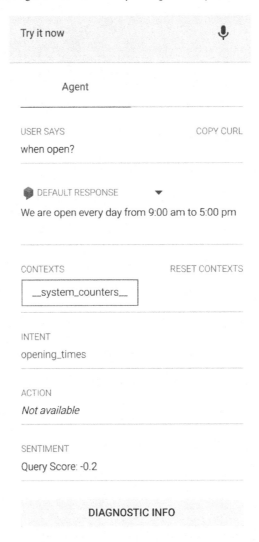

In this agent, we can create multiple intents. Dialogflow will understand which intents to use and respond to the user's question.

Now, let's create a new intent for ordering pizza. Click on **Intents** from the left menu and click on **CREATE INTENT**. The following screenshot shows some expressions you can use:

Now, provide a single response to the question (you can add more responses if you wish):

Upon saving your intent, your agent will be retrained. Let's test our agent:

Note that the user's phrase was different than it was in the training phases, but Dialogflow still understands the intent and gives the correct response.

If the user needs to provide more details, such as different toppings for the pizza, then Dialogflow will need to use entities that haven't been created yet. So, we will need to create an entity.

From the left menu, click on **Entities** and then **CREATE ENTITY**, as shown here:

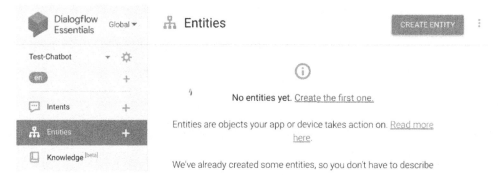

We will use `topping` as the entity's name. Check the **Define synonyms** box; this will help us find synonyms for each word. The following screenshot shows some examples of synonyms for `topping`:

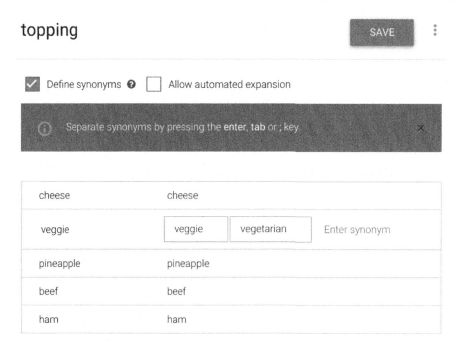

Click **SAVE**.

Let's go back to our intent to order pizza and create a new training phrase with some details of ordering such as "I want to order cheese pizza."

Here are some additional expressions for ordering a pizza:

Note that when we type two, it automatically detects the entity:

@sys.number is a built-in entity in Dialogflow that captures/recognizes the numbers in the dialog. There are also other built-in entities that can recognize emails, addresses, phone numbers, and other details. Check out https://cloud.google.com/dialogflow/es/docs/reference/system-entities for more built-in entities. Here are some examples:

English (en)	@sys.cardinal	ten	10
English (en)	@sys.ordinal	tenth	10
English (en)	@sys.number-integer	12	12
English (en)	@sys.number-sequence	1 2 2003	123
English (en)	@sys.flight-number	LH4234	LH 4234
English (en)	@sys.unit-area	ten square feet	{"amount":10,"unit":"sq ft"}
English (en)	@sys.unit-currency	5 dollars 25 pounds	{"amount":5,"currency":"USD"} {"amount":25,"currency":"GBP" }
English (en)	@sys.unit-length	ten meters	{"amount":10,"unit":"m"}

In our case, we are building entities, so we will need to map some words to an entity. This will allow us to see which part of the sentence is related to which entity. Simply select a word or a phrase from the expression that we used in the **Intents** section and assign it to the entity that's been created, as shown here:

After selecting the entity, you can select other words or phrases from the training expression and map them to that entity:

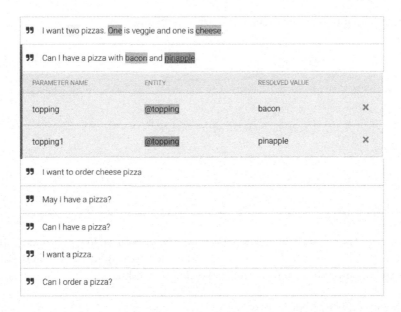

In this example, we have two different entities – `@sys.number` and `@topping`:

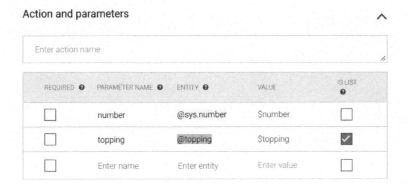

We can also change or modify the response with more dynamic answers:

Click the **SAVE** button to train the agent and test/try the chatbot:

If the user provides information about the topping for the pizza, we need to reinforce the extra question to gather that particular information. Click the checkbox next to **topping** in the **REQUIRED** section and click on **Define prompts**, as shown in the following screenshot:

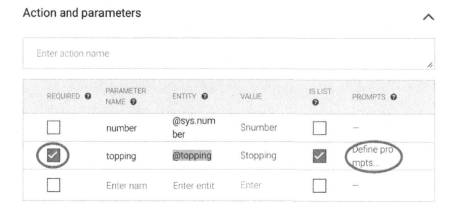

Add a question that the user will be asked, as shown here:

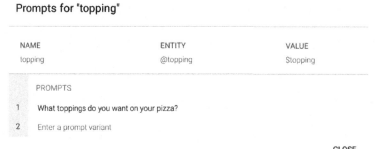

Click **Close** and save the agent. Note that you can add more prompts as well. Now, let's test the agent, which doesn't know anything about the topping:

With that, we have a very simple chatbot with basic functionality. But in real life, we would want to keep asking the user if they have any other questions *or* if they would like to add some other items to their current order. In our case, we have a chatbot where users order a pizza. In addition to asking about the pizza and its toppings, we can ask them if they want another pizza *or* if they want to add some drinks. This feature is called a **follow-up intent**. To enable this feature, click on **Add follow-up intent** next to the **order_pizza** intent, as shown here:

So, if a user wants to continue to add another pizza, they can simply answer **YES**. Click **YES** to add the follow-up intent:

Click on the **order_pizza - yes** section; you will be taken to a page where you can modify the section's content.

In our case, we will change the name of the intent, leave all the training phrases as-is (they are good enough to use in our case), and add a response that states `Great! What topping do you want on your pizza?`. Then, click **SAVE**:

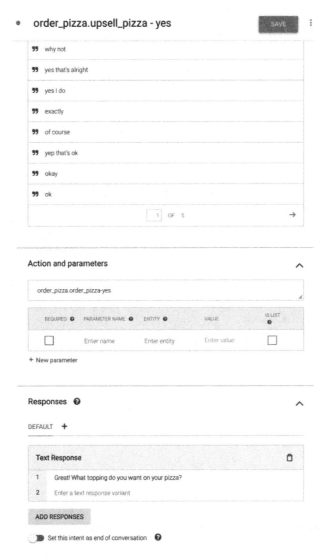

But what happens if the user answers **NO** to this follow-up question (Do you want to add more pizza?)? In this case, we would like to ask if they want to add a drink to their order. As we did previously, from the follow-up intent, select **NO**, click on the sub-intent and change its title (optional), leave all the training phrases as-is, and type the answer, as shown in the following screenshot:

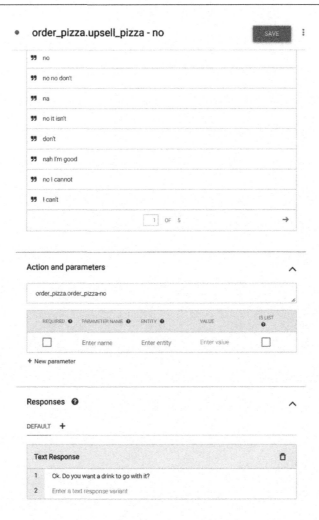

After saving the agent, you can try to chat with the bot. You can keep adding follow-up questions or new intents based on your designed conversation architecture.

Summary

In this appendix, we provided examples of how to use various Google Cloud ML APIs, including the Vision API, NLP API, Speech-To-Text API, Text-To-Speech API, Translation API, and Dialogflow API.

Index

Q

R

S

#

Packt.com

Subscribe to our online digital library for full access to over 7,000 books and videos, as well as industry leading tools to help you plan your personal development and advance your career. For more information, please visit our website.

Why subscribe?

- Spend less time learning and more time coding with practical eBooks and Videos from over 4,000 industry professionals

- Improve your learning with Skill Plans built especially for you

- Get a free eBook or video every month

- Fully searchable for easy access to vital information

- Copy and paste, print, and bookmark content

Did you know that Packt offers eBook versions of every book published, with PDF and ePub files available? You can upgrade to the eBook version at packt.com and as a print book customer, you are entitled to a discount on the eBook copy. Get in touch with us at customercare@packtpub.com for more details.

At www.packt.com, you can also read a collection of free technical articles, sign up for a range of free newsletters, and receive exclusive discounts and offers on Packt books and eBooks.

Other Books You May Enjoy

If you enjoyed this book, you may be interested in these other books by Packt:

Practical Deep Learning at Scale with MLflow

Yong Liu

ISBN: 9781803241333

- Understand MLOps and deep learning life cycle development
- Track deep learning models, code, data, parameters, and metrics
- Build, deploy, and run deep learning model pipelines anywhere
- Run hyperparameter optimization at scale to tune deep learning models
- Build production-grade multi-step deep learning inference pipelines
- Implement scalable deep learning explainability as a service
- Deploy deep learning batch and streaming inference services
- Ship practical NLP solutions from experimentation to production

Machine Learning on Kubernetes

Faisal Masood, Ross Brigoli

ISBN: 9781803241807

- Understand the different stages of a machine learning project
- Use open source software to build a machine learning platform on Kubernetes
- Implement a complete ML project using the machine learning platform presented in this book
- Improve on your organization's collaborative journey toward machine learning
- Discover how to use the platform as a data engineer, ML engineer, or data scientist
- Find out how to apply machine learning to solve real business problems

Packt is searching for authors like you

If you're interested in becoming an author for Packt, please visit authors.packtpub.com and apply today. We have worked with thousands of developers and tech professionals, just like you, to help them share their insight with the global tech community. You can make a general application, apply for a specific hot topic that we are recruiting an author for, or submit your own idea.

Share Your Thoughts

Now you've finished Journey to Become a Google Cloud Machine Learning Engineer, we'd love to hear your thoughts! Scan the QR code below to go straight to the Amazon review page for this book and share your feedback or leave a review on the site that you purchased it from.

https://packt.link/r/1-803-23372-9

Your review is important to us and the tech community and will help us make sure we're delivering excellent quality content.